Patriotism was everywhere—this was total commitment and effort. Factories were turning out war matériel. C. H. Masland was no longer making carpet but was now producing tents for the army and parachute backpack covers . . . . People were really angry. Young men were expected to be in uniform. Mom said that they were called "slackers" if they were not. My father said the stupidest thing the Japanese could have done was to attack Pearl Harbor. He said it united a d͟i͟s͟u͟n͟i͟t͟e͟d͟ ͟U͟n͟i͟t͟e͟d͟ ͟S͟t͟a͟t͟e͟s͟

By Col. Robert W. Black

RANGERS IN KOREA
RANGERS IN WORLD WAR II

A RANGER BORN

BORN

A Memoir of Combat and Valor
from Korea to Vietnam

Col. Robert W. Black

PRESIDIO
PRESS

BALLANTINE BOOKS • NEW YORK

A Presidio Press Book
Published by The Random House Publishing Group
Copyright © 2002 by Col. Robert W. Black

Presidio Press and colophon are trademarks of Random House, Inc.

www.presidiopress.com

ISBN 0-345-45326-3

Manufactured in the United States of America

First Edition: August 2002
First Mass Market Edition: November 2003

OPM 10 9 8 7 6 5 4 3 2 1

To my beloved daughter, April Black Croft.
So she knows.

Contents

CONTENTS

Acknowledgments

To write a book is a considerable expenditure of time and effort. The author may believe in the work, but it takes the support of family and the editor to bring the effort to a successful conclusion. I am most fortunate to have a beloved friend, lover, wife, and proofreader, Carolyn Black, and my Ballantine editor, Chris Evans, who have both given their enthusiastic support. I also express my appreciation to my soldier friends who have served with me in Army khaki or green and talked of our experience in words that begin, "Remember when . . ."

Introduction

"Once a Ranger, always a Ranger." I first heard those words more than a half century ago when I began the Ranger course of instruction at Fort Benning, Georgia. It takes considerable effort and will to achieve membership in this highly trained, all-volunteer military brotherhood. The reward is forever knowing that you were part of the best. The Ranger experience provides a lasting "belief in self" philosophy that is a shield against adversity.

To be a Ranger is to be unique. No military organization of the United States has the history of the American Ranger. We existed for over 165 years before the United States came into being. The Rangers fought six wars on American soil before the Declaration of Independence. In the Revolutionary War, Ranger units and Ranger leaders often made the difference between defeat and victory, submission and freedom. In the wars that followed, they continued to lead the way. The Rangers are a river of courage flowing through American history.

Ranging was a product of the American experience brought about by the vastness of our land and the method of war as practiced by the Native American. In the early 1600s when Capt. John Smith wrote the words "I ranged that unknown country," war was the centerpiece of life for many Indian tribes. They were masters of small-unit tactics, the raid, and the ambush. It became evident that to survive in the new world, the early colonists required a new breed of fighting men, ranging outward in search of the enemy. The Ranger was born.

Throughout years of conflict in America and across the

world, the volunteer spirit of the Ranger instilled in men the truth that "It is all in the heart and the mind. . . . You can accomplish anything." That belief became the core of my being. It would not survive if it were arrogance. It is a willingness to meet the challenges of life and a determination to fight for what you know to be right no matter the odds or who the adversary might be.

Many men who have never heard the song of the bullet have written well-researched accounts of soldiers at war. I enjoy those, but reserve a special affection for the writings of those who have lived the experience. As one who loves history and despises the frequent revision of it, I have long enjoyed the firsthand accounts of the Rangers who went before me. From the 1600s onward, men who were American Rangers have left behind a record of the events that shaped their lives and the conduct of their wars. Rangers Benjamin Church, Robert Rogers, Noah Smithwick, Samuel Reid, Rip Ford, and James Altieri are among those who have told us of their lives as American Rangers. Some of them wrote of their misadventures as well as their adventures—I like that. It is enough of a challenge to be a Ranger without also being an angel.

A Ranger Born was written as an account of the events that had the most impact on my life. Growing up during the Great Depression and World War II had a profound impact on me. It was my privilege to fight two hot wars and one cold war for my country. It was my disappointment that the goal for the United States in both Korea and Vietnam became something other than victory. Victory is the only end that justifies the sacrifice of men at war.

If war had been the only challenge I faced, life would have been much simpler for me, but tragedy denied an ordered structure to my life and career. Grief tested every aspect of my being. It was in this challenge that I learned that the Ranger philosophy goes far beyond military usage. The words "It is all in the heart and the mind. . . . You can accomplish anything" are an azimuth to follow in life, and one that guided me safely through.

Ranger Robert Black

A RANGER BORN

Prologue

It was a time of intensity, a grim night game where the stakes were life and death. We spent hours in patient movement under cover of a light wind and a thick cloak of darkness, first walking, holding on to the cartridge belt of the man to our front, and then crawling on our stomachs to quietly penetrate the Chinese positions. We were now beyond their forward line, but the Chinese had the numbers and employed a defense-in-depth. There would be another Chinese line of fortifications and another beyond that. In foxholes, bunkers, and trenches, men in quilted uniforms would be straining their senses searching the night against the possibility of our coming. A rifle stock knocking against a stone, a loose sleeve catching on a bush, or water sloshing in a half-filled canteen could betray our presence. I could not see the American to the front of me or the one to my rear, but they were there within reach of my hand or foot. We were tied together by training and tradition, bonded in a unique brotherhood of warriors.

The still of the night was broken by a sharp cry in an Oriental tongue. We froze in position. Overhead came the pop of a flare, then the hissing sound as it came to earth swaying beneath its parachute canopy. To retain night vision I closed one eye at the first sound of the flare. Turning my head in a barely perceptible motion, I saw the outline of a Chinese bunker to my right. Movement of a few yards would enable me to feel the edge of the opening and drop a fragmentation grenade into the firing slit. It was a temptation to be avoided. The flare burned out and the Chinese soldiers began talking

1

in a conversational tone. We touched each other in signal and crawled silently onward. Ours was a mission of stealth, to penetrate enemy lines and lay mines along the trails used by his supply columns. The Chinese were veterans who would stay in Korea until they were dead or badly wounded, or until the war ended. They were skilled at the art of patrolling and made it a game of one-upmanship, frequently tailing American patrols and following them quietly through the night. When the American patrols returned on the same path, the Chinese would ambush and strike. That would not happen this night. Months of selectivity and arduous training had molded a band of American paratroopers who volunteered to seek and endure to an even higher level of combat skill. We had become the masters of night warfare. There was no one on our trail because we checked it. We were difficult to ambush, as our routes were carefully selected and our procedures practiced until they were routine. We always took a different route home. The Chinese were unaware of our presence that night. Soon, though, enemy soldiers who thought they were secure would die. That's the calling card of the American Airborne Ranger.

EARLY LIFE

1

A Ranger Young

All things have a beginning; mine was the fifteenth of June 1929. As soon as the United States learned of the event, it went into that cataclysmic period of despair known as the Great Depression.

I was the descendant of a long line of citizen warriors. On my mother's side, they came from Holland in the 1600s and settled in the area of Bergen County, New Jersey. Later they moved to New York City and intermarried with the Scots and the Welsh. My father's line was German. Coming through Philadelphia in 1713, they meandered through the Cumberland Valley, down the Shenandoah, and settled in the Yadkin River area of North Carolina. In the Revolutionary War, my ancestors fought the British and paid the price of freedom. One died in an infamous British prison called the Sugar House. Another was murdered by Loyalists when he came home from the Battle of Guilford Court House. In the Civil War, my great-grandfathers fought each other, the one from the North serving from Bull Run to Antietam. He was an engineer and while under fire laid a pontoon bridge across the Rappahannock River during the Battle of Fredericksburg. The one from the South was an infantryman and fought at the Battles of the Wilderness and Cold Harbor. Captured in 1865, he ended his military career as a prisoner of war. An uncle sailed around the world with Teddy Roosevelt's Great White Fleet, and my father served in the navy in World War I and survived an attack on his ship by a German submarine. His ship, the USS *Pocahontas*, was homeported in New York, where he met my mother.

My mother was named Emma; she was my rock and I adored her. Brooklyn-born and raised in poverty, she was an angel who could curse like a trooper. Until age eight, I thought my name was "Ya goddamn dope!" but it was always followed by hugs and kisses.

I never heard my father say anything stronger than "cripes," but he was a hard and dangerous man. He was a crack shot, who as a boy kept fresh-killed meat on the family table. North Carolina relatives told us that when my father was in the third grade, he was badly beaten by a teacher. He went home, got a .22-caliber rifle, stood outside ringing the school bell with bullets, and called on the teacher to come out. The teacher went out a side window, and my father did not go back to school. He was quick with his temper and his fists. In later years I asked my uncle what my grandfather had been like. "Oh, he was a hard man," he responded, "knock ya flat as quick as look at ya." Perhaps it was inherited, as that description fit my father.

A college degree was rare in the early twentieth century. Sober, hardworking, and determined, my father had come far on a third-grade education and correspondence courses. His name was Frank Black. As the chief engineer of C. H. Masland's rug mill in Carlisle, Pennsylvania, he felt mathematics was the only study worth pursuing. After dinner, his standard direction was "Get your nose in a book," meaning a thick book of fractions and equations. Years later, after his death at age eighty-five, I found that book in our family library. On a page therein scrawled in a childish hand was the inscription "Fuck you, Frank Black!" I hated math and became determined to live my life without it. Fortunately, my mother taught me to love other books. I would sneak away to enjoy Dumas and Sir Walter Scott. I doted on the gunfire and flashing swords of Rafael Sabatini's Captain Blood and Scaramouche.

My father loved the outdoors. In 1932, when there were fourteen men lined up for every job and many farms were for sale, he used his grand salary of fifty dollars a week to buy a farm. It consisted of 146 acres, located between the two historic Pennsylvania towns of Carlisle and Gettysburg. We lived in a big stone house that dated from the early 1800s. We had a wooden house nearby for tenants and a large Pennsylvania bank barn, which had been built in 1854 by experienced carpenters. The frame was made of great logs held together by thick wooden pegs.

I grew up in a wonderful outdoor life of woods, streams, and mountains. My bond with my father was hunting together. I was shooting from the age of nine. I also had ample opportunity to visit the Gettysburg battlefield, where my parents and I were present in 1938 for the seventy-fifth anniversary of the battle. My father told me it would be the last gathering of Civil War veterans. It was hard to believe that those old men had ever been young. We watched as President Franklin Delano Roosevelt (FDR) dedicated the peace light. The battlefield fascinated me, and I discussed it with those adults who would share time with a child.

We had a tenant house. One of the renters was a combat infantryman, a sergeant from World War I. He talked with me of battles and on occasion allowed me to wear the steel helmet he had brought home. I listened with rapt attention when my father or "Old Sarge" would talk of wartime experiences.

My brother and sister were older, so they went to the higher-grade schools in Carlisle. I was dispatched to a one-room country schoolhouse where eight grades were taught in the same small room by the same teacher. The Depression had its grip on the nation and poverty was rampant.

This was a time when workingmen were told "Don't need ya." There was no unemployment compensation, and the pink slip in the final paycheck was a fearful thing. The adults called it "the crash" and "hard times." For many people it was a time of endless struggle, an era when idealism faced reality and died. My father said people were not interested in ideals, they wanted a job. He was not for Roosevelt; he said FDR would oppose an idea until it passed and then claim it as his own. That sounded very slick to me.

My loving mother sent me off to my first day in school

wearing a white silk shirt and an outfit called "Little Lord Fauntleroy." I found my companions were farm boys who went barefoot spring, summer, and fall. Some wore Farmer Brown bib overalls without shirts. Many girls wore dresses made from the covering cloth of feed and flour sacks. The cloth was produced in simple prints to entice farm families to buy the product.

When they saw me, the country boys could hardly believe their good fortune. Now they had something more in their lives than endless arguments over whether a John Deere farm tractor was better than an Allis Chalmers. To most of these boys, tractors represented the ultimate wealth. The older boys were already manhandling plows in furrows behind teams of horses and had a personal reason for wanting tractors. This was rural Pennsylvania. The same families had lived here for generations and intermarried. My family were outlanders in this society, and in the first grade I was a "city slicker." Some of the older boys took me around the back of the school where two outhouses were located, one for girls and one for boys. I was invited to look through a knothole in the boys' two-holer and, when I did, a boy inside pissed in my face. I fought and was soundly whipped. When I got home, I got a whipping for my torn clothes. It did no good to complain of mistreatment by fellow students. The answer was "Fight back!" I quickly learned never to complain of mistreatment by a teacher. Parents and teachers had an inseparable union. Complain about a teacher and your parents would flay your backside. My eyesight was going. I could not read the writing on the blackboard from my seat. I was terrified. Any boy who wore glasses was looked down upon, teased, and tormented as "four eyes." I understood that once you got that nickname, you were branded. It lasted for life. I could not tell my parents that the world was becoming blurred.

I fought, was whipped, and fought again. I learned the hard way the importance of an attack philosophy. I also found if I took the blows, hung in there, and kept fighting, that I had more respect for myself. By the eighth grade I was

King of the Hill. I kicked the ass of every boy in school that year and would not hesitate to give equal treatment to a mouthy girl.

Girls were strange. They could milk cows, churn butter, and even cut the lawn, but they could not fork hay or properly leap from the barn rafters into a straw mow. They were scared their dresses might lift, as though I cared. Not one in twenty of the girls owned cap pistols or a BB gun, yet they always wanted to play with us boys. They could never keep a secret no matter how dreadful the oath they swore. If we raided an apple orchard or put something on the railroad tracks, they would always tell. There was some rule that said girls had to stay clean. They had to sneak off to do everything, probably even to go to the toilet. Parents kept them under tight control. Older boys told me it had to do with something called "sex."

When I was a child, sex was never openly discussed by my parents. Once my mother and father had guests and the Virgin Islands were mentioned. Wanting to impress everyone, I piped up with "I know what a virgin is!" The adults were stricken dumb. Noticing that I had their undivided attention, I trumpeted, "Shirley . . . was a virgin until Harry . . . took her into the woods." I learned in a hurry to stay out of adult conversations.

This was subterfuge on the part of my parents. They knew about sex; they had to know about it. Any book my mother tried to keep from me had to contain "sex." One day I saw my mother reading a book called *God's Little Acre*. "Oh, this is so suggestive!" she would cry, but she could hardly wait to get to the next page.

A key element of education in a one-room country schoolhouse was corporal punishment. We were whipped for the slightest offense and sometimes were instructed to go into the woods beside the school and cut the switches we were beaten with. Any boy with self-respect carried a pocketknife, and lying that I did not have one was no help. There was always some girl who wanted to hear us yelp. I was caught reading *Tom Sawyer* during the period when another grade was reciting. The teacher made me hold out my hands and hit them again and again with a ruler. Most of us did not see a ruler as a measuring device. It was an instrument of torture.

It took a skilled liar to avoid punishment, and I practiced whenever possible. A boy gave me a condom and I felt like a big kid to own one. Unfortunately, I left it in the pocket of my overalls. My mom was doing the Monday washing and the Prudential Insurance man had stopped by to make collection, as was done in those days. While my mom talked, she ran her hand around the tubful of water and came up with a wet rubber draped across her finger. She was terribly embarrassed. As soon as the man left, she asked me if I was responsible. I lied that I was not. When my father came home, she gave him four types of hell while the poor man reeled in shock. It was not long before they both turned on me, and I babbled a terrified confession. My father handled the whipping with my mother cheering him on.

It remains my contention that a boy should be allowed some latitude as a liar in early years, otherwise he will be unable to deal with the opposite sex in later years.

My mother dreamed of going to Hawaii, but would never get there. Most people did not have the money to travel anywhere. We only went to visit relatives. Dad would pack us all in the car and we would drive to the area of Winston-Salem, North Carolina. This was a visit of adults and there was little for children to do. I have a memory of going out on a sidewalk to play. An elderly man came walking in my direction. His skin was very dark. When he came close to me, he left the sidewalk and walked in the street. The experience stayed with me. Adults did not act like that. I did not understand why an old man would give up a wide sidewalk to a child. Everyone in my country school had the same color skin that I did. Sometimes I would hear about a black family that lived near Mount Holly Springs, six miles away. People talked about them like a tourist attraction. "Oh yeah, we got some coloreds. There's them Gumbys live over at Mount Holly."

The Depression was a terrible experience for much of America. Fourteen million men were without jobs. They and their families lived in silent sadness and chewed poverty at mealtime. Anyone lucky enough to have a job worked hard to keep it. Entertainment was simple. In the 1930s and '40s, the family radio was our lifeline to the world. When I was very young, Saturday morning brought me the children's program *Let's Pretend*. Growing older, I eagerly looked forward to *The Green Hornet*, *The Shadow*, and *I Love a Mystery*. Radio allowed, indeed forced, listeners to use their imagination. I was terrified when Orson Welles did the program on the invasion of the Martians. We tuned in late and, like many others, thought it really was an invasion from outer space. I begged my father to shoot me before the Martians came. As I recall, he took a long look at me and seriously considered the idea.

There were simple country festivals with chicken corn soup, fiddlers, and cakewalks. Money was raised for the one-room country schoolhouse by holding box socials. Older girls coming on marriageable age would make a lunch for two, put it in a cardboard box, and wrap it with a pretty ribbon. The identity of the girl who made the box lunch was supposed to be a secret, but the girls usually told the boys they most liked the color of the paper or ribbon they used. The young men would then bid auction-style for the opportunity to sit and eat with the girl they liked.

A well-known song was "Brother, Can You Spare a Dime?" but thanks to my father's effort and foresight and my mother's thrift, we were doing well. We had a five-acre truck patch where we grew a wide variety of vegetables. We had hogs and chickens and steers for butchering. I learned how to capture a rooster, put his head on a stump, and chop it off with a hatchet. If they were then put on the ground, they would run around for a bit before they flopped over. The chicken was then put in hot water. It was a stinking job to pluck the feathers. Pigs were shot between the eyes with a .22-caliber rifle, their throats cut, and then they were hung up to be butchered. The saying was that we used everything but the squeal. There was nothing squeamish about farm life at this time. Farmers knew how to butcher an animal, and their women knew how to can fruit and vegetables. If you wanted to survive, you did what it took to do so.

President Franklin Roosevelt was a god to millions of poor and desperate Americans. When I would visit the homes of other boys, it was not unusual to see his picture cut from a magazine, framed, and hung on the wall, or in poorer houses tacked there. He made the federal government a part of people's lives with a variety of "alphabet" government assistance programs. They often seemed radical to a population that had grown up in a self-sufficient "sink or swim" society. Unemployment compensation and a program called Social Security began. Some adults said the notion of the government taking care of people would grow until people expected it.

There was the National Recovery Act (NRA) and a works program called WPA. Farm boys said WPA meant "We poke along." Many young men who were without work joined the Civilian Conservation Corps (CCC). They lived in barracks or tent camps in a quasi-military-style life. My friend Old Sarge got a job supervising one of the work gangs. This was good for him as he now had money to buy a pint, and it was legal and available. For Old Sarge the real horror was not the Depression but Prohibition, when the law said a man could not legally buy a drink. Prohibition ended in 1933, and Old Sarge told my father that if he could live through that, he could live through any depression.

With axe, saw, pick, and shovel, the men of the CCC cleared the logging roads in the mountains. They cleaned debris from springs and streams, cut firebreak lanes to reduce the threat of woodland fires, and planted millions of trees. The people of our area had high respect for the CCC. When Old Sarge saw me, he said that his men were toughening up and learning to work things as a team. He felt war was coming, and his men were learning teamwork that would be helpful to a soldier.

Anyone who grew up in this time knew the country song

"You Are My Sunshine." The song was played in endless repetition and I was sick of it. A young man whose family farm joined ours had a passion for my sister and, while working his fields, would bellow that song at her.

The Russians invaded Finland. The radio, magazines, and books told us the Russians were bad. People cursed the Russians and praised the Finns, who were fighting gamely.

A family named Whitmore lived about three miles up the road. They had a boy my age named Buck and a Model-A Ford built like a box. On Saturday they drove fourteen miles to Carlisle for a movie and groceries. Buck and I would strap on our six-guns; I wore two cap pistols, slung low and tied down. The movies we were going to see were black-and-white Westerns. I never cared for singing cowboys like Gene Autry or Roy Rogers. Occasionally they would sing to girls, and that made me uncomfortable. I liked Johnny Mack Brown, Bob Steele, and Tom Mix. They would punch bad men and could draw their pistols quickly. Their pistols were marvelous weapons that could fire a hundred shots without reloading.

Some cowboy star had a sidekick called "Lucky." I thought that was a wonderful name and tried hard to get my parents to call me "Lucky." They refused—no one would call me "Lucky." Later, I tried "Bugs." I even painted it on a sweatshirt so everyone would know what they should call me, but no one paid any attention. Years later I would be known simply as Ranger Black. I'm rather glad Bugs never caught on.

2

World War II

I was twelve years old. It was a Sunday morning in December. I was standing alone in the living room. The freestanding Philco "Green Eye" radio was playing, when an announcer broke in to say that Pearl Harbor was under attack by the Japanese. I had no idea where Pearl Harbor was and thought the Japanese were little yellow elves who made five-and-ten-cent store items. I did not understand what was happening, but my parents were in the kitchen and rushed to hear the news. The war now consumed the thoughts and conversations of the adults in my life. They huddled around the radio listening to the frequent reports. My brother, Frank, soon went to the army. My sister, Virginia, had married, and her husband, Paul, went to the navy. People were flying the American flag, and my mother hung a small red, white, and blue banner in the window; it had two blue stars, signifying that two men of the family were in the service.

Girls were an increasing problem. Initially they were in the way and messing up boy games, but they seemed to improve with age. I began to have uncomfortable thoughts and stirrings in my body and to see these creatures in a new light. Any farm kid knew about copulation—the barnyard was full of it. I'd watched chickens and ducks, sheep, goats, hogs, cows, and horses go at it. I understood what testicles were for. We had a bull with big ones. I would shoot him in the balls with my Red Ryder BB gun just to make him mad. It did. My father knew that bulls kill, so we kept ours in an eleven-by-twelve-foot enclosure surrounded by four-inch pipe set in concrete. Having a spark of mercy in his soul, my brother, who is ten years older than I, had once thrown a fifty-gallon steel drum into the cage so the bull would have a toy. In an awesome display of power, the bull mangled that steel drum. The bull only got out of his cage for sex.

I knew about sex, but I did not know about foreplay. Stallions don't care about foreplay, nor do bulls, rams, boars, or roosters. So I had no mentor. I had this terrible need that was giving me hot and cold sweats. When I was twelve I knew it was time for action. I sat in my school seat looking at a girl who was doing a recitation—I knew this girl. When we were six years old we were in the barn together. She had shown me hers and I showed her mine. Our relationship was cool after that. Now she had protrusions from her chest, and I had a need. As she returned to her seat, she passed my desk. I reached out and touched her arm.

"How about a fuck?" I inquired with hopeful passion. There was a quick intake of breath, followed by a giggle as she hurried away. I turned to see if she was considering my proposition while she took her seat. With her hand cupped in front of her mouth, she began to whisper to her girlfriend, who whispered to the student next to her. I watched in horror as my needful request spread among the twenty-eight students. I heard the mocking laughter and felt the eyes of my world ridiculing me. Red-faced with shame, I shrank down in my seat. It was a devastating experience, and I became terrified of contact with girls. My life improved greatly when a classmate demonstrated a technique he called "jackin' off."

If girls made me uncomfortable, guns did not. We had more guns around our house than a German rifle squad. My father would hit me if I pointed a gun at any person. "Never . . . never point a gun at someone unless you mean to kill them," he told me, "and then, don't miss." I breezed through the transition from cap pistols to BB guns. I meant to kill Bucky Whitmore, and we had BB-gun fights until I got shot just under my left eye. My mother was furious at me and put a stop to our private war. I progressed to .22-caliber rifles, shotguns, and a lever-action 30-30. Slaughtering groundhogs, squirrels, and rabbits and hunting deer, I moved up the game ladder. It was not uncommon to see boys carrying guns in the fields and forests of Pennsylvania. At the base of the mountain about two miles behind the farm, there was a stream where giant hemlocks grew in profusion. The stream split in two here, forming an island. An old tree, a forest giant, had died and fallen, forming a natural bridge over the water to this sanctuary. Fallen needles from the hemlocks and great patches of moss formed a carpet. There were trout in the stream, and the water sang as it passed among the stones; this was a place of rest and refuge. I frequently came here with my rifle. I thought of this island as my own, my private place, my kingdom. At various places in the woods there were natural springs of cool, clear water. Hunters left coconut shells or blue agate cups for drinking, and if they were absent, I could always cup my hands.

Prior to the Depression, a neighbor farmer had planted a thirty-acre field of pines in the hope of selling Christmas trees. By the time they came to size, hard times were on the country and people needed what little money they had for food and clothes. The trees grew, and by the time I came along, they were tall and sheltering. I could lie on my back in the softness of the pine field and watch the cumulus clouds roll overhead. They looked like travelers searching for adventure across a bright blue sky. We had two dogs that were my ever-faithful companions. The female was a collie, and the male was a mix between collie and Newfoundland. My parents had no imagination when naming dogs and called them both "Teddy." My brother named the female Mary Louise Black and the male George Melvin Black. Mary Louise was smart enough to hunt for game and George Melvin was big enough to kill it. Our dogs lived outdoors and free, never tied. The only time they came in the house was during a snowstorm. They hunted game, baying through the mountains after deer, bringing dead rabbits home, and fighting ferocious battles with sharp-toothed groundhogs.

I was walking up the road to our farm when I heard furious barking and snarling in the woods below me. A pack of strange dogs was attacking George Melvin and, though greatly outnumbered, he was fighting gamely. Though he was bloodied, my dog was backed up against a tree and sometimes rising up to lash out with his fangs. I picked up a length of deadwood and attacked from the rear, putting the enemy dogs to flight. George Melvin chased them a short distance, then returned to me and pressed close as I hugged him. He licked my face and I shared his pride in our joint victory. A big dog was the best friend a boy could have.

There were always farm chores to do. I began milking cows at age eight, bringing in the bucket, straining it through a cloth to remove any filth that was on the cows' udders, and putting the milk in cans. Like the generations before us, we did not know about bacteria, but we stayed healthy. We had a springhouse where cold water was channeled and the milk cans stayed cool. The next morning there would be a thick coat of cream at the top. Mom would skim off the cream to be used when baking.

There was planting and harvesting of our large truck patch. Fieldstones could break an expensive farm implement. My father wanted every stone of size removed from the fields so this land could be plowed by a tenant farmer and put into corn or wheat. The work was never done.

A boy named Duke lived about two miles away. Duke was sixteen and could drive his father's old truck. One day he took me along when he went swimming at a lake. A raft was moored out in the center of the lake and we swam out to it and relaxed in the sun. Duke saw some older girls on the beach and swam back to shore. Some time later I decided to swim back in, but en route I developed a cramp in my leg and began to go under. I was drowning, but I was too embarrassed to call for help. I would call out "Hey, Duke!" and go down. I saw the water closing above my head and the sunlight shining through it from above. I was finished and I knew it. Fortunately, one of the girls was a trained lifeguard. She must have cut the water like a mermaid, as she soon was at my side, with Duke and another girl following. They towed me to shore and pumped the water out of me. I was thankful, frightened, and disgusted with myself for allowing the fear of embarrassment to almost kill me. From this experience I learned two things that became a part of my nature. I vowed never to allow fear of embarrassment to stop me from what needed to be done, and I learned to profit by, but not worry about, the close calls in life. No matter how close disaster, disease, or death comes, if they don't get you, don't worry about it. "Never sweat the close ones."

The war raged. The Germans invaded Russia. I thought this was good, because we hated the Russians for what they had done to Finland. The adults informed me that this was in the past. Now the Russians were our friends. I was confused. The Russians were bad, and now they were good? What if they went bad again? Had the Germans ever been good? I put that question to Old Sarge, but he said not in his experience. I quickly learned that hating Germans, Italians, and Japanese was the right thing.

At the beginning of World War II, the threat of bombing and invasion of the United States was considered real. Rural communities in the United States had blackouts and air raid drills. My father was issued an oversized, white steel helmet. It had a triangle painted on it and the initials CD for Civil Defense. Dad had something to do with air raid protection. What Japanese or German bomber had the range or desire to reach central Pennsylvania in 1942 was not mentioned. I joined the Boy Scouts and went six miles to Mount Holly Springs for an air raid alert drill in which I would be a messenger. Mount Holly Springs had a population of some fifteen hundred people, a grocery store, and a free library, so someone believed that German and Japanese bombers could hardly wait to attack. The headquarters of the Mount Holly Springs defense effort was at the fire station, and the blackout was scrupulously observed. I was eager to carry a message to someone that enemy bombers were on the way, but nothing happened. Some of the men were doing something with a woman on a porch across the street, and she made enough noise to drown out any Stuka or Aichi Type-99 dive bomber flying over Cumberland County. I asked Old Sarge what type of enemy aircraft would bomb us. He said all the German planes he saw in World War I were Fokkers. At least, I think that was what he said. The threat of bombardment in rural Pennsylvania quickly faded. It was not long before people went back to turning on their lights at night and leaving the shades up.

Patriotism was everywhere—this was total commitment and effort. Factories were turning out war matériel. C. H. Masland was no longer making carpet, but was now producing tents for the army and parachute backpack covers. Soon they added lathes and were manufacturing barrels for 90mm guns. Poverty was replaced by sudden wealth, as there were jobs in the workforce or military for everyone. Farm women sewed the army tents at Masland's and were paid piecework. My father commented that these women made more money than he did. People were really angry. Young men were expected to be in uniform. Mom said they were called "slackers" if they were not. My father said the stupidest thing the Japanese could have done was to attack Pearl Harbor. He said it united a disunited United States.

Children were told that collecting scrap was important to winning this war. The disposal of trash had always been a problem for farm families, so they threw it out along the road on someone else's property. About a half mile from our house there was a place along the road where people had discarded unwanted items for years. Now I searched this refuse area for old pots and pans and worn-out tires. I would load these into my child's wagon and pull it to a country store that collected refuse that could be recycled for the war effort. My scrap collecting was both patriotic and self-serving. My pots became B-17 bombers, and I received a few cents to buy penny candy.

We all had ration books. I understood why gasoline was scarce but could not understand the lack of butter for my bread. Before the war we bought butter from stores; now it was rationed. Every time I asked for some, I was told that butter was for the boys at the front. I grew up thinking that a soldier in the United States infantry ate a tub of butter a day. We had a hand-crank churn and filled the glass container with the cream strained from the daily milking of our cows. Before the cream turned into butter, you had to crank that handle for a week. Often it was the wrong color and taste. It seemed that if I was not milking cows, I was churning butter or shelling corn. My right arm was developing muscles like Popeye the Sailor Man.

Puberty was at hand in more ways than one. My face was a mass of pimples. When I opened my mouth to speak, I never knew if my voice would be tenor or bass. Pictures of pinup girls were appearing, designed to raise the morale of servicemen away from home. I don't know what they did for the servicemen, but they certainly gave me a rise. *Life* magazine published a full-page photo of the beautiful actress-dancer Rita Hayworth. She wore a slinky and revealing negligee, kneeling on a bed, her full breasts straining against the cloth. If Rita had done her part, by the time we went to war in Vietnam, I would have fathered an army for America larger than that of the Chinese.

World War II dominated my life. I wore glasses now and I absorbed the war, reading all I could about the weapons and aircraft of our men. My brother, Frank, was an Army Air Corps enlisted man in the Aleutian Islands, and my brother-in-law, Paul, was on a supply barge in the Pacific. A young man who had been a neighbor of ours was shot down and killed over the Ploesti oil fields. Sometimes there was crying among the families whom my mother and father knew. Blue service stars were changing to the gold that symbolized men killed in action. Student pilots occasionally landed Piper Cub training aircraft in our fields. On one occasion, Medical Service school students from Carlisle Barracks marched past the farm on a training exercise. On one morning of dense visibility, a four-engine B-24 bomber lost in the fog nearly crashed into our farmhouse. It was an exciting time. My classmates shared my enthusiasm. For a boy growing up during World War II, it was not a question of if you would go into the service, only which branch of service you wanted to join.

The nearest theater was fourteen miles away in Carlisle. Sometimes when my father took my mother to town for shopping, she and I would go to the movies. As a special treat, she took me to see *Northwest Passage*, starring Spencer Tracy. It was the story of a raid by Rogers' Rangers in the French and Indian War. The concept of skilled woodsmen creeping up on the enemy fascinated me. I begged for the book of the same name by Kenneth Roberts and devoured it. The thought of being a Ranger began to grow. I was reading everything I could in magazines about Rangers in combat. Some Rangers participated in the Dieppe raid. Rangers were the first ground-force Americans to fight in Europe and the first American infantry to kill the enemy there and suffer loss. I followed their exploits in North Africa, Sicily, and Italy, and on D day, 6 June 1944, when Rangers climbed the cliffs to destroy the German guns. My brother had sent home some items, including a copy of Army Field Manual 22-5, *Infantry Drill Regulations*. I began to memorize this book.

In ninth grade I went to school in Carlisle. Having been scorned in the country as a "city slicker," I was now referred to as a "country hick." That did not last long. My brother had been a weight lifter. His best friend, Jake, lived beside the school and had a basement full of weights. Jake was in the Merchant Marine. When he was home between sailings, I got permission to use his weights at lunchtime. I usually stunk of sweat when I got back to class, but my strength was considerable. Strength promoter Charles Atlas had a newspaper and magazine ad that showed a ninety-eight-pound weakling having sand kicked on him at the beach. The weakling's girlfriend was embarrassed until he got muscles. I never got to an ocean beach in my youth, but I was taking no chances. At a time when few boys lifted weights, I pumped iron.

Suddenly the war was over. When the news came over the radio, only my mom, sister, and I were home. I took my shotgun, went outdoors, and fired a couple rounds in the air. I was glad my brother and brother-in-law would be coming home, but so disappointed that I would not get to go. I was fifteen years old. My brother had gotten a commission as an infantry lieutenant, but before he saw action the war ended. He ended his wartime service as an athletic and recreation (A&R) officer at Camp Atterbury, Indiana. Everything had gone to the military. With the end of the war and the discharge of millions of men, war surplus matériel was being sold for pennies, trashed, or acquired by what was called "midnight requisition." Our attic began to look like a sporting goods warehouse. I could outfit teams.

My father and mother were dead set against football. "Your brother broke his collarbone" was their endless theme, and they would not allow me to play until my last year of eligibility. Football is war without guns. I loved the tests of strength and agility, the uncompromising demand for excellence by the coaches. There were no contact lenses or face guards in the football programs of my era. I was cursed with myopic astigmatism, and without my glasses, things had a tendency to blur. When my parents finally allowed me to play high school football, I settled for playing the line at the tackle position. I played offense and defense in a sixty-minute ball game. I loved the down-in-position conversations I had with opposing tackles. Usually these were cordial exchanges such as, "I'm gonna kick your fucking ass, you sum-bitch," or "How did you like that, shit-face?"

My tactic on defense was to drive over, under, or through the opposing tackle, get into the other team's backfield, and feel around until I located the kid carrying the football. It worked well. But on one occasion I ran up against an opposing tackle who would later play for the Naval Academy. He planted me like a hammer plants a nail.

I sang in the high school choir, and we went to sing at a black church. The congregation was wonderful, so kind and appreciative. An experience like that stays with you. When you get to know people, you know them as individuals and like them or not on that basis. Sports brought the races into contact with each other. When you are a team, everyone on your side is part of the team. In football I played left tackle, and the right guard was black. In one game I overshifted on a play. The opposing tackle blocked me to the outside and there was a hole five yards wide. Just as the opposing half-back entered this open space, our right guard came from the opposite side and spread him out like butter on a pancake. I was learning that being good at what you do has nothing to do with color of skin.

I resented parental control and became increasingly sassy to my father. Finally he'd had enough, and one morning began to punch me in the face. At this point I began to realize how strong I had become. He was my father and I would not hit him, but I knew I could have and he knew it also. That made him even angrier. I blocked the punches as best I could, but he was wearing a ring and it left some cuts. The bruises and cuts stayed with me for a few days. I told my schoolmates we had been in a car wreck.

Those who saw my report card would have thought the alphabet begins with a D. I was reading army field manuals. I rejected any form of math and, due to my years of not wearing glasses, was far behind in most subjects. I learned to type. Later in life I felt that was the most important thing I learned in school.

3

This Is the Army

FORT BRAGG, NORTH CAROLINA, JUNE 1950

The wide, white, porcelain-coated, cast-iron mouth of the urinal yawned before me, its bottom covered by a golden pond of piss. The drain was clogged with urine-soaked cigarette butts thrown in by careless fellow soldiers. A fly lit on a wet, gray stub, rubbed its feet together, buzzed contentedly, then flew at my face.

"Duty," said Robert E. Lee, "is the most sublime word in our language." Marse Robert and I had differing definitions of duty. His was to serve his cause—mine was to slave at it. My duty began with my name appearing on duty rosters tacked to the bulletin board of Headquarters Detachment, 82d Airborne Division. It was usually found under such descriptive headings as Kitchen Police, Ash and Trash, Night Fireman, or Barracks Guard, which translated to Latrine Orderly.

I was a private first class, the bottomland inhabitant of an army division headquarters, where everything flowed downhill. I had an assigned job as a file clerk in 82d Airborne Division headquarters, but that was an army ruse. Army administrators of this period had an unsatiable lust for typists. My effort to avoid mathematics in high school by taking typing courses had betrayed me. And so, one of the finest riflemen (in my opinion) in the army was dragooned into an office already filled with skilled clerk typists who outranked me. Everyone else in my section was a corporal or higher, and corporals did not pull "duty." Some of them were "jocks" on Special Duty (SD) to play sports. They could not possibly work. The commander wanted to win the division championship in their sport, and they must practice. Though I was assigned as a file clerk, along with the privates from other administrative sections, my duty was to be a soldier slave.

Outside the latrine window the band of the 82d Airborne Division struck up the division song, and the words began to roll in my mind: "We're all-American and proud to be. We are the soldiers of liberty. Some ride the gliders to the enemy, others are sky paratroopers."

Somehow I did not feel military pride while facing the clogged urinal. If I felt proud later, I could catch up on the song. The band played it over and over, every morning as they marched about the division headquarters area beginning at a time that soldiers know as O-dark-thirty.

After cleaning out the urinal, I hurried to wash my fingers and looked into the mirror above the sink. I could not believe that the person looking back at me had volunteered to be a soldier, enlisting as Regular Army, Infantry Unassigned. Gazing wearily at my sad face, I muttered, "How the hell did I get here?"

I was still studying army field manuals in my brother's collection and devouring the great books that were coming out of the experience of war. I read Irwin Shaw's *The Young Lions* and cried because I had missed my war.

On my seventeenth birthday, I joined the Army Reserves. During my first year at summer camp at Indiantown Gap, Pennsylvania, I was the only recruit in the 313th Infantry of the 79th Infantry Division. Everyone else was a World War II veteran, and I was their prize. The combat-experienced noncommissioned officers talked with me by the hour, patiently instructing. They also harassed me in many ways. I loved to march, and throughout my life the sound of boots crunching in unison on gravel has been music to my ears. Initially I did not know how to skip and change step, and they withheld that information from me. The sergeant marching to the front would change step, and I would run in small steps in order to get back in unison with the others. Then he would change step and I would run again. They finally wearied of this and set me right.

Sergeant Will Farver would sit on his bunk, empty a beer, place it on his footlocker, and say, "There's another dead soldier." Farver was an expert with a 60-millimeter mortar. I was enraptured as he told me about his unit trapping a column of German soldiers on an open road and of the terrible effect his mortar fire had on them. Sergeant George Sponsler was a crack shot. Men said that he had cornered a German platoon in a bunker and, as they tried to escape, killed them one after another, piling them up in the doorway until the remainder surrendered. The combat-experienced sergeants taught me much about the technique of war. They taught me that in the attack to keep moving forward, pinning the enemy with fire. They taught me to dig deep when in defense. They warned me about leaving footprints, making noise, or carrying shiny objects when on patrol. They told me to always keep my mission in mind. These men had seen friends torn apart by bullet and shell. Time and again they reminded me to hate my enemy in war and leave the loving of them to those who don't know the hell of the battlefield. It was all heady stuff for a boy who dreamed of being a soldier.

They also taught me about being a man by wreaking havoc with my ego. Sometimes the sergeants would take me to town. They drank beer, and to prove I was tough, I drank beer also. I began to show off by coming back to the barracks and making a running dive for my steel cot. One night the stay-behinds took the side support springs out and replaced them with light cords. When I leaped onto my cot, the mattress collapsed and I plunged through to the floor. They laughed till their sides ached. When I learned caution and crept beneath my covers, I found they had folded the top sheet in half in the technique called "short sheeting," and I could not extend my legs. After they had their fun, they always taught me how they had done it. I was privileged to have the private instruction of these men who were experienced in barracks life and war.

I tried to outdrink them and became terribly sick on beer. I collapsed on a sidewalk, vomiting in the gutter, feeling an agony I had never known and hoping for death. I have never enjoyed the taste of beer since. While at Indiantown Gap, we often went to Oh Yes Hotel in Ono, Pennsylvania. I had a good singing voice, and while the sergeants drank, I sang with the band, songs such as "Sentimental Journey" and "Shanty Town."

On graduation from high school, five of my friends and I decided to join the army. There were no Ranger units in the army after World War II, but there was the opportunity to be a paratrooper. When we met at the soda fountain or poolroom, the five friends talked about what it would be like to jump from an airplane. When I told my father that I planned to join the army, tears came to his eyes. My mother did not want me to enlist, but both of them knew their youngest child was living a dream and needed a solid dose of reality.

4

Brownshoe Days

When it came to signing our enlistment papers, two of my five friends joined the air force. Three of us joined the army, and two of us were assigned to the same basic training platoon with G Company of the 39th Infantry at Fort Dix, New Jersey. When I went through my army physical, several doctors were examining men, poking and prodding their bodies. "Look at this," called my doctor to another, "I've never seen one this hard!" I blushed and was considerably embarrassed until it became apparent he was talking about my abdomen.

We had to work our way up to the rank of private. Until we completed basic training, we carried the lowly designation of recruit (Rct). I cringed when I put that on the return address of a letter. I knew much more about military life than my fellow trainees, so I was designated platoon guide and wore a temporary black armband with sergeant's stripes. My cot was near the platoon sergeant's room so that he could issue instructions and chores through me when he had other things to do. I was fanatical and ruthless in the pursuit of what I perceived as duty. Told to have the weeds cut when the sickles were locked away, I had my fellow recruits use mess kit knives to cut them. More than once I was challenged and fought, but managed to hold my position.

My platoon sergeant was astounded that I knew the field manual on drill and ceremonies better than he. I could recite much of it from memory. He took me on a tour of other barracks and won some bets from sergeants there. My platoon sergeant would say, "Tell them how to fix bayonets, Black." I would snap to the position of attention and, shouting the

28

commands, would recite, "War Department Basic Field Manual FM 22-5, Infantry Drill Regulations, August 4, 1941, chapter 3, paragraph 57, Being at order arms. One. FIX, two. BAYONETS. At the command BAYONETS if the bayonet scabbard is carried on the belt, move the muzzle of the rifle to the left front and grasp the rifle below the stacking swivel with the left hand; grasp the bayonet with the right. . . ." When sergeants heard my recitation, they would frequently go slack-jawed and mutter, "Well, I'll be gawd damned!"

The sergeants were pleased they had a recruit who cared. Most of them were given to complaining that "the army ain't like it used to be." Now and then when they had some beer in them they would add wistfully, "It never was."

Our steel helmets had a plastic liner in the same shape as the helmet; this was our usual headgear that we wore to and in class. It was sometimes difficult to stay awake in droning lectures, especially after the noon meal. The cadre carried wooden swagger sticks with a .30-caliber shell casing on the butt end. If a man began to nod, he would be hit over the helmet liner with the butt end of the stick. It was like a ringing of large church bells in our skulls.

One day as we were in formation, the platoon sergeant gave an improper command. Without thinking, I bellowed "AS YOU WERE," countermanding his order. For a recruit to countermand the order of a platoon sergeant was unheard of. It simply was not done. He was on me with shock and fury. I learned in a hurry that being right is no protection. I lost my arm brassard rank and was sent to the rear of the formation. Fortunately, the man who replaced me had an ass that waddled when he marched. The platoon sergeant also remembered the money I was winning for him. I was soon back out front.

When I was selected as guidon bearer for the company, I felt as though Gaius Julius Caesar had personally appointed me as Aquilifier carrying the eagle of a Roman legion at the right front of the column. With my head full of dreams of glory, I saw myself at the forefront of a charge, waving the

Infantry's blue swallowtail guidon of Company G 39th Infantry and inspiring my faltering comrades to victory. I was soon to get a dose of reality.

My sheltered upbringing had not prepared me for some of my experiences in the army. Within a week my wallet was stolen. When I went to the shower I would place the wallet under my pillow. The thief saw me do that and I lost all that I had. Twelve dollars was a considerable amount of money to a recruit making seventy-five dollars a month. Military units live or die on the trust men have for each other. When a barracks thief was caught, he was given no mercy or opportunity for legal maneuvers. The training cadre informed us that we were expected to handle these matters within the family of our platoon. They told us that it was not unusual for people to get hurt falling down stairs from the second floor.

We caught our thief as he attempted to steal a wallet from a footlocker. We beat him to the floor, kicked him, and then put his hand on the open footlocker from which he had attempted to steal and slammed the lid. The platoon cadre took him away and we never saw him again. There were no thefts in our barracks thereafter.

Some of the men did not shower—they had grown up filthy and stank. These men got a GI shower. A number of us would strip them and drag their nude bodies to the shower. They were forced to lather with carbolic soap, and we then scrubbed them with the stiff bristle scrub brushes that we used on the floors. We had two men who underwent that treatment, but they only needed it once.

Mail call was the highlight of the day. My first letter from my girlfriend was fifty-three pages in length. We were so filled with love for each other. I wrote her that I expected to rise to be a general, and we would be married and have a great life. Due to a hurried call to a formation, I left my unfinished letter lying open on my bunk. While inspecting the barracks, a corporal read what I had written and gave it to the platoon sergeant, who read it aloud at the formation. The platoon laughed at me and I was terribly embarrassed.

Sometimes after mail call, a man would not go to the mess hall to eat. He would lie on his bunk, often with tears in his eyes, staring into space, and snarling at anyone who asked him a question. He had received the letter we called the "Dear John." His girl back home would not wait—she was breaking off the relationship. It seemed that girls went through a course of instruction on writing Dear John letters, since practically all such letters began with the words, "This is the hardest letter I have ever had to write." We took pity on those who received this shock and consoled our own private fears with the words "Not my girl." My Dear John had the standard opening and followed with the words "I've met another red-haired boy named Bob that I love very much. . . ." It was short and direct, and a knife pierced my heart. The hurt was years in healing.

That evening we were marched to the theater, where a recruiting team from the 505th Parachute Infantry Regiment of the 82d Airborne Division showed a film and gave a presentation on basic airborne training. These paratroopers wore jump boots that gleamed like polished jewels, their uniforms fit them like another layer of skin, and their jaunty overseas caps had the red, white, and blue patch that featured a parachute and glider. Some of my companions said anyone who volunteered was crazy. I hurried to sign up.

Marching, weapons training and firing, and first aid were among the subjects that filled our days. We enjoyed the venereal disease films. We did not care about the disease. Venereal disease was what other people got, those people who came from a bad home. The VD films always featured short-skirted women that we wished we could go to bed with. "Take a prophylactic," warned the films, but few men wanted to squeeze a substance up the head of their penis.

Each Friday night we had a GI party when we scrubbed the wooden barracks floors on hands and knees. Saturday morning was standby inspection, standing stiffly at attention beside your bunk while company officers made detailed examinations of equipment and personal cleanliness. I respected sergeants; I thought they were demigods. But officers were creatures descended from heaven. When an officer halted before us, we brought our rifles to a diagonal position, known as port arms, and released the rifles into his grasp just as his hand touched the stock of the rifle. Anyone who held on to the weapon was in trouble. If the officer dropped the rifle, he was embarrassed and we were inwardly wild with joy. The belief was that if they dropped the rifle, they had to clean it. I never tried to drop a rifle on an officer. I looked upon them as being the ultimate authority of heaven. You do not drop a rifle on God.

A first lieutenant inspecting my rifle asked me to recite a general order, one of those standard instructions soldiers were required to learn before doing guard duty. I knew them well, but I was so afraid of making a mistake before him that I could only stammer. He was a kind man. He asked me where I was from and gave my brain a chance to thaw before I answered his initial question. Not every officer took that approach, and no self-respecting sergeant would.

Winter was coming on, and it was a cold one with an early snow. As we went on bivouac, the icy winds howling about us were fit companions to the studied, often painful movement of our bodies. We slept in small two-man tents called "pup tents." Our sleeping bags were the World War II variety consisting of two army blankets in a canvas shell. They were designed for survival, not comfort. The nights were worse than the days. One night the water froze in the canteen I had beside my sleeping bag.

Basic training ended and I was promoted to private, making $82.50 a month. My buddy from back home was assigned to the 2d Infantry Division. I was selected to go to leaders' course. For the next six weeks I experienced the initial steps of learning to be a leader of men. It is one thing to have rank, it is something else to be a leader. Leadership is an ancient and honorable art with principles that while simple are all too often forgotten or put aside by men who may rise to high rank.

Since there was no algebra or Latin in leaders' course, I graduated as the outstanding student of my class. The man who was my primary competition and I were running neck and neck until the last exercise in patrolling. Our mission was to lead a combat patrol against an enemy outpost. He led his men along the slope of a hill. Unfortunately for him, it was the wrong side of the hill. He was seen by the opponents long before he got to the objective, and they were ready for him. I looked for the worst possible terrain, a route that most people would not choose. We waded through swamps and chest-deep water and came out where the "enemy" did not expect us. My company commander said he would recommend me for Officers' Candidate School, but I wanted to go airborne. I felt that with my talent I would be at least a captain in another year.

The sunshine of my glory did not prevail for long. When the course ended, there was a brief period over the Christmas holidays before the next course of instruction would start at the Airborne School at Fort Benning, Georgia. I was retained at Fort Dix and carried in the dreaded designation of "holdover." As platoon guide with an arm brassard in basic and in leaders' course, I had not pulled the many odious duties the army had for a young soldier. Now the full weight of bureaucratic attention fell upon me. I quickly learned how lowly a private is. Every day I was scrubbing pots and pans, cleaning latrines, or caring for barracks fires. I had applied for Christmas leave, a leave I was supposedly entitled to, as I had had none after basic training. However, my name did not appear on the list.

The morning before Christmas was bitterly cold. I was cleaning ashes from the coal-fired furnaces of the barracks, putting them in tall ash cans, and taking the cans to the street for pickup. It was heavy lifting in that awful cold. Weary, I decided to accomplish the dual purpose of resting and warming my body. I raised my body and sat down with my rump in a can of warm ashes. Charles Dickens was only half right—it was the worst of times and the worst of times. Misery was in my soul. A taxicab driver making a pickup yelled, "Merry Christmas, Soldier!" "Go to hell!" I yelled back.

There is a God, there must be, for shortly thereafter

another soldier came by and told me my name was on the bulletin board for leave starting that day. Sergeants of the period usually had some means of making extra money. Some had automobiles. When going on leave, they would take the less fortunate who were heading in the same direction and who could pay. I learned of a sergeant going to Pittsburgh. Since Carlisle was on his route, for the outrageous sum of seven dollars he gave me a lift. Four other soldiers were crowded in with us.

Christmas was the great celebration at our house, the gathering of our family. Mom cooked and Dad took photographs. My brother and my sister were both married and parenting little children. Beginning in 1947, in addition to my presents, my mother put a Christmas card under the tree for me. It was a card with a beautiful inscription about a little boy grown to a man, and a mother's memories. She kept that card and would add the numerical description of the year. She did this until her death in 1963. If I could not come home for Christmas, my location in the world would be shown beside the number of the year.

5

Airborne, All the Way

At the Airborne School, sergeants were demons from the underworld. Many were from the poverty-stricken coalfields of Ohio and Pennsylvania, the Deep South, and the hills of Appalachia. I learned that Harlan County, Kentucky, was the birthplace of many sergeants. There was a saying of the time, "You found a home in the army." This was certainly true for these men. They had power and they used it.

We came into Airborne training through Headquarters and Service Company. The top sergeant of a company is the first sergeant. Way out of their hearing, we called them "first pig" or "first hog." The first sergeant of Headquarters and Service Company was Charles Craig, known throughout the army as "Charming Charlie." Craig was reputed to be the push-up champion of the army. It was said he could do five hundred push-ups. Craig and his subordinates were terrors who drove us relentlessly. Inside our barracks, we would hurry to put our uniforms and equipment in order, knowing that at any moment the stentorian roar of the first pig would come.

"BY THE TIME I COUNT TO TEN, I WANT EVERY SWINGIN' DICK STANDING TALL OUT HERE IN FORMATION. . . . WUN . . . TWOP . . . THREEP . . ."

"SHIT FIRE!" a sergeant would scream at me. I tried my best to comply.

There was no "consideration-of-others" training in the brownshoe army that I entered, and Airborne was run-run-run. Any deviation from instruction brought instant retaliation. The push-up was the ever-present remedy "HELL-DAMN, DROP AND GIVE ME TWENTY-FIVE!"

a sergeant would bark. To be facedown, pushing away the world, was routine.

Sergeants were innovative with the English language. Craig would stand us tall, and anyone who displeased him would hear his bellowing voice shouting: "DADDY-DADDY-DADDY-BULL PUSSY! GET YO' SELF UP IN THAT TREE AND FLAP YO' ARMS LIKE A BIG-ASSED BIRD!" No matter the heat or cold, training went on, beginning with the early-morning five-mile run. It was not truly running. We moved in what was called the "airborne shuffle," more comparable to a jog, and sang Jody Cadence (see the glossaries at the back of this book for an explanation of this and other military terms). We jogged along the Chattahoochee River and Lawson Airfield. A hill there was torture to many men, but not for me. This was soldiering, and I loved it so.

Various devices were used to train US Army paratroopers in World War II. They were so effective that most have stood the test of time. We practiced entering a shell that simulated the fuselage of an aircraft. Benches lined each side and there were two steel cables overhead, one on each side of the aircraft. We would sit on the benches and practice the command sequence of parachute jumping until it became routine. We would rise from the sitting position on the command "Stand up and hook up." Facing in the direction of the aircraft door, we hooked our static line snap over the cable that ran from the front to the rear of the aircraft and made certain the snap had locked in place. Since we were unable to see the arrangement on our backs, the command "Check equipment" had us examining the parachute arrangement of the man to our immediate front. "Sound off for equipment check" was followed by a down-the-line shouting of "One OK. . . . Two OK, etc." The next command was "Close up and stand in the door." With the hand toward the interior of the aircraft holding the static line, we would shuffle close to the door. The lead man would throw his static line toward the front of the simulated aircraft to keep the line clear for those who would follow. He would turn into the doorway in a crouching position, eyes on the horizon, arms spread downward in the diagonal, and hands on the outside of the aircraft door. On the command "Go!" the first man sprang outward. We hurried forward through the door, jumping with hands on each side of the reserve parachute that we wore on our chests. As we jumped, we turned our bodies toward the rear of the mock aircraft. The speed of the aircraft and wind from the aircraft propellers, called "prop blast," would accomplish this turn on an actual jump.

Falling through space, a body quickly reaches 125 miles an hour, or about sixty yards a second. Hopefully, we would not be long at that speed. The static line extended from the cable and would tear the backpack cover from the rear of our parachute. The backpack was attached to the top of the nylon parachute by cord, and the extension of the connected static line and backpack would begin to pull the parachute open. When static line, backpack cover, parachute, and body were fully extended, the cord at the top of the parachute would break free and the twenty-eight-foot-circumference parachute would open. Four webbed risers secured our harness to the chute. By pulling down on those in the front, side, or rear, we could guide the parachute. Preparing to land, we would bring our chins down, elbows in, knees bent, and seek to collapse and roll sideways into the impact—this was appropriately called a "parachute landing fall," or PLF.

Initially we practiced the maneuvers on the ground, including inside the harness sheds, where we donned the sturdy webbing and jumped from platforms. We became accustomed to the harness and the fall. Part of the parachute webbing runs between the thighs. It was not advantageous to have the testicles caught beneath that webbing. On long tables in long buildings, we learned to pack the parachutes we would use in jumping. The theory was, "If your parachute does not open and you fall eleven hundred feet to the ground, you packed the parachute, so don't go running to the army to complain."

While putting the back cover on my parachute, I noticed the imprint of the manufacturer, "C. H. Masland and Sons,

Carlisle, Pa." I felt the warm glow of home. Carlisle, Pennsylvania, was always close to a soldier. The Medical Service
school had been at Carlisle Barracks for many years, and the
wheeled ambulances and first aid packets that soldiers carried were developed in my hometown.

Some men did not complete basic army training—a
greater number did not complete Airborne School. It was
physically and mentally demanding. The mental challenge
was to control the natural fear that was a clarion call to save
one's life. If nature had intended us to jump from great
heights, we would have been given wings or a spectacular
ability to bounce.

Most who did not complete Airborne School quit on the
thirty-four-foot tower. Thirty-four feet does not constitute a
great height until you are standing in that open door in harness, uncertain of the fact that when you jump, your fall will
be checked and there will be a ride down a wire to a berm.
The mind says, "That ain't gonna happen—you're gonna
die." But most of us can't stand the thought of quitting, so
we made the jump and endured the disparaging comments
on us and our ancestry by the watchful-eyed sergeants. They
always followed their colorful critique with the opportunity
for more push-ups.

We progressed to the 250-foot towers that had been purchased from the 1939–40 world's fair and have long been the
primary landmarks of Fort Benning, Georgia. One by one
we donned parachute harnesses and were hauled to the top
with an open chute surrounded by a ring spread above us.
About six feet from the top, the machinery would stop and
we would hang there in the silence of breathless anticipa-
tion. Then came a whir of machinery. We rose the remaining
distance and the parachute released from the ring. We pulled
mightily on the risers in a hurried effort to steer the parachute away from the tower. The landing never pleased the in-
structors. "Drop like a scalded dog!" and "Get your face in
the clay!" were routine admonitions. As soon as we shed the
harness, we stood tall, got reamed out, and went facedown

in the dirt. The starting position of the push-up was known as the "front leaning rest." What a misnomer that was!

My first parachute jump was from a twin-boomed C-82 aircraft. A parachute harness was not designed for comfort. Legs spread wide from the constriction of the tight harness, bent over from the weight of equipment, we hobbled to the flight line and pulled ourselves up the ladder and through the open door of the C-82. Never having flown in an airplane, I felt like a dazed lamb being led to slaughter. As I began my climb, I patted the metal skin of the aircraft and said, "Well, baby, I'm going up in you, but I'm not coming down in you." It became my superstition to pat the plane and say those words before every jump. Like most superstitions, it took more effort to break than begin.

The jumpmaster on my first jump had an 11th Airborne Division patch on his right shoulder; he had served in combat with this famed division. It was said he had forty jumps, maybe more. We took some comfort that he had survived. Above the roar of the engines, his orders were crisp and clear. As we flew through fear-filled skies, he stood in the open door of the aircraft and was the epitome of courage and élan. We took heart from that and looked to him as a buttress against our fears. Men tried to look unconcerned, but avoided each other's eyes. The soldier next to me was a mountain boy from Tennessee. He began to sing "Rock of ages, cleft for me. . . ." The man on his right screamed, "Shut the fuck up!"

Most of us probably felt we were going to die, but we knew we had to jump anyway or be shamed. When the moment of truth came, the jumpmaster turned his face to us, and we quailed before his piteous gaze. His entire being defined fear. He looked at us with terror in his eyes. His lips moved as though in prayer. Then his eyes closed, and it appeared that he fainted and fell out the door. An agonizing groan arose from all of us who witnessed this. Then training took over. We hurried to the door and outward into space. I felt the fall and then the snap and pop of the parachute opening above my head. It worked. It really worked. The two most gratifying experiences in life are sexual release and to have a parachute open safely over your head. If only we could combine them.

All around me were the camouflaged parachutes of my classmates swaying to and fro. Joyful shouts came from men pulling on their risers to guide themselves from collision. We were jumping the T-7, a World War II–model parachute. On opening, the sensation was that of being on the end of a cracking whip. Metal D rings on the harness would slap against the side of our steel helmets with a sudden clang. Our shoulders would be bruised from the sudden shock. We called these purple marks "riser burns." Though our steel helmet chin straps were of a style that cupped the chin, helmets occasionally flew from our heads during this opening shock. Those on the ground below had to be wary of this rain of steel.

The parachute did not descend in a straight line to earth. Like the pendulum on a clock, each man swayed beneath one. But this oscillation was far more violent than a clock pendulum's. It was possible for the parachute to touch the earth while the paratrooper was still in the air along a horizontal line. When that occurred we were slammed to earth, and men were frequently injured.

I made an acceptable landing, ran around my parachute to collapse it, removed my harness, rolled my chute, and moved hurriedly to the waiting trucks. Another wave of aircraft was coming in, and I found that trying to dodge a falling steel helmet was a challenge. My jumpmaster from the 11th Airborne was standing by a truck. As I drew near, a jumpmaster from another aircraft approached him and said, "Well, did you scare the hell out of them?" "I sure did" was the proud reply.

I began to think about the correlation between leadership and acting. This sergeant had just taught me that training can overcome fear. Acting is often used by leaders to make their point. Properly used, dramatics and even props are useful. George Patton had one style of acting and Omar Bradley another. Bradley was no good-old-boy simple soldier, but that was the image he used. MacArthur was a master of dramatics and used a corncob pipe as an easily identifiable prop. Ridgway carried a hand grenade on his pack harness. Four-star generals don't need hand grenades.

I never saw a man freeze up in the door of an aircraft. By the time we flew, we had jumped so often from the towers that training took over. The parachute jumps proceeded in routine fashion. The more frequently we do something properly, the easier it becomes. Jumping frequently was enjoyable. Later, I hated those long intervals when funding cutbacks meant we could jump only once every three months. An ever-increasing fear would build in me and not abate until the parachute opened above my head.

The last week of Airborne School was devoted to glider training. We used Waco gliders that would carry a ten-man infantry squad and flight crew. A jeep and a 75mm pack howitzer were also standard loads. The gliders were made of fabric over aluminum struts. A plywood floor covering with tie-downs was used when hauling equipment. Many men were more frightened of flying in gliders than of parachuting. We were only along for the ride and had no control of events in a glider. Glider flights were seldom smooth, and vomit on the floor was not unusual. We were cautioned not to step on the fabric skin of the aircraft. Imagination ran rampant when we received that warning. There was not much to be seen as a passenger of a glider, save to look over the pilot's shoulder at the towrope that ran to the pulling aircraft. When the release was made, the nose of the glider would sweep up, then we would begin our descent. We were glad to earn our glider wings and have that experience behind us. Some time later a glider crashed, killing all on board. Other means of transportation were being developed and the army discontinued the glider program.

Graduation was a thrill, though none of my family were present. I did not expect them to drive down from Pennsylvania. The roads of the period went through every town and stoplight, and southern towns in particular had police forces that looked for cars with license plates from Damnyankee land. My paratrooper wings felt good against my chest, but they were dull in appearance. No one liked the army-issue dull wings, but supply sergeants at the Airborne School sold commercial models that were bright and shiny. The Corcoran jump boot was a symbol of paratrooper pride. We had our khaki shirts and our Eisenhower jackets tailored skintight. We wore jaunty overseas caps whose design reminded lustful men of basic parts of a woman. They were called "cunt" caps. Enlisted men's caps had colored piping on the edge that indicated the branch of the army the individual was assigned to—blue for the infantry, red for artillery, for example. Each hat also had a round red, white, and blue patch that featured the parachute and the glider. These hats could be easily folded and tucked under the belt. Some men sewed a silver dollar under that round patch, making their hat a weapon. For a young man in good physical condition, the US Army uniforms of that period were superb. When worn by a paratrooper, they were classic. Naturally, the army changed them.

6

Enlisted Life in
the 82d Airborne

On graduation from jump school, I was proud to be a soldier, prouder still to be a paratrooper, part of the 82d Airborne Division, America's guard of honor. Somewhat behind schedule for becoming a general, I was promoted to private first class. In the reality of a Fort Bragg latrine, it all seemed like a grim joke, one I had played upon myself. I finished cleaning the porcelain of the urinal, then picked up a blitz cloth and clean rag to begin polishing the horizontal brass pipe that supplied the urinals' wash-down water. Anything brass had to be polished. That commandment was right up there with "Thou shalt have no other gods before me."

My link with the sanity of the outside world was a Philco portable radio about the size of a toaster. It was maroon in color and covered with that remarkable new substance called "plastic." The radio rested safely in a sink. With the division band now playing in the distance, I turned the radio on, found some music, and began the rest of my latrine duties.

I was scrubbing a brown stain from the inside of a toilet bowl when the music from the radio stopped and an announcer brought the news that changed my life.

"An estimated ninety thousand North Korean troops supported by tanks, artillery, and aircraft have invaded South Korea. The South Koreans are retreating. Hurried consultations are under way in Washington, and American military forces are being put on alert. . . . Stay tuned for further developments."

It was war! I threw the bowl brush in the air and danced

43

around the latrine. The 82d Airborne Division was America's guard of honor, its first line of defense. We would be on planes going overseas within hours. I would be a soldier. I would fight for my country!

But nothing changed for me. The 82d Airborne Division stayed at Fort Bragg. No one had told those of us at the bottom that the 82d Airborne Division was the strategic reserve for the United States. If the Communists were willing to pick a fight in Asia, they might do so in Europe. Historically, Americans have considered Europe more important to their interests than Asia. Therefore, the 82d Airborne Division would stay at Fort Bragg, to be used in Europe if needed. How could God permit this?

I had to live with the possibility that men in the National Guard and Reserve might get to war before me. The radio announcement that thrilled me was grim news to others. The army is like a rubber band. It stretches out in time of need to fulfill its mission and contracts in peacetime. This contraction wreaks havoc on the lives of patriots who answer the call to colors. Men called to active duty usually lose their civilian jobs. Reserve officers could not count on remaining in the army. At the end of World War II, men who were colonels one day were corporals the next. Those who are regular army have some protection, though their careers are stunted. It is the reserve officer, the temporary sergeant, the citizen soldier who carries so much of the brunt of our wars, who gets the boot.

Only nine years after Americans proclaimed "Remember Pearl Harbor," they had forgotten the painful lessons of being unready for war. There is an old rhyme that soldiers know:

> God and the soldier we adore
> In times of danger, nothing more
> When the danger is passed and all is righted
> God is forgotten and the soldier slighted.

When the Korean War began, the United States was not ready to fight. The twelve-million-man military, the eighty-nine-division army of World War II, had melted away under the leadership of President Harry Truman. The post–World War II army consisted of nine under-strength divisions. Infantry regiments were reduced by a battalion, and battalions were minus a rifle company. Despite protests from army leaders, the Truman administration and Congress provided little money for training or equipment.

Secretary of State Dean Acheson made a speech in January 1950 in which he outlined the American defense perimeter. It did not include Korea. Russian dictator Joseph Stalin and his North Korean allies saw this as an opportunity to strike. War was brought on by lack of a clear defense policy and military unpreparedness.

We attended "why we fight" classes, but I acquired a broader view of the war from magazines and newspapers at the Fort Bragg library. I was hungry for knowledge, as most of us knew nothing of Korea. I learned that Korea is a peninsula about 500 miles long and some 200 miles across at its widest point. In the north, across the Yalu River, is Manchuria, and in the south some 120 miles from Pusan is Japan. Throughout history, Korea was frequently a battleground as forces invaded from Japan or China. Japan annexed Korea in 1910 and ruled until World War II ended in 1945. The Communist-led Soviet Union had very little to do with the defeat of Japan, but they paid the heaviest price in the war against Nazi Germany, suffering some twenty million dead. The Soviets therefore insisted that they occupy part of the defeated Japanese empire. Trusting to the good intentions of our former ally, the United States agreed to divide Korea along an imaginary line on the ground in what was believed to be temporary occupation duties. This device of the mapmaker was the 38th parallel. North of that line, the Russians set about building a well-trained and well-equipped army. The American military effort in the south was halfhearted at best. Korea was not considered important.

Two of the eight divisions in the North Korean army were composed of experienced soldiers who had fought in China under Mao Tse-tung during the Communist defeat of the

Nationalist Chinese. The plan of attack on South Korea was devised by Russian advisors.

As the North Koreans drove southward, the action of the United States was initially to respond with air forces. Soon American ground forces were committed. Small numbers of ill-trained army-of-occupation troops from Japan were thrown into the cauldron of war and fared as badly as the South Koreans. The Korean War became a race for time, but that was not evident at the lower echelons of the 82d Airborne Division.

I was sitting on my cot with my Philco portable radio beside me when an officer unexpectedly entered the barracks. Someone cried TENCH—HUT! and I leaped to my feet. The radio bounced to the floor and shattered the case. All of us stayed frozen in the position of attention. The officer saw what happened and expressed regret, but did not offer to pay for a new radio. My link with the outside world was broken. I did not have the money to replace it.

My life as a soldier slave continued unabated. Whitewashing rocks was a passion of the army. Rocks were used to decorate the bases of signs or walkways, and no rock must be left in its natural color. It was hard to be patriotic when painting rocks. At night, some men would go to visit girlfriends or take their chances in the bar and hooker section of Fayetteville, North Carolina, known as "combat alley." Those of us on the bottom rung spent most of our nights in our undershorts and T-shirts, sitting on our footlockers, spit-shining boots and polishing our brass. This was "brown-shoe" army life. Our boots were cordovan color, and we used cans of Kiwi polish to make them shine. For most men, the top of the shoe polish can contained water, but others used Mennen's Skin Bracer to bring forth that final gleam. Some believed that a better shine was achieved by lighting the shoe polish with a match. This Kiwi flambé frequently burned their fingers. Wrapping a piece of linen cloth around the forefinger, we would touch it to the shoe polish, working the polish into the firm leather toe and heel of the boot, and then touch some water to the spot. With a clean section of wetted cloth, we would again use the covered forefinger to polish boot and heel to a glasslike finish. The edges of the sole and heel were then coated with heel dressing to make them shine. The Corcoran jump boots were the paratroopers' pride. Step on a man's boot and you had a fight on your hands; catch a nonjumping soldier in Corcorans and he was left barefoot. Paratroopers bloused their trouser legs, holding the blouse along the top edge of the boot with rubber bands or condoms. To make the blouse hang horizontal, some men even used tire chain made into a ring.

Only paratroopers bloused their trousers. Other soldiers wore theirs straight. These nonairborne people were called "straight-legs" or "legs." These creatures did not jump from airplanes, and therefore it was assumed that they were without courage. I remembered the line infantry sergeants in the Army Reserve who taught me so much about war. I had a cousin who had fought in World War II with the 3d Infantry Division. The experiences he related were actions of brave men. Though I had my doubts about calling other soldiers derogatory names, I was young, cocky, and tended to run with the pack.

Every trooper had at least two pairs of jump boots, three if he could afford them. The best and most highly polished pair was kept in the shoe line under the cot for inspections. This line included a seldom-worn pair of traditional shoes, called "low quarters," and a pair of shower thongs. The inspection jump boots were never taken to the field (on military exercises), where they might be scratched. The field pair of boots was hidden in the cloth barracks bag tied at the head or foot of the cot. The barracks bag was the single private item of the soldier, a place for dirty clothes. Looking inside the barracks bag was not part of a just inspection by an officer.

We shined the brass of our belt buckles and the brass US and crossed muskets of the Infantry that we wore on the collar. To do this we used a rag and a substance called Brasso or a cloth called a blitz cloth. Brass- and shoe-polishing equipment were essential items for a soldier of this time.

Just as in basic training, Saturday morning was barracks inspection. That meant scrubbing the barracks floor on Friday night. Everything that could shine, did. The olive drab woolen army blankets were stretched taut across our cots. Bouncing a quarter on your blanket was a good test to make certain it was sufficiently taut. Uniforms were hung in a prescribed sequential order with the wire hangers two fingers' width apart. The footlocker was open, with shaving gear on display. No one used what was displayed. It was only for inspection. It was a lot of work getting your bunk area ready for Saturday morning inspection. Some men slept on the floor on Friday nights.

Those of us who were clerks did not get the chance to fire weapons as often as those in the parachute infantry regiments. Due to lack of funds, weapons were also limited in number until the war came. I loved being on the firing line at the range. Although I was a natural left-handed shooter, the army made me fire from the right shoulder. Army rifles ejected cartridge casings, called "brass," to the right. When finished shooting on the firing line, we would pick up ("police up") the brass.

One story going around was that during a movie at the post theater a woman in the film had shot her lover and cried out, "Oh, I have killed him. What shall I do?" Some paratrooper yelled out, "Police up your brass and move off the firing line!"

0430 hours. The heavy hand of the charge of quarters (CQ) roused me from a sleep of exhaustion. The nerve center of a company or detachment was the office known as the orderly room. At night, some corporal or sergeant would have the duty known as charge of quarters. When the company commander, first sergeant, and company clerk went home, the charge of quarters would stay in the orderly room, answer telephone calls, pass on messages, and perform routine duties, the most demanding of which was to rise early and make certain the cooks and kitchen police (KPs) were prepared to begin their duties. The mark of servitude for a KP was a towel tied to the foot of his cot, which allowed the

CQ to enter the dim visibility of the barracks at night and rouse the unfortunate for his work.

With repetition comes routine. As a fixture in the kitchen seemingly as permanent as the sinks, I had a well-established routine. Having showered and shaved the night before, I would put on my oldest and dirtiest fatigue uniform and head for the mess hall. Army mess halls came in two sizes. One was a very large facility called a consolidated mess where some 800–1,000 men of a battalion might eat, and the other was the smaller company mess that fed approximately 200. The smaller arrangement was favored by the troops, as each unit sought to have the best-decorated mess hall and serve the best food.

Soldiers who ate garbage when growing up would complain about army food. I enjoyed army "chow," though there was some adjustment. I had never seen potatoes as part of the breakfast meal and, since I was raised in the North, had no understanding of or desire for grits. The army never served the scrapple that Pennsylvania farm boys loved. Looking for ways to conserve money, the army tried various cost-cutting programs. TAKE ALL YOU WANT, BUT EAT ALL YOU TAKE read a sign that hung in the mess hall. The cooks tried to enforce this and prove their authority by yelling at us lower ranks when we still had any scraps left on the aluminum tray. I enjoyed the food, but I hated army cooks.

Before I started my regular kitchen job, I had other duties. In many units the kitchen police had to start the fires in the stoves and have them ready for the cooks. We also peeled bags of potatoes or broke hundreds of eggs into bowls, where they could be speedily used. People of little authority often abuse what they have, and many of the cooks I knew were among the worst. After the fires were built, they assigned jobs to the KPs. The best job was that of dining room orderly (DRO). This soldier set the tables: wiped off the oil-cloth-covered tables, and put out napkins, silverware, and pitchers filled with juice. He brought coffee for the cooks and looked after the senior sergeants, who had a reserved dining section. To be DRO was the dream of every KP. I never had that job.

As cooking for several hundred men requires the use of many large utensils, another KP was assigned to "pots and pans." A scrubbing sink and a rinsing sink were his world. A third KP had "trays, silverware, coffee mugs, and glasses." This was the first stop in the kitchen police system and the one I habitually occupied.

It is a long day, starting at 0430, that is, "four-thirty A.M. National Guard Time" we would say. All day long it was work and sweat in the humid atmosphere of the kitchen. We also sweated to prepare for the nightly inspection by the duty officer. One officer would eat a randomly selected meal in the mess hall each day to ensure that the troops were being well fed. Then the duty officer for the night would make an inspection of the mess hall at the close of our workday.

On the days I did my job as file clerk, I would find large stacks of onionskin file copies waiting to be stuffed into their appropriate folders. Given my other duties and an avalanche of army paper, I could never keep abreast of the work. I had a macabre fascination for the death files. They usually contained gruesome details about some trooper whose parachute had not opened, resulting in him falling hundreds of feet to his death. Many mishaps were possible in parachuting. One man had the top of his parachute catch on a snap on his field pack. No one knew how he got into that position, but he never had a chance to pull the ripcord on his reserve chute. The main parachute of an experienced jumper failed to open; it streamed upward in what was known as a cigarette roll. He pulled the ripcord on his reserve parachute, and it entangled with the main. Observers related that he maintained perfect body position and was trying to sort out lines all the way to earth. As a paratrooper, I would have been better off not reading those files.

A Coke and a hot dog at the post exchange and a movie at the post theater were my primary entertainment. The film *Battleground*, a story of the 101st Airborne Division at the Battle of the Bulge in World War II, was a powerful war film, one of the best ever made. It was a vivid reminder that there was a war being fought in Korea and I was not part of it. Could I stand up to what those men of World War II had endured—could I measure up? I had to know.

Payday. As a PFC, I now received $95.55 per month. If I held that rank for ten years, I would make $132.30 a month. As a paratrooper earning hazardous duty pay, an additional $50.00 per month was added. Those who had contact with lepers received the same amount. We stood in line before the pay officer, saluted, and watched with great anticipation as our meager dollars were counted out before us. Next, we ran the gauntlet of a series of "collection tables." Projects to improve the mess hall or company area required money. The Red Cross, Community Chest, and every other charitable organization in the nation was in the soldiers' pay line. It was expected that you would contribute; to not do so would mean that your commander could not report 100 percent participation, and that would reflect badly on him. It meant you had no unit pride. It also meant you went even deeper on the shit list. Seething with anger, we paid. Waiting like vultures at the end of the pay line were the army bankers, sergeants who would lend money at the middle of the month to the lesser ranks. The interest rates were outrageous. It was three dollars for two or twenty dollars for fifteen.

Payday meant crap games. These were usually on the top floor of the barracks so there would be early warning in case an officer came. An olive drab army blanket draped over a footlocker and a pair of dice were the tools. The technique was to roll the dice on the blanket and bounce them off the footlocker.

Hoping to improve my meager fortunes, I entered a crap game. In three passes I lost my month's pay. I went downstairs and borrowed ten dollars from a friend and lost that in one pass. For an entire month I could not go to a movie or buy a Coke. Fortunately, I could eat at the mess hall, but it was a month of hell. I never tried serious gambling again.

7

A Ranger Born

Throughout July 1950 the war raged in Korea, with the North Koreans driving southward while the United States hurriedly sent troops who tried to stave off disaster. Other nations were sending small increments of troops and the fighting became known as a United Nations effort, even though the South Koreans and the United States were providing most of the men, and the money and materials were primarily coming from the United States. Our government spent a lot of time on mobilizing world opinion.

The North Koreans were a small but well-trained army. Special units often dressed in white civilian garb would infiltrate American positions, passing through our lines with the thousands of refugees who were on the roads fleeing south. In the rear areas, these units would reassemble and strike at communications centers, rear-area headquarters, and support units. Meanwhile, the main force, often led by Russian T-34 tanks, would attack in the front, flow around, isolate, and destroy any strong points. These tactics resulted in the primarily American and South Korean forces being driven southward into an area roughly the size of the city of Los Angeles. This was known as the Pusan Perimeter.

On 15 August, marines and soldiers of the US 7th Infantry Division landed in an amphibious end run, 170 miles behind enemy lines at the port city of Inchon. On the sixteenth our forces in the Pusan Perimeter attacked north, and by the twenty-sixth of August linkup occurred and the shattered North Korean army fled north. The consensus opinion of American politicians, military leaders, and the press was that the war would end before Christmas. I felt a sense of keen frustration at being denied my war.

We got the hopeful word early at 82d Airborne Division headquarters, and it soon spread like a whirlwind throughout the division. The word was "Rangers." The North Koreans' success at infiltrating units through American and South Korean positions had inspired Gen. Douglas MacArthur to develop an all-volunteer American unit that would strike the enemy behind their lines. In Washington, D.C., army chief of staff Gen. J. Lawton Collins decided to call for volunteers to undergo Ranger training. He also decided that every man who volunteered for the Rangers had to first be a paratrooper.

Throughout history, the Rangers have been small, highly select units. The army needed less than a thousand volunteers for the Rangers from the 82d Airborne Division. But before the process ended, five thousand regular army paratroopers of the division volunteered. I promptly went to my section sergeant and announced my intention to volunteer. Suddenly friendly, he initially tried to dissuade me. When that failed, he angrily told me to forget my request. I was in a critical position and was not going anywhere. I could not believe what I was hearing. How could a lowly file clerk be critical to the success of the 82d Airborne Division? I was critical because my departure would mean one less bare sleeve or one-striper to pull all the odious details. That meant some of his pets would have to do dirty work. Despite his objection, I put in my request. I paid dearly for it. Administrative supervisors have ways to delay, string out, and thwart the desires of those under them.

I knew the Korean War and I were made for each other. I had to find a way to get into this war. Seated at a long table with several large stacks of onionskin file copies to my front, I pondered the problem. There had to be a way out. An electric anger charged my brain and translated to action. Without conscious thought, I picked up the top file copy, crumpled it into a ball, and threw it in my wastebasket. The action was satisfying. I filed papers until anger returned, then crumpled another file copy and threw that away. This was revolutionary; it was sheer genius. I was amazed at the speed with which I could reduce a pile of file copies by the simple act of discarding them. I felt secure, as there were few times someone asked for file copies. What began as an occasional paper quickly grew to a hail of crumpled onionskin documents in my trash can.

This expeditious procedure lasted only a few days. An officer, an aide to the commanding general, put a paper on my desk and said, "File this." I glanced at it and saw it was a letter from my commanding general to his commander. This was their affair and of no interest to me, so I crumpled the letter and threw it away.

Some thirty minutes later the officer returned and said, "I need that file copy back." Now the enormity of what I had done came home. I was terrified. "Wha-wha-wha-what paper, Sir?" I stammered.

He was stunned, "The one I just gave you!"

"I-I-I, d-d-d-don't re-re-member any pa-pa-paper, Sir," I stammered and lied.

The mind has a tendency to block memory of a horrible experience that threatens us. The next thing I remember is coming back from noon chow. The section sergeant had my trash can on his desk. He would reach into the can, take out a crumpled ball of paper, use both hands to stretch it open, and lay it on a pile that rose ever higher.

I now passed beyond the glazed eyes of the section sergeant. He was stricken dumb by the administrative horror of my action. Marched before my commanding officer, I awaited my fate. Imagination ran rampant. Would I be shot into my coffin? Would the division band play? My company commander seemed more puzzled than angry.

"You know, you are not going to make corporal," he said. "You have been a good soldier. Why would you do such a thing?"

"Because there is a war on and I want to fight," I replied. "I want to be a Ranger, Sir."

"Son," he said with a wry grin, "you are going to get your wish."

Later, when I knew bureaucracy better, I came to the conclusion that the Adjutant General (AG) Section felt it best not to have people thinking they did not properly supervise their men. They had the general's letter. It was best to keep this quiet and let me go. It was probable that no one would ever again ask for the missing file copies. I learned later that some other men who volunteered for the Rangers also had a difficult time getting free. One man went absent without leave (AWOL) when his unit would not let him go. Others were given extra details and told they were letting their units down.

The Rangers would form, train, and fight as companies of 107 men and five officers. I was interviewed by Capt. James Herbert, who would command the 8th Ranger Infantry Company (Airborne). He never mentioned file copies or typing. He was interested in my knowledge of basic soldiering and my spirit. I was accepted and, along with other volunteers, was soon en route to Fort Benning, Georgia, and the newly formed Ranger Training Center.

To be a Ranger is to become part of a unique American military experience. Before there was a United States, this land was known as America. European settlers who came to this land in the 1600s found it far different from their previous experience. Europe was small. This new land was vast beyond the imagination, with great forests, rivers, and bays. There were no roads and no cities. In Europe, armies stood shoulder-to-shoulder and fired at point-blank range. In the new world, the European settler lived in terror of the Native American. The Indian would not stand and be butchered, and they did not move in vast armies. They primarily traveled in small war parties, did a thorough reconnaissance, and then made a swift attack and withdrawal. They were masters of the ambush and the raid. The early history of the European colonist in America was written in their blood and terror. Some men became better adapted to this new environment, men who were able to endure great hardship. They were at home in the forests. They studied the tactics of the Indian warrior and added to it the discipline and better weapons of the European settler. Soon they began to range outward to provide early warning of Indian attack and take the battle to the Indian. "This day ranged 15 miles," read an early report. The American Ranger was born.

The Rangers fought a half dozen wars before the United States came into being. John Stark, Nathan Hale, George Rogers Clark, Daniel Morgan, and Francis Marion were among Ranger heroes of the Revolutionary War. The Texas Rangers were initially a military force. Northern and Southern Rangers fought each other in the Civil War. Rangers led the way across the continent.

The Rangers were seldom of the regular army. They were volunteer citizen-soldiers, frequently fighting in the area of home. The result has always been a love-hate affair on the part of the conventional army. Since the French and Indian War, conventional generals have been trying to do away with the Rangers, but the Rangers keep coming back because they are needed. In World War II, when America wanted a force similar to the British Commandos, Gen. Lucian Truscott reached into American history and named these brave volunteers "Rangers."

My new comrades and I arrived at the Ranger Training Center in the Harmony Church area of Fort Benning, Georgia. This was some eight miles from the main post, a small collection of World War II barracks secluded to minimize distraction from training. Previous interviews had helped determine what positions we would occupy. I was assigned as a Browning automatic rifleman to the 3d Squad of the 3d Platoon of the 8th Airborne Ranger Company. The BAR, as this weapon was known, dated from World War I. It was first used there by my old outfit, the 79th Infantry Division. The BAR was a heavy brute, weighing twenty pounds without the sling and carrying a magazine containing twenty rounds of .30-caliber ammunition. Rifle companies of infantry battalions were twice the size of our 112-man Ranger companies, but we had two automatic rifles per ten-man squad while they had one. In fact, we had a wide variety of weapons that we could draw upon, depending on our mission.

My platoon leader was 2d Lt. Berk Strong. He had earned a Combat Infantry Badge in the South Pacific as an enlisted man serving as a scout. Berk Strong had a baby face. He looked younger than his men, and we were initially suspicious of him, wondering if someone so young appearing would measure up. We found that below that baby face was the heart of a lion.

Our platoon sergeant was Bill Cox. We called him "Wild Bill." He was mother, father, teacher, boss, and friend to us. When I think of what a sergeant should be, I think of Bill Cox.

We were issued weapons fresh from the box, wrapped in heavy waxed paper and covered in the heavy grease called cosmoline. It was a difficult job to clean the weapons, and I was amazed to see our officers working at our sides, an action that was unheard of. The Rangers really were different. The reality of that opinion quickly proved itself.

Training for combat began promptly and continued without letup. Little attention was paid to polish and shine. We were experienced soldiers and knew how to keep our barracks and equipment clean. There were no standby inspections, no Friday-night GI parties, scrubbing of barracks floors, or polishing brass. We fired .45-caliber pistols and submachine guns, carbines and M1 rifles, Browning automatic rifles and .30-caliber machine guns, 2.36- and 3.5-inch rocket launchers, 60mm mortars, and endured the earsplitting crack of 57mm recoilless rifles. We ran obstacles and had map-reading courses. Our day began with a five-mile run. We marched to and from our training areas, and some 50 percent of our training was done at night. In the blackness of a Georgia wood at midnight it was routine to collide with a tree. When we were not moving it was difficult to tell men apart from the scenery. Sometimes we would relay a signal to move out and find we were talking to a tree. It took a lot of practice to move and fight as a team at night.

Our morning runs were filled with the leader's song and our responses:

> Here we go . . . HERE WE GO
> All the way . . . ALL THE WAY
> Gotta run . . . GOTTA RUN
> Every day . . . EVERY DAY
> Airborne! . . . AIRBORNE!
> Ranger! . . . RANGER!
> Chorus: "I wanna be an Airborne Ranger,
> 　　I wanna live a life of danger. . . .
> 　　Airborne! . . . Ranger!"

Now came word that the Chinese army had crossed the Yalu River and dealt the Americans, South Koreans, and other United Nations forces a stinging defeat, driving them southward. We now knew we would fight.

The men who prepared us for battle had learned their trade in the OSS (Office of Strategic Services, predecessor to the CIA), First Special Service Force, and Rangers of World War II. Our teachers included Edwin Walker, Francis Dawson, Bull Simon, and John Singlaub, names well known to those who go behind enemy lines.

We practiced laying mines and setting booby traps. Demolitions was a favored class. We used plastic C4 explosive that could be rolled in strips or in a ball safely. We would throw balls of C4 at each other. It became dangerous when a detonating cap was added. We blew up stumps and trees and telephone poles, then progressed to preparing bridges and buildings for demolition. Since these were often too valuable to destroy, we searched the woods for old unused structures. A number of old outhouses scattered about the woods of Fort Benning did not survive these excursions.

The 1st, 2d, and 4th Ranger Companies had completed training and were en route to Korea. Ranger training at Fort Benning was now operating in high gear. The 3d, 5th, 6th, 7th, and 8th Ranger Companies were undergoing training at the same time. These were independent companies whose common bond was "Ranger," but rivalry between companies was fierce.

We were men who had volunteered for the army, the Airborne, the Rangers, and for combat. In the Rangers we were treated like responsible men. We were treated with respect. Those who did not measure up disappeared. A vehicle with a white flag followed marches and was present in training areas. If a man felt he could not continue or wanted out, he would get on that vehicle. He and his equipment would be gone from the barracks before we returned. A "washout" board of officers eliminated those who did not measure up to Ranger standards. Many of the men who did not succeed as Rangers did well elsewhere.

Our officers trained with us, leading us in all aspects. Company commander Capt. Jim Herbert was born in West "by God" Virginia. West Virginia is a mountainous state. We came to believe Captain Herbert was born marching and climbing. We fervently wished that he would tire, but he just kept marching, marching, and marching, with us behind him.

Many of us were suprised to find that our first sergeant in the 8th Rangers would be Charles Craig from the Airborne School. Most of us expected we would soon be facedown in the dirt, but now he was one of us, training at our side.

We were more than a band of brothers. We were a bond of brothers. The sharing of military experience bonds men in layers of loyalty. The thirty-three-man Ranger platoon was my immediate family. The rest of the company were close relatives who lived nearby. The men of other Ranger companies were extended family. Anyone not Ranger was an outlander. To move from one platoon to another, from one barracks to another in our company would be to build a new set of friendships.

In our barracks world we moved like fish swimming in a school. We were constantly surrounded by other men. We lived and traveled together, yet we were closer to some than others. Though we did not all like each other, we were a team. Privacy was a recent invention of the civilian world. It did not extend to the military. We showered, shaved, and shit before each other. When nude, we looked at each other's eyes—not thighs.

We practiced individual exercises with rifles and squad exercises with logs. We did hand-to-hand combat and ran obstacle courses that were ever increasing in difficulty. The Rangers taught a man to believe in himself. We would begin by crossing a log that was two feet off the ground, then move to ever-higher levels. If you could run across a log two feet off the ground, you could do it at five feet; if you could do it at five feet, you could do at ten and higher, much higher. We had our own obstacle course that included a maze of torturous devices that carried names such as the belly buster, the tough nut, the dirty name, and the Tarzan. One of the toughest was climbing the outside of a three-story structure, crossing a two-cable bridge more than twenty-five feet above the ground, scaling a wall nearly twenty feet high and jumping from it, climbing another tower, and doing a gut crawl over loose logs that threatened to spin away from the body. We did these things step-by-step until we could do them carrying weapons and equipment at the rapid pace the army calls "double time."

Much of our time was spent in day and night cross-country movement. Patrolling is the fine art of the infantry soldier. It is a technique of small groups of men moving by stealth on a reconnaissance or combat mission. The object of patrolling is to conduct a raid, learn what the enemy is doing, or bring back a prisoner. For centuries the patrol has been a specialty of the American Ranger.

We did speed and distance marches cross-country and on roads with our weapons on our shoulders, our bodies laden with packs, belts, and canteens filled with the necessities of war. Ammunition, water, and food rated highest priority. The goal was to be able to move forty to fifty miles cross-country in twelve to eighteen hours. The time difference was determined by the ruggedness of the terrain. We were practicing to move rapidly over long distances and do it behind enemy lines. The marches were often "tactical," which meant that the appearance of anyone or anything not of our unit would send us hurrying to concealment. If we were on a road and a truck came along, we cleared the road and melted into the earth. Much of the training included exhaustion followed by stress. We would march hour after hour until our minds felt numb and our bodies ached, and then be presented with a problem calling for instant action.

I learned that it was possible to sleep while marching. On a night road march, I saw a bright light in my eyes. I came awake to find myself leaning against the front of a two-and-a-half-ton truck. When the driver came down the road, my brother Rangers had quickly gone into concealment. Fortunately, the driver saw me, stopped, and watched in amazement while I marched into the truck's bumper. Occasionally a squad or platoon would be marching while asleep. When the head of the column stopped, there would be a clang and clatter as the line of men collided with those in front and steel helmets and weapons came together.

The only training that prepares men for combat is realistic combat training. The conditions of the battlefield must become routine to the soldier. Training exercises using live ammunition were a significant part of our experience. We used our weapons as we closed on the objective, and we participated in live-fire exercises in urban warfare, practicing house-to-house fighting. We made attacks on fortified positions with artillery and close-air support.

We followed the progress of the war with great interest. In December 1950 the Chinese were still driving southward, crossing the 38th parallel and moving on the South Korean capital of Seoul. There had been a false opinion among American political and military leaders that the Chinese would not fight and, if they did, would be easily defeated. It was incorrectly believed that the Chinese had nothing but numbers. President Truman, the Joint Chiefs of Staff, and General MacArthur were all wrong. Americans learned the hard way that vast numbers of the Chinese were battle-experienced soldiers who had fought against the Japanese and for or against the Nationalist Chinese. They had skilled commanders who frequently outmaneuvered their American adversaries. The Chinese were superb infantrymen, accustomed to hardship. Unlike roadbound American forces, the Chinese would cross the most difficult terrain. Unhampered by constraints caused by the loss of life, they lost thousands upon thousands of men to disease, winter cold, and the magnificent performance of our air force, navy, and marine pilots, who pounded them with unrelenting fury.

The greatest weakness of the Chinese was their inability to logistically support their armies. Their greatest strength was a will to win. Our situation was the reverse. We had the greatest logistics in the world, but our political leadership did not have the will to win. At that time we had nuclear weapons, but so to a lesser extent did the Soviet Union. The big bomb was considered another weapon of war, and the Chinese were aware of its power, but they rightly gauged that America would not use this advantage. American soldiers and the American public did not know that from the moment the Chinese entered the war, political knees began to buckle in Washington, D.C., and in Europe. Fear of a war that would spread to the Chinese mainland and bring the Soviet Union into an attack in Europe made Korea not worth the effort. This fear paralyzed the Truman administration.

Despite strong protests from General MacArthur, American political leaders began the practice of granting the enemy safe haven in his homeland. Though the Chinese were at war with us, they maintained the fiction that only Chinese volunteers were fighting in Korea. This made it easier for American politicians to not order strikes at China. Undisturbed at home, the Chinese could freely wage war against our men in Korea. The Truman administration did not seek victory. From the time of the Chinese entry into the war, the goal of President Harry Truman and Secretary of State Dean Acheson was a negotiated settlement.

Consisting of experienced soldiers who were all repeat

volunteers, the Ranger companies quickly melded into efficient teams. The Infantry School at Fort Benning had school troops whose purpose was to portray the enemy. They knew we were coming, the approximate time, and they knew the terrain. As they moved to ambush us, we moved faster than the timetable and ambushed them.

When the marches were not tactical or we were returning to barracks or around campfires, we sang. There were some fine voices in the 3d Platoon of the 8th Rangers. One of them belonged to a man who introduced himself as "Harry Trout from Childress, Texas, gateway to the Panhandle." Another singer was Eugene Conrad Rivera, whom I came to know as E. C. We three would share the lead in singing. Around the campfire we often sang:

> I'm a Ranger born
> I'm a Ranger bred
> And when I die
> I'll be a Ranger dead.

> Take down your service flag, Mother
> Replace the blue with the gold
> Your son is an Airborne Ranger
> He'll die 'fore he's twenty years old.

A Ranger company had three 33-man platoons assigned but, during training at Fort Benning, the 8th Rangers had a fourth platoon that consisted of black Rangers. These men were preparing to go to the all-black 2d Ranger Company, which was attached to the 7th Infantry Division in Korea. We did not have time to concern ourselves with men of other platoons, regardless of race, but one memory of the 4th Platoon stands clear.

We were marching home through the darkness, looking forward to cleaning our equipment and getting some rest. The 4th Platoon was last in line and, as we closed into our area, they sang together:

* * *

The 4th Platoon now says farewell
Parley vous
The 4th Platoon now says farewell
Parley vous
The 4th Platoon now says farewell
The rest of the company can go to hell
Hinky dinky parley vous.

It was done in flawless harmony and brought laughter to the lips of exhausted men.

As a youth who loved history, I was taken by the salad bowl mix of ethnic representation. We had Rangers whose ancestors came from all races and lands. Our ranks included American Indians whom we were glad to have with us on this warpath. We did not celebrate our differences; we were all Americans and our strength was in unity.

Realistic training for war is serious and sometimes deadly. Nine Rangers would be killed in training during the Korean War. Our training included methods of getting into enemy territory by air, land, and water. Every Ranger had to be able to swim. We learned how to take ponchos (our primary rain gear), cross rifles on them, and make a raft that would keep our equipment and ammunition dry as we swam in undershorts or nude behind them. That worked well when the temperatures were mild. One of our tests was to swim a Fort Benning lake known to generations of infantrymen as Victory Pond. We did this in early January of an extremely cold winter. When we arrived at Victory Pond, a cold wind was snapping at us and the edges of the pond were coated with ice. To strip and make that swim was a terrible experience, one never to be forgotten by those who participated.

We expected to parachute into action and continued airborne training. Our final week of Ranger training was called Hell Week. It began with a low-level night parachute jump by five Ranger companies. The 8th Rangers were jumping from the twin-boomed C-119 aircraft known as Flying Boxcars. Going out the door from the dimly lit aircraft was like stepping into a dark room without a floor.

Everyone was training for combat. The air force pilots flew at less than 200 feet, then pulled up to 400 feet for the jump. The air force gauged the altitude on this jump a bit too closely for our liking. I felt the drop, the snap, and the opening shock, immediately did the required look upward to check my parachute canopy, and was slammed to earth. The tactical silence was broken by curses and expressions of pain from the many who were injured.

We assembled and a roll call was taken in the darkness. Ronald Sullivan's name was called. Initially no one answered; then a voice said, "He's around, I talked to him." It developed that no one had talked to Sullivan after this jump. His parachute failed to open and he fell to his death, impaled by a pine tree. The 8th Rangers promptly made another parachute jump. This jump had the dual purpose of honoring one of our own and helping control our own imaginations. It is not wise for paratroopers to think deeply about possibilities.

We practiced overwater movement. The bridge over Upatoi Creek served as the side of a simulated ship. Cargo nets were thrown over the side of the bridge. We would descend the nets into rubber assault boats and paddle our way to the objective, which was usually on a cliff that had to be scaled using grappling irons, climbing the cliff face hand over hand with weapons and full equipment. We were in superb physical condition and took this exercise with a levity that angered Lieutenant Strong. He marched our platoon into the water and had us doing close order drill, up to our hips in water. We marched up and down that creek until there were no more grins on our faces.

I began to form friendships. Nick Tisak, the other BAR man of my squad, was from Ambridge, Pennsylvania. A tall, quiet, deeply religious man, Nick had joined the marines at age sixteen. After the marines, he joined the army and became a paratrooper. A number of Rangers age nineteen or twenty had done World War II duty with another service. E. C. Rivera was from Santa Fe, New Mexico. He left high school at the end of the war to enlist and had been a cook in the navy, serving on an LCI (landing craft, infantry). Rivera later said that he was a high school dropout before the term was invented. After World War II, when the army depended on volunteers, they decided to accept any sailor who enlisted in the army at the equivalent rank he had held in the navy. This created a circumstance where galvanized sergeants were yelling at confused recruits to get up the ladder (stairs) to the top deck (second floor of the barracks). A wall was a "bulkhead," and "avast" replaced "halt!" as a command. The army was forced to form a special training unit to teach these "swabs" how people talked on land. After this training, Rivera had been assigned to the 82d Airborne Division band as a trumpeter, but he wanted to soldier. He had managed to transfer to the 325th Airborne Infantry, who sent him to radiotelephone school. He had just returned to his company when he learned about the Rangers; he volunteered. His company in the 325th Airborne Infantry took revenge by putting a box of Brillo pads in his hand and lining up all their field ranges (stoves) for him to polish. E. C. Rivera would begin his Ranger experience as the 3d Platoon radio operator. He was a very special person, a happy warrior with a sparkling wit.

I enjoyed the company of Jimmy White. He was from Florida. Jimmy was the youngest and the smallest of us. He was concerned about having what it took to succeed as a Ranger. I did not doubt him because he never faltered. Jimmy was in my squad and we marched and trained side by side. This man was proof that big courage can come in a small package. We called him "the Little Tiger."

Having no other entertainment, Rangers argued frequently. There were southern men ready and eager to refight the Civil War. Few men from north of the Mason-Dixon Line knew or cared about that distant cataclysmic conflict, but it still raged in the hearts of some Rangers from the South. My great-grandfathers had fought on both sides, and I honored them both. I was glad the North had won the war, as I saw no future in two separate nations, and no one wanted to be a slave. Some men from the South saw the war as a northern invasion, with southern men fighting for their homes and families. A few of these men had a tendency to use the words "damn" and "yankee" as though they had an eternal linkage. Our platoon medic, Gil "Doc" Gregory, was from South Carolina. With a war raging in Korea, we got into a fight in the chow line about the Civil War.

As the only man in my company who wore glasses, I was called before a medical board whose members were prepared to end my rangering on the grounds that I might break or lose my glasses in combat and put other men at risk. I begged to be allowed to stay with my company. I wanted to go to combat and go with the friends I had trained with. This board was accustomed to having people before it who were trying their best to stay out of the war. My plea to go fight as a Ranger impressed them greatly. They admonished me to keep spare eyeglasses with me and wished me good hunting.

Each company has a small swallowtailed flag that the infantry calls a guidon. It is the cloth identifier of the unit. Our blue infantry guidons contained the crossed muskets of the infantry, a parachute, and the word "Ranger" with our company number. We felt great pride when we marched behind that banner to form with our sister companies for graduation. The Korean War Rangers were the first men in history to complete the Fort Benning Ranger Course. We were awarded a cloth, shoulder arc-tab that had a black background and ranger in gold. We sewed this tab high on the left arm of our uniform.

Our next destination was Colorado, where we would undergo mountain and cold-weather training. On any such move by the army, a small group of men, called the "advance party," is sent ahead to prepare the way, to ready barracks, and be capable of serving as guides.

The remainder of the men of the 3d, 5th, and 8th Ranger Companies spent days packing equipment and cleaning barracks. We then marched to the railroad yard, where a long line of olive drab passenger and baggage cars waited to take us west. In my young life, the railroad was the steel ribbon pathway to adventure. It was the railroad that united the separate states, that moved freight and passengers long distances. Travel by rail was heralded in our literature and frequently a part of the songs we sang. The great steel dinosaurs thundered through the night, and the mournful wail of a steam engine whistle remains at the center of my nostalgia. On several occasions my mother had taken me to Brooklyn to visit her sisters and see the Brooklyn Dodgers play baseball. When we went to New York, we rode the Tuscan-red cars of the Pennsylvania Railroad. The Pennsy was so vast and powerful that it set the standard for the world's railroads; this railroad "ran on the advertised," leaving and arriving on the time it promised. The dining cars featured white linen, heavy silver, and monogrammed china.

An olive drab troop train had none of these features. The cars were gutted of anything that resembled comfort. Their interiors featured rock-hard seats and tiers of wooden bunks without springs or mattresses. Our sleeping bags were spread out on the boards. The dining area was an empty baggage car where the cooks set up field stoves, a row of insulated Marmite cans, and various food and trash containers. We stood in line and ate from our mess kits while trying to keep our balance in the swaying cars.

Singing was a convenient way of passing the time, and bawdy songs were popular:

> Sweet Antoinette
> Your pants are wet
> And it ain't sweat . . . I bet
> In all my dreams
> Your bare ass beams
> You're the wrecker of my pecker . . . Antoinette

We rattled, squeaked, and swayed across the southern states, spending an inordinate amount of time crossing a barren wasteland without a sign of life. The vastness of the State of

Texas was imprinted on our minds and bodies. It was night when the train arrived at Colorado Springs, Colorado. We moved by truck to barracks at Camp Carson, worked long hours in stowing equipment, and then fell on our cots grateful for a few hours of restful sleep.

8

The Colorado Mountains

Reveille came early, and as we fell into formation we stared in wonder at the magnificence of the Rocky Mountains. Most of us from the eastern United States had never seen mountains that reach for the sky. The air was clean and crisp, but movement seemed slow. Our morning five-mile run was a disaster. We were in superb physical condition, but our lungs were not acclimated to the high altitude and lack of oxygen. We did not stop, but we suffered mightily until our bodies adjusted to the rarefied air.

We drew new equipment. Our beloved Corcoran jump boots were put aside and we were issued square-toed mountain/ski boots that were heavily cleated, came above the ankle, and were topped off with half-leggings. We were issued rucksacks, thick mittens, parkas with fur-lined hoods, arctic sleeping bags, and two-man tents that had a self-contained floor. Our issued supplies indicated that a cold and wet time lay ahead.

We were not long in barracks when the order came to prepare to move. We began to climb into the mountains. Once again the long marches began. In Georgia we traveled on the horizontal. In Colorado the marches were vertical. On snowy mountaintops around Pikes Peak and the Garden of the Gods, along the mountain trails to Camp Hale, the former training ground of the 10th Mountain Division, we learned to live and fight in mountains and snow. We were taught the techniques of mountain climbing and moving equipment over arduous terrain. Again we practiced patrolling. Having experienced moving through muck-filled swamps, we now found ourselves struggling through deep snowdrifts.

A can of Sterno was our stove. Our lightweight mountain rations included packets of dehydrated Lipton chicken noodle soup—this was a personal favorite. I would melt a canteen cup of snow, add the soup, and smack my lips as I savored the steaming broth. We frequently patrolled into Rock Creek Canyon, where the temperature on one occasion was reported at twenty-four degrees below zero. That golden soup was a highlight of my day.

It was not long before we stopped using tents. They were impediments to rapid movement. We found that we could spread out our ponchos on the ground, put our sleeping bags on top, and wrap the poncho around to aid in keeping us dry. Staying dry bordered on the impossible. Snow was everywhere.

While marching and climbing I tried to think of ways to improve my comfort and efficiency. Innovation got me in trouble. We were soaked to the skin when we stopped to bivouac for the night, but I was determined that I would sleep dry. I remembered that somewhere in Boy Scout training I had been told that if wet clothes were removed and placed in the bottom of the sleeping bag, the body would be warm and the clothes would tend to dry from the body heat. When we stopped for the night, my brother Rangers stayed dressed in wet clothes, wrapped themselves in their sleeping bags, and were soon asleep. I carefully removed my wet boots and uniform, put them in the bottom of the sleeping bag, and followed them with my nude body. I had scarcely zippered the bag when the voice of Platoon Sergeant Bill Cox split the cold night air.

"Everybody on your feet," yelled Cox. "We're moving out—right now!"

The company disappeared before I could get dressed. I was grateful that I could track them in the snow, but it took a lot of hustle to rejoin them. From that point on I followed the actions of my fellow Rangers.

Our mountain bivouac areas were occasionally so steep

that it was difficult to find a level place to rest. On one very steep slope, I tied the top of my sleeping bag to a tree. Gravity pulled me into a contorted ball toward the bottom of the bag. I was too tired to care and slept soundly. Young joints get stiff but recover quickly.

A mule-pack outfit still remained at Camp Carson, the last vestige of horse cavalry days. Mules had been used to transport equipment and supplies long distances in the China-Burma-India theater and in Italy in World War II. Therefore, army wisdom dictated that we should learn how to harness and pack our food, water, recoilless rifles, and mortars on these four-footed wonders. We kept our rifles with us at all times, but any soldier who carried the baseplate of a mortar or a recoilless rifle any distance would welcome a mule.

The soldiers of the 35th Quartermaster (pack) Company were the end of an era. They, along with men of a small artillery unit, were the last mule skinners of the army. These men had faces of the outdoors, chiseled into ravines and ridgelines by wind and snow. Their skin was the consistency and color of old leather. These mule skinners were old soldiers, old horsemen, who had spent much of their lives in a saddle. They rolled when they walked and looked uncomfortable on the ground.

The mule skinners taught us how to put various items of equipment on the mules. Back on the farm a halter was a halter and a bridle was a bridle; in the army we had the Halter Bridle M1917 and the Halter Tie Rope M1912. We loaded equipment on a Phillips Cargo Pack Saddle, which was also known as the China Special. It had a frame of steel arches that was well padded and had two cinch straps under the mule's belly.

We tied our equipment on the mules with half-inch Manila rope and were taught a wide variety of hitch knots. These knots carried exotic names, including the Wyoming diamond hitch, the squaw hitch, the single diamond hitch, the Sweeten diamond hitch, and the Nagle hitch. We were taught single-tie slings, double-tie slings, and cross-tie slings. We learned as many knots and ways of loading cargo as a sailor. Those Rangers who had previously been sailors or Boy Scouts did the best at knot tying.

A mule is a hybrid animal, the usually sterile offspring of a male donkey and female horse. Army mules were usually trained to move in a single file behind a bell mare and her rider. Their training for battle included gunfire, smoke, whistles, and aircraft. They were taught to cross fallen trees, narrow bridges, and ditches. Normally, mules marched at four and a half to five miles per hour.

Some of my city-born brother Rangers kept referring to these animals as "horses." I had been raised around horses and mules, and knew there was a considerable difference. Horses have a beauty and majesty about them; they grow to be big and powerful. Some people believe that horses are affectionate, though when they give you a lick with that big tongue, it is really the salt on your arm or neck they want. Horses are fright animals with a small two-sided brain. Once when ring-riding my horse we passed a small flowerpot sitting on a post. We rode counterclockwise a dozen times passing that flowerpot without a problem. The first time we rode the other direction, the opposite side of his brain registered the flowerpot as a threat and he leaped five yards sideways.

If a horse seems as affectionate as a dog, a mule is as independent as a cat, a cat that will stomp you and kick your remains into the next county if you are not careful. A mule is tougher than a horse and can work harder and longer. Mules are sly, crafty, and treacherous. If a mule does not care to work or even move, emergency action is required. Our farm mules were named Jack and Jill. When Jack did not want to work, he would freeze up solid like a bronze statue on a courthouse square. I can still see our tenant farmer as he reached for a billet of wood that he kept handy. "All right, you son-of-a-bitch," he would say. "You are gonna work or I'm gonna lay you up alongside the head." Jack had learned that our farmer was a man of his word. The sight of that club was an inspiration to duty.

Some country-raised Rangers believed that if you twist a

mule's tail, it will control his brain. But if a mule's brain is at the rear, so are two dangerous hooves. Back on the farm, I found that the best way to handle a recalcitrant mule was to bite his ear. Old Jack had a fine respect for my teeth. When he wouldn't move, I would seize an ear and bite hard. After a while his knees would begin to tremble and small sounds that resembled a moan would come from his throat, his rib cage would begin to twitch, and soon all parts would begin to function.

Of course the mule skinners knew about the ear-biting practice. They made it clear that there would be no "earing down" with their mules. "Never look a mule in the eye," said our instructor at Camp Carson. That was something new to me. When questioned, he explained that the mule would then know he was smarter than we were and that would change the relationship.

We practiced with our mules, leading them about, then packing them for a long trek up Cheyenne Mountain. There was a great deal of shouting and cursing, and an occasional bray as Rangers and mules became acquainted. I had a docile beast and a ringside view of pandemonium. When the confusion ended and the dust settled, we moved out in a long line of men and mules. As the climb began, my mind pondered the instructor's words. Growing up on the farm, I had never looked in a mule's eyes. Why do that when I could look at that photo of Rita Hayworth and masturbate to exhaustion. Though I lacked proof, it was not possible that a mule was smarter than I. After all, I reasoned, the heaviest load was on his back—not mine.

At the earliest opportunity, I turned to examine my four-footed companion. He was a typical army mule without a distinguishing mark, save for the U.S. brand on his flank. The army did not expect him to be smart. All that was required was that he work until he dropped. That thought gave me a feeling of kinship with the mule.

I had to know if he was smarter. Taking a deep breath, I leaned close and went eyeball to eyeball with the mule. His eyes were large and round, dark and deep, and as impenetrable as the surface of an ocean. I took a long look into nothingness. No spark of intelligence glimmered in those depths, no passion, hopes, dreams, or ambitions. He was just a dumb-assed army mule. Suddenly the mule's ears went flat and he seemed to explode. I watched in horror as all four feet left the ground and went horizontal. Then, while still airborne, he launched a devastating kick rearward. His mouth flew open, exposing broad, knifelike teeth. There was a defiant bray and a savage jerk of his head that pulled the lead rope from my hand. Spinning about, he charged down the mountainside, taking with him much of my equipment and food.

Sergeant Cox made several loud observations about my ancestry. That sped me on my way in pursuit, but it was an hour of strenuous exertion before I caught up with that mule. There was no time to express my feelings with a club or chew his ear. I had to rejoin my platoon, or Wild Bill Cox would bite part of my anatomy. I was contrite. The mule accepted my apology and we resumed the climb. I could not find the opportunity to be alone with that mule, and I wanted that desperately. I wanted to tie his lead rope securely to a stout tree, savage his ears, and bring the reasoning power of a thick club to him. But he was US Government property. A private, even a private first class, can get in big trouble harming something that belongs to the government.

Just as we needed them, the mules were taken from us and we climbed into the high mountains. The weather turned bad, with alternating sleet and snow, preventing the air force from dropping supplies to us. We learned to go a long distance on a cup of snowmelt coffee.

When we returned from the mountains, I was promoted to corporal. I felt vindicated. All those people back home who thought I would never amount to anything would have been astounded to see me wearing two stripes. There was little chance they would, as we were soon back on the trail, climbing ever higher into the wonderful world of white that is the Rocky Mountains in winter. On some clear nights, when our world was roofed by a billion stars, we could look down to the ground far beneath and see the lights of Colorado Springs. Someone said it had a population of some 33,000 people and a lot of good bars.

The final touch to our training was a fifty-mile march carrying up to ninety pounds of gear. Fortunately, we encountered no storms. We had some light snow, which was sufficient to hide patches of ice. The footing was treacherous, and this made the march even more difficult. When our barracks came into view, tired men quickened their pace. To be dry, warm, and rested seemed the greatest of all rewards.

Hurry up and wait is a part of army life. After our mountain training was completed we spent our time doing light duty of two hours' physical training a day, and cleaning and packing equipment for shipment to Korea. Suddenly we had the luxury of free time. My friend Len Wiggins was built and looked like the Greek god Apollo. He taught me that being quiet can say a lot. Len, a superb soldier, was raised in the vicinity of New Bern, North Carolina. On 8 March 1865, my southern great-grandfather, Sgt. John Wesley Black, Company I, 42d North Carolina Infantry, had been captured by General Sherman's troops in the preliminaries of the Battle of Bentonville, not far from Len's family home.

Len and I used our free time to go mountain climbing and enjoyed the outdoor challenges we faced. Many men were going to Colorado Springs each night. When our advance party had arrived in Colorado, two Rangers had gone to a downtown bar, where they were heavily outnumbered and beaten up by air force people. Now the Rangers went hunting, and they were not merciful.

E. C. Rivera and a few other Ranger friends of mine already had girlfriends. I wanted a girl badly, so I went to Colorado Springs with Ranger corporal Howard Weitzell. He was an older man with much more experience in life than I.

The men of the 3d, 5th, and 8th Ranger Companies found bars that suited their needs. Rangers proudly wore their uniforms to town and were very supportive of each other if a problem arose. Weitzell took me to a nightclub called the Navajo Hogan. He was dating the club stripper, a brunette named

Judy. We settled into a ringside table where we could watch her nightly performance. When he learned that I did not like beer, Weitzell introduced me to a gin drink called a Singapore sling. I drank those until the world took on the rose complexion of that drink. Alcohol and I were never meant to be companions. When drinking, I became loud and nasty, and it was not hard to find a fight at the Navajo Hogan.

After a few drinks I had the notion that it was my duty to defend the sacred soil of this watering hole. When a customer became unruly, I would remove my glasses, take the offender by the scruff of the neck and the seat of his pants, and hustle him to the street. On one occasion I had one drink too many. I lost my grip on a man and he spun around, using his fists to do a staccato drumroll on my head.

The stripper, Judy, was the root cause of much trouble. One evening she was in the company of a large man when I said to her, "Judy, would you care to join us at our table?"

"Fuck you!" she replied.

"Well, fuck you, too," was my clever response.

She turned to her companion, looked up, and said, "Are you going to let him talk to me like that?" I arose from the table to do battle and found myself looking at his belt buckle.

"Ranger!" I screamed in terror. I heard a thundering of jump boots, and the big fellow found himself surrounded by a half dozen warriors. "Well?" I inquired, my heart thumping with relief. He looked around and underwent a sudden change of mood.

"Let me buy you men a drink," he said hurriedly. All of us went off to the bar, leaving Judy stamping her feet in rage.

One night, fraternity men from a college arrived at the Navajo Hogan. They were drinking heavily, growing loud. We Rangers resented their presence. We were serving our country and they were not. While Judy was doing her bump and grind, a college man reached across the rail and tore away a pastie covering one of her nipples.

No conversational reprimand occurred. Three of us hit this man from different angles and the slaughter began. Women screamed, men grunted and bellowed, and all over the night-club was the thudding sound of fists on flesh. One fraternity brother charged me, bent low, and swung at my abdomen and groin. I took a beer bottle from a table and hit him over the head. He cried, "Oh! Oh!" and fell to the floor.

Actions such as these are usually brief in nature, and this was no exception. Those fraternity brothers who could fled the scene. However, a number could not. The Navajo Hogan looked like an untidy morgue, with the prone bodies of the college men scattered about. The sirens of the Colorado Springs and military police vehicles grew ever louder, and we knew it was time to evade the reach of the law.

I did not succeed. Fleeing down an alley, I found myself trapped in a tactical maneuver known as a "double envelopment." The military police had come out on the losing end of some early encounters, and now they traveled in packs like wolves. Just how vicious and uncivilized they were, I was soon to learn.

When they took me to their den, I began to speak loudly of the rights of an American citizen and made some physical moves to demonstrate my strong beliefs in those rights. The military policemen were not in a mood to debate, and I was struck on the head with a nightstick. When I awoke, my revolving eyes slowed and focused on the military police bulletin board. Across the top was a line of cloth airborne hat patches, the circular red, white, and blue with parachute-and-glider insignia that we wore so proudly. When the military police would take one of us down, they would "scalp" us by tearing off our paratrooper symbol. Only loose thread remained on my cap.

I received a chewing-out for this incident but nothing more serious. The army had put considerable time and money into developing my aggressiveness. Now it was payback time— the army was shipping me to a war. An aching head and a large lump was sufficient punishment.

The troop train gave us a sudden transition from the winter white of Colorado to the green of California. We underwent the inoculations and administrative processing for overseas shipment at Camp Stoneman. We were only a few days in California. Our pay records had not arrived from Fort Benning, but at this point my needs were very small. That was not so for some of my buddies, including Rivera, who did escape and evasion to San Francisco and met a lonely woman with money. Soon our three Ranger companies took the ferryboat *Sacramento* to the port of San Francisco. Staggering under heavy loads of weapons and equipment, we climbed the gangway of our troopship. E. C. Rivera had a happy smile on his face, but was late for formation. First Sergeant Craig put him on permanent kitchen police duty with the navy for the voyage. Craig was unaware that Rivera had been a navy cook. It was not long before E. C. was baking sweet goods, broiling steaks, and living like he was in officer country.

KOREA

9

On the Way

The *General William F. Hase* was a 17,250-ton troopship. As we sailed away on this ship of gray, an army band played "So Long, It's Been Good to Know You." The army bands of Fort Benning and Camp Carson had also played that song as we departed from their locations. Some Ranger said that the next time a band played this song for us, our caskets would be lowered into the earth.

Countless Americans have sailed to war. Those sailing from New York to fight in Europe remember the Statue of Liberty. Those of us who have sailed from San Francisco to fight in Asia and the Pacific remember the Golden Gate Bridge. The giant structure seemed alive with a steady stream of traffic. It would be some time before most of us would again see so many automobiles, and for some it was their last sight of life in the United States.

A troopship is an instrument of torture. Canvas cots suspended from chains hung in vertical rows from the steel bulkheads. They were arranged eight cots high with so little space between that we had to slide into these cots sideways. The canvas on the cot above would sag under the weight of its occupant, leaving only inches of free space. Troop compartments were barren of any aspect of comfort, and the stench of oil was nauseating.

The pitch and roll of the ship's movement was an immediate cause of misery. Men were vomiting before we left the harbor. I found this amusing. As we entered the ocean waves, I walked among my retching comrades with an air of smug superiority. The latrine resembled a scene from

Dante's *Inferno*. The combined stink of vomit, feces, urine, and oil was an assault on the nostrils. Men knelt over commodes and urinals, heaving putrid streams from their bodies; others staggered about groaning and cursing, trying to push their comrades from position and, failing that, throwing up on the deck or other men. Their faces had the wan and pasty look of the dying, and some were proclaiming that they only wanted life to end.

Robed in the arrogance of youth, I stood in this latrine, took an orange from my pocket, peeled it, and began to eat in front of these seasick men. Within moments my stomach revolted and I was among them, pushing and shoving as I frantically searched for a place to empty my guts.

I was sick for several days as our gray ship carved its way through the deep swells of the Pacific. We sailed alone and, when I began to care about my surroundings, I was astounded at the vast, rolling, empty sea. The Pacific Ocean is gigantic and our travel was slow. There was ample time to think about what lay ahead. Our future was in battle and some of us would die. It would, of course, be someone else who would give his life, but there was always a nagging voice that predicted personal doom. Surrounded by hundreds of other men, we visited private islands of thought. A person can be mighty lonely in a crowd.

Within the platoon, our bonding ebbed and flowed according to our interests of the moment. I shared Pennsylvania memories with Nick Tisak. Len Wiggins and I talked about climbing together. Doc Gregory and I learned to talk rationally about the Civil War; and Howard Weitzell knew about women. I sang and laughed with E. C. Rivera and Harry Trout. Ken Erb, Wendy Washburn, Jimmy White, and John West were men I enjoyed talking with. On shipboard, Tony Velo and I shared our dreams. Tony Velo's dress uniform fit like another layer of skin. He was immaculate in his appearance, a handsome young man whose ambition was to open a clothing store. We were a happy few, all brother Rangers, intensely proud of our volunteer spirit and the hardship and challenge that we endured to be part of this unique bond.

There are other justly proud American units whose men have done all that is possible for our nation, but none of these units have histories that predate the founding of the United States. From the earliest days of American history, Rangers have led the way. We shared the common bond that the American Rangers are a river of valor through time. Even during the immensity of World War II, only some five thousand men carried the proud title of Ranger. Now we would enlarge this magnificent tradition on the battlefields of Korea. Honed to a fine edge of physical fitness, we spent many hours on shipboard doing a variety of physical exercises. We cleaned and recleaned weapons and reviewed tactical procedures.

Sharing the crowded confines of our troopship was a battalion of US Marines. They were well trained, physically fit, and intensely proud of their great tradition. As a small service relying heavily on navy funds, the Marine Corps did not hide from the public eye. Marines are not given to adopting the military fad of the moment, and they project a constant image of hard training. The eagle, globe, and anchor that they wear are earned. One of their traditions seems to be to speak badly of the army at every opportunity. Of necessity, the army is much larger than the marines, and not all army units are going to measure up to the caliber of the more carefully selected marines. Nevertheless, many units of the army can stand tall in any company. The US Marine division fighting in Korea did a superb job on their part of the battlefield, but there were six US Army divisions and several Republic of Korea divisions spread across the front, and where the front moved depended upon everyone.

The marines of this battalion thought of themselves as elite troops. They looked with disdain on the army. We Rangers did not look upon the marines as an elite organization because there were divisions of marines, and a division might be 17,000 to 20,000 men. We felt that anyone could get into an outfit that large. Five companies of Rangers fighting in

Korea meant a total of some 750 Rangers fighting to the front of all the army divisions on line. "Now *that* is elite," we told them.

Words flew back and forth. Ranger Chet Wolfe would taunt the Marines with the old Texas Ranger slogan "One riot, one Ranger." We did not intermingle, and walked stiff-legged around one another with hackles raised. We were young, proud, and ready to fight. The uneasy peace was broken when it was announced over the ship's loudspeakers that a movie would be shown belowdecks. Anxious to see the film, we Rangers stood in line waiting and waiting, expressing our impatience by lowing like cattle. At length a hatch opened and a marine sergeant informed us that there was no room for anyone else to see the film, which was already in progress. Much more familiar with shipboard life than we, the marines had entered the compartment by another hatch and were sitting there, smug in the satisfaction that they had outwitted men of the army. This was a miscalculation.

A very large Ranger took that marine sergeant by the throat and we charged into the theater with fists and boots flying. There were no niceties of combat. Although smaller in number, we had the advantages of surprise and that most of the marines were sitting. They fought a delaying action, regrouped, and counterattacked. Other Rangers arrived and we committed this reserve force to action. We were all having a great time until the voice of authority crackled from the loudspeaker. The captain of the ship sent Ranger and marine officers to the scene of the fray and both sides were required to shut up, cool off, and sit down crowded together. The movie was restarted. I don't recall the title. The film was anticlimactic. Many men wore the marks of the fight for several days. Oddly, the fight resulted in a mutual respect and bonding. Marines and Rangers started talking to each other and searched for other men from the same town or state.

We sailed into Yokohama harbor at night, my heart filled with the romance of this great adventure. I was up under the stars standing alone in the bow of the ship with the wind in my hair and the salt spray in my face. To be young, confident, and have life and the world before me was a wondrous thing. Alone, looking at the twinkling lights of the Japanese shore, I sang the words of a popular song of the period, "You ask where I live, here's the answer I give. . . . The four winds and the seven seas."

Yokohama harbor was crowded with commercial shipping, some from the Soviet Union and China. The battalion of marines left us at Yokohama. They were bound for Korea by some other means. The *Hase* steamed out of Yokohama and set sail for the great Japanese seaport of Kobe. We now had ample room aboard the ship and access to many compartments we had not previously seen.

At times in the army, men in transit would be separated from their pay records. The army knew the man was present for duty, but the necessary paperwork was not. To resolve this crisis, the army would pay the soldier ten dollars a month until soldier and pay records were reunited. Soldiers called this rapidly disappearing payment "a flying ten."

It was our misfortune that we were existing on flying tens when we learned that we would be allowed on shore at Kobe. Determined to have one last fling before battle, we searched the ship for items of barter. We took blankets, sheets and pillowcases, tools, and anything that could be secreted beneath an army overcoat. As we staggered down the gangway, we looked like an army of the obese.

I trailed after Ranger Weitzell looking for adventure and not knowing how to get there. Weitzell had been stationed in Japan previously and knew some of the language. A number of Japanese boys were standing about. Weitzell told me they were guides to the whorehouses. One of the boys led us to a nondescript house with sliding panel doors. We were greeted by an aged crone, who was wearing a kimonolike garment and bobbing and bowing. Weitzell told me this was the "mamma-san." We removed our layers of loot, took off our boots before stepping on the rice mat floor, and were ushered inside.

Like Indian traders, we sat on the floor with our piles of goods before us. Several girls were brought forth for our selection, and we made our choices. Weitzell bargained with the mamma-san and procured a Coke for me and a beer for himself. The mamma-san directed a girl to bring me a dirty bottle of what she called "Coka." We were then led to separate compartments by the girls we had selected. There is no memory of the Japanese prostitute who gave me knowledge of the sweet mystery of life. I am grateful that she gave me nothing else. It was good to have this knowledge. I had a spare watch with a cracked crystal, which I traded to learn some more.

We returned to the ship. I was still in uniform, but some of the Ranger brethren came back practically nude or in Japanese apparel far too small for their American frames. Some only returned to hunt for additional trading material. They were not allowed down the gangway, but several who were well lubricated with alcohol tried to go hand-over-hand down the mooring ropes. They were frustrated by the large circular shields that formed the rat guards and fell into the harbor.

10

Korea and War

We sailed into the Korean port of Pusan, gathered our gear, and disembarked into a place of filth and pandemonium. Pusan had docks inhabited by hordes of Korean civilian laborers. Dressed in soiled white, many carried huge loads on their backs by means of a crude but effective carrying device called an "A-frame." I saw a railroad train completely covered by this mass of humanity. It looked like a caterpillar being devoured by maggots. Pusan had the smell of a giant latrine.

Our three Ranger companies next boarded an LST (landing ship, tank) and sailed from Pusan for the port of Inchon, scene of Gen. Douglas MacArthur's end run amphibious invasion that set the stage for the North Korean collapse. On arrival, we marched to truck convoys to be taken to the various infantry divisions to which our companies would be attached. The word "attached" meant with and under the direction of, but not part of. Every American army division in Korea now had an Airborne Ranger company attached to it. The 1st Ranger Company was with the 2d Infantry Division. The 2d Airborne Rangers were the only all-black Ranger unit in history; they were with the 7th Infantry Division. The 3d Ranger Company went to the 3d Infantry Division. The 4th Rangers were with the 1st Cavalry Division, while the 5th Rangers joined the 25th Infantry Division. My 8th Ranger Company boarded trucks and moved to join the 24th Infantry Division. At this time, the 24th had never been stationed on the mainland of the United States. It was one of the divisions whose roots were in the Hawaiian Islands, and the taro leaf of those islands was its insignia. Men of the 24th Infantry Division had been in Korea since the earliest days of the American involvement. They were now fighting in Central Korea.

We were on these trucks, not knowing where we were going or when we would get there. We only knew we were going into war and we trusted our leaders. As the day ended, we traveled through the rubble that was the South Korean capital of Seoul. Our forces had recently retaken the city. What we saw was utter devastation inhabited by furtive figures scurrying about. The trucks drove through the night, at length stopping along the road beside some railroad tracks. Those of us in the lower ranks had no idea where we were. We dismounted in darkness and put out security. A Ranger from my platoon was searching for straw to make his rest more comfortable. Some unit had been in the area before and had used an open communal latrine. Walking in darkness, the Ranger pitched headfirst into the hole and was covered with feces. Normally an immaculate soldier, he was now doomed to several weeks of ridicule. Spreading our ponchos on the ground and placing our sleeping bags on them, we quickly went to sleep with Mother Earth as our pillow. I was awakened for guard duty before dawn and took up station at the corner of a deserted Korean thatched-roof hut. I peered into the blackness, feeling the responsibility of my comrades' lives on my shoulders. Save for the occasional call of a bird, the night was quiet. The breeze came in gusts, and one of them brought the distinct smell of garlic. Because garlic was part of the diet of an enemy soldier, my imagination began to travel its own path. I disengaged the safety on my BAR and strained my senses, listening for the man or men who were obviously creeping toward me. These were terrible hours of tension, but the enemy did not come. In the welcome light of dawn I looked about and saw a bundle of garlic hanging from the eaves of the house directly above my head. Imagination can be the worst enemy of a soldier.

We were located at a railroad stop called Sangczon. The railroad was not in service, but we soon were. The 24th Infantry Division had as its infantry fighting arm the 19th and 21st Infantry Regiments and the 5th Regimental Combat Team. We would see service with each of these regiments.

Prior to these missions we would assemble behind our lines, blacken our faces and hands, and check all weapons and equipment. I cleaned my Browning automatic rifle and my .45-caliber pistol. I checked each round of ammunition before it was loaded into a magazine for the BAR or a clip for the pistol. We passed boxes filled with cast-iron, corrugated fragmentation grenades. Each fragmentation grenade weighed some 22 ounces and was filled with two ounces of TNT. The safety pins were pulled by hand and required a pull of 10 to 35 pounds. Film heroes of the period gave us many laughs when they were shown pulling the safety pins on grenades with their teeth. When the safety pin was pulled and the safety lever released, the grenade would explode in four to five seconds. The theory was that if the grenade was thrown too soon, it might be thrown back. It took a patient man to stand there with a live grenade in his hand. As a javelin thrower, I had a powerful arm. Most of the time I relied on being able to out-throw my opposition.

Most men took four, but some selected six or more "pineapples," as they were known. We were briefed and, when possible, we rehearsed the mission. Any equipment that would rattle was taped down; even the metal identification tags we wore around our necks were taped to prevent any sound. Our canteens were filled to prevent any sloshing noise. We wore soft caps to reduce the noise of movement. To preserve our night vision, we would permit no light after darkness fell that could harm our night vision. The unit through which we would pass usually provided a guide to lead us through their lines, so we could avoid their barbed wire, land mines and napalm "foo" gas mines (see Glossary: Korean War), and booby traps. As we crossed into no-man's-land, the men in foxholes beside the trails turned their faces toward us, their eyes conveying thoughts, one of which was probably "better you than me."

Ours were combat patrols looking for trouble. As such,

they usually were of platoon strength—thirty-two enlisted men and one officer. On occasion the raids would involve the entire company. Sometimes we quickly encountered the enemy, and at other times we would spend hours moving through the darkness, searching. There were no night-vision devices at the time. The leaders set the direction by compass heading, pacing, and stars. We frequently moved slowly, each man holding on to the cartridge belt of the Ranger in front of him in a technique we called a "daisy chain."

Trying to get through enemy positions to strike their rear, we would often crawl for long periods. The night battlefield was an eerie place. To expose Chinese movement, American searchlights would bounce light off low-hanging clouds, creating an artificial moonlight that was not helpful to those of us in enemy territory. Conditions of low light were best for our operations. Daisy chaining through the darkness, we would freeze in position at the pop that signified a parachute flare was about to ignite. The flare would hiss and sway until it fell to earth. I would close one eye to preserve my night vision and scan the lighted area to search for the enemy with the other. I often felt a temporary feeling of imbalance after a flare burned out.

We fought the enemy through the night. As a result of our airpower, night was the time the Chinese were most active. We often encountered their specialized reconnaissance units. In our hit-and-move forays in the blackness of night, there was little accounting of the damage we were causing. On some raids Rangers were wounded. To have a man wounded on a night action behind enemy lines created great difficulty. "Cat" Berry of my platoon was shot through the thigh and Doc Gregory felt the arterial blood spurting. Kneeling in a rice paddy in the darkness, Gregory used Berry's belt to put a tourniquet on the leg. Doc pulled hard, breaking the belt buckle with the force of his pull. But he stopped the bleeding. Tom Nicholson was also severely wounded. We always brought our wounded home, carrying them on our backs when necessary.

Sometimes we were on the Chinese before they spotted

us. Some of my comrades have said they killed with the knife; I was not faced with that necessity. On some nights an alert sentry would shout a challenge, unintelligible to us. Gunfire would be followed by hot pursuit, and we would "How Able"—haul ass, breaking contact as quickly as possible. Our leaders, Lt. Berk Strong and Sgt. Bill Cox, always put Rangers with Browning automatic rifles (BARs) at the tail end of the column for these circumstances. It became normal for me to act as a "tail-end charlie" during our patrols. These were nights that drained our strength. Once we had passed through our own lines and into our assembly area, the men collapsed. It was not only the physical exertion that took a toll but the constant strain on the senses. Trying to locate the enemy before they found us drained our energy.

We were gypsy warriors, cooperating first with this infantry regiment and then with that. As attached troops temporarily serving with another unit, we were sometimes forgotten when ammunition, food, and water were being supplied. The supply people of the regiments were very busy or, as sometimes happens in war, the information had not been passed down that we were with their unit.

A Ranger company had a considerable supply of weapons from which to draw for tailoring a mission. On many missions we operated as high-firepower rifle platoons carrying automatic carbines, BARs, .45-caliber submachine guns, and M1 rifles. We had two BARs per squad, Nick Tisak and myself. We each had an assistant who, in addition to his own ammunition load, carried spare ammunition for us. Light machine guns, rocket launchers, recoilless rifles, and demolitions were available as necessary for the task we were engaged in.

As we became more accustomed to life with grenades and men began to be less careful with the safety pins, some men tried loosening the pins and using adhesive tape from the medics to keep the safety lever in place. I thought it took just as long to take the tape off as to just pull the pin. I tried holding a live grenade for a few seconds in the hope of having it explode in the air. One of them went off quicker than I expected and made me think about quality control at the factory. I went back to bending my grenade safety pins wide and throwing long.

I saw a small mule and, aided by our interpreter, tried to bargain for it with the farmer. Sergeant Cox put an end to my enterprise. There would be no private transport in the 3d Platoon. We had trained with mules at Camp Carson, but no mules were available to us in Korea. The mules were back in the United States living better than we were. In Korea we packed everything on our backs, with everyone carrying extra ammunition for the mortars and machine guns. It was the norm to climb those mountains carrying 100- to 110-pound loads.

Occasionally some of us would visit other units in search of ammunition or food. While doing this, I saw General MacArthur pass by in a jeep. It was a thrill to see this famed leader. He was relieved as United Nations commander on the eleventh of April 1951. We had no knowledge of the battle that was going on at the highest level. Whatever his faults, MacArthur wanted to win the war and hurt the Chinese whom we were fighting. With the complaints of our allies droning in his ears, President Truman and his advisors had already decided that Korea was not worth the possibility of a larger war. They had determined that Korea would be evacuated if military operations were unfavorable to us. All of us fighting in Korea were putting our lives on the line for a cause that had already abandoned victory. We were fighting for a better negotiating position.

It was a shock when General MacArthur was relieved of overall command and replaced by Gen. Matthew Ridgway. At the time of MacArthur's relief, General Ridgway had been serving under MacArthur as commander of ground forces in Korea. Our army was in retreat when Ridgway took command on the accidental death of Gen. Walton Walker. Ridgway changed the concept of our effort. At the time the Chinese entered the war, the North Korean army had been crushed. The American mission at that time was to gain ground to the Yalu River. The powerful Chinese blow sent

American and allied forces reeling backward in the longest retreat in US Army history. This was a new enemy, and new tactics were called for. The capturing of ground now was of less concern than slaughtering the vast number of Chinese. Ridgway made good plans that were approved by MacArthur. The Chinese were stopped and bloodied, and a limited movement north began.

Prior to MacArthur's relief, Ridgway had Operation Ripper under way, which had recaptured Seoul and brought us to a line called *Idaho* just south of the 38th parallel. We then continued the attack to Line Kansas, which brought us some ten miles north of the 38th parallel. When General Ridgway replaced General MacArthur as overall commander, Gen. James Van Fleet became the commander on the Korean peninsula. General Ridgway understood the reason MacArthur was relieved and followed the instructions he received from the Truman administration. Van Fleet was a general we loved, a man who sought victory in Korea. Van Fleet was a strong supporter of the Rangers.

It soon became obvious that the Ranger experience in Korea would have some variation from that which caused the public to remember the Rangers of World War II. Any who recall the WWII Rangers will remember the climbing of the cliffs at Pointe du Hoc on D day, 6 June 1944. There was nothing that dramatic for the Rangers in Korea. Our Communist enemy did not have sophisticated command and control facilities to be destroyed. There were no rail lines to be cut and, after Inchon, no amphibious invasions. The Chinese relied on large numbers of dedicated and disciplined men, ably backed by mortars and artillery. The Chinese might use bugles and drums in lieu of radios, but they were a formidable foe. The Ranger actions in Korea were the highest form of the art of patrolling.

It was difficult and demanding for even small numbers of men to get through the successive lines of the enemy. The Chinese numbers were far beyond that which the Germans or Japanese could muster in World War II. Few names of towns or cities in Korea were familiar to the American public. The people back home could not identify with a big fight at Hongchon. The World War II Rangers who fought in the high mountains of Italy at Monte Cassino would have been closest to the Korean War Ranger experience. The terrible winters of Korea and the monsoon rains were additional problems. No one knew the hardship and suffering in those Korean nights unless they were there.

Men in war need to strip away the propaganda and preconceived notions about the enemy. To think of the Chinese only as numbers is a critical mistake. They are a proud people and the product of an ancient culture. Their military leaders had absorbed lessons learned over thousands of years of warfare. "Know the enemy and know yourself," wrote Sun Tzu, who lived 400–320 B.C. The Chinese soldier was usually a man of the soil, accustomed to outdoor life. He was no stranger to hardship. To limit the effectiveness of our airpower, they remained hidden during the day and moved and attacked at night. Marches of twenty miles or more were routine. They were very adept at camouflage and concealment. Their reconnaissance elements were active during the day and night, while their larger forces remained hidden, readying themselves for the night attack. A very close relationship developed between leaders and men. Chinese soldiers were well briefed on their missions.

A key aspect of both North Korean and Chinese tactics was to get forces to the rear of an American position and isolate the American unit from supplies and reinforcement. Then the night attack would come from the front and flanks. Frequently attacking along the seams of unit boundaries, the Chinese sought to fragment the defense, to break it down into small elements often of platoon size. Then the Chinese would overwhelm the smaller American force with the sheer weight of their infantry assault. Attempting to retreat often meant being ambushed by the infiltrating force.

We found that the Chinese had a large amount of American equipment. We were fighting in Korea with much the same matériel that had been used in World War II. In its perceived role as the arsenal of democracy, the United States had delivered large quantities of war matériel to the Nationalist Chinese. When the Nationalists were defeated by Mao's Communist forces, vast stocks of war matériel were captured. Additional matériel had been taken from South Korean and American units that the Chinese had hammered on their entry into the war. We began to retake some of this American matériel back from dead and captured Chinese. One favorite weapon was the American Thompson submachine gun. A Prohibition-era favorite of the warring gangs of Chicago, the ten-pound, nine-ounce Thompson was effective at close range. It fired .45-caliber ammunition from twenty- or thirty-round detachable boxes.

In mid-April 1951 we began a series of daytime missions that gave us a different view of war. Chinese supply lines were overextended. The enemy was withdrawing northward, screening their movement with skilled reconnaissance units. We were unaware of this action at the time, but our senior commanders believed that the Chinese were preparing a major attack. In our sector of the 24th Division's front, the American advance had paused briefly while events developed. It was our mission to determine the situation in our sector.

On a sunny spring day, the three platoons of the 8th Rangers moved from concealed positions, passed through friendly lines, and proceeded on different routes to different objectives. Prior to departure we were teasing Tony Velo. He had a little Beretta pistol that he treasured, and he had worked on it till the weapon glowed. Most of us who carried .45-caliber pistols as a side arm thought the Berreta was useful only for shooting flies, but Tony loved that pistol. Jimmy White confided in me that he had been detailed to carry extra ammunition for the platoon machine gun. Though he would still be with the platoon, he would not be with our squad. He was very concerned about not being with those who were closest to him. It was a separation of only a few yards, but it seemed a world away to Jimmy; I understood his feeling. In battle you feel lost without your friends nearby.

In the 3d Platoon, our lead scout was Pete Torres. He was called "Silent Pete" for his ability to move ghostlike through rough terrain. Torres was followed by some men with automatic rifles, Lieutenant Strong, and radio operator E. C. Rivera. Stepping cautiously, wary of mines, we moved down a wooded ridge and into intermittent brush and broken ground. We then moved toward Hill 299, which rested between the lines and took its name from its elevation on the map. Now and then we could see the high ground that marked the Chinese main line of resistance (MLR). The only Chinese we encountered were rotting corpses, charred black by napalm.

Thirty-three men were on this patrol. If we encountered the Chinese, we had little doubt that we would be seriously outnumbered. The morning wore on, with the heat and the expectation of battle rising. Our scouts were not finding the enemy—but war is filled with expecting one thing and finding another. Emplacements were there but not the enemy. We thoroughly scouted the area, found it deserted, and decided it was time to return to friendly lines.

Tree- and brush-covered ridgelines ran from the hill, and one of these flanked open ground with woods to either side. We were moving down this ridge when the sound of nearby gunfire from the woods closest to the Chinese lines grabbed our attention. Flushed like a covey of quail, a small number of US soldiers came running out of the woods across the open field directly to our front. They were men of the 19th Infantry Regiment Intelligence and Reconnaissance (I&R) Platoon who had been conducting a reconnaissance when they were located by the Chinese. Lieutenant Strong snapped an order and we dropped into firing position, flipping off the safeties on our weapons. The Americans had no sooner reached the woods on the other side of the field than a torrent of Chinese soldiers poured out of the woods in hot pursuit. The discipline instilled during our training held firm. Not a single shot was loosed until the Chinese were in the middle of the open area. Lieutenant Strong gave the command, "Fire!" In Ranger lore, what followed became known as the (Hill) 299 Turkey Shoot. The enemy did not have a chance, which is the best way to fight a war. We were good shooters and the roar of our fire was deafening. I was one of six BAR men. Firing from the prone position with a bipod supporting the rifle barrel, we had a shooter's dream. An observation aircraft later estimated that seventy dead lay in the field. Other Chinese had followed their comrades to the edge of the woods, and we now began a firefight with them. Some of their bullets struck home. First to be hit was Pete Torres, who was shot through the face. The sight of Pete, his face covered with blood, numbed my mind. He lost so much blood that I felt certain he would die. Gil "Doc" Gregory was hurrying to his side. Training took over and I continued to fire. I learned later that the bullet went in on the high side of Pete's right eye, exited under his left jaw, and lodged in his shoulder blade. Doc Gregory extracted the bullet using a pair of fingernail clippers.

Eventually we achieved fire superiority and were able to force the Chinese to withdraw. Seeing this, Lieutenant Strong ordered us to pursue. With adrenaline flowing, we attacked. We encountered a fortified bunker that stalled our advance. I heard Strong's voice yelling, "When I throw the grenade, everyone goes!" The Chinese position was destroyed. Firing from the hip, we then continued our advance. A Chinese soldier rose up to throw a grenade, but just as his arm went back, Ranger Bill Williamson shot him and the grenade exploded in the Chinese position. As we drove into their line, the Chinese realized that they were confronting a small force and began to flank us. Now they became the attackers. Mortar rounds were dropping around us, and machine-gun fire and shrapnel were hitting our men. Jimmy White, our Little Tiger, was killed either by a grenade, mortar round, or a mine, something that exploded at his feet and tore life from him. The Chinese attempted to block our route of withdrawal, and bullets came at us from all sides. Rangers Washburn and Waldecker were hit. We knew, when surrounded, to concentrate our fire in one direction and break out. With Strong and Cox leading, we fired and ran, fired and ran.

Like angry hornets, they pursued us while we moved as rapidly as we could, dragging and carrying our wounded with us. A Chinese machine gunner was covering an open space from long range, which we had to cross. Several of us noticed a peculiar circumstance. If an unhurt man was crossing the field, the gunner would attempt to shoot him. If someone was carrying a wounded man, the Chinese soldier did not fire. Was this a Chinese Beau Geste, a gentleman warrior on the other side? Was he changing belts of ammunition or firing elsewhere? It was best to take no chances and run like hell.

As we retreated we continued to suffer casualties. Most of us could run, but Tony Velo was seriously wounded, hit in both thighs by automatic weapons fire. We had tourniquets on both of Velo's legs, but his blood kept dripping. The men to my front took turns carrying Velo on their backs, his hands tied across their chests. We moved rapidly, the scouts running ahead while several of us with automatic rifles covered the rear. As we moved more to the center of the open land between the armies, the Chinese ended their pursuit. To make better time, we followed a dirt path used by local farmers and woodcutters; narrow and thick with dust, it ran uphill and down. I followed closely behind the men who were taking turns carrying Velo. As I moved along I could see the bright drops of Tony Velo's blood settling into the dust of the trail.

Exhausted, we reached our lines. Other soldiers came to help with our wounded while the remainder of us rested on the reverse slope of the ridge. After a time Sergeant Cox took us to a truck on which Tony was lying. "Take your last look at Velo," said Cox, "he's dead."

Sometimes when looking toward rear areas I would see a helicopter with a stretcher affixed to each side—they were not for Rangers. We had no helicopters and no stretchers. In all our fights behind enemy lines, the practice of carrying out our wounded on our backs was routine. Helicopter evacuation for our casualties could not take place forward of friendly lines. It was too dangerous for the helicopter. Many a man risked his life to bring out a wounded companion. When possible, we brought out our dead as well. We had a deep appreciation for the quiet South Carolinian medic Gil Gregory. He was nurse, doctor, first-aid station, and hospital to us. Above the roar of battle the cry of "Medic!" was often heard, and Gil was always there for the 3d Platoon. I never asked him what the Geneva Convention contained about medics going armed. The North Koreans paid no attention to such rules and would not hesitate to kill a medic. On day missions Gil carried extra mortar or machine-gun ammunition and was armed with an M1 rifle. For night operations he carried a lightweight .45-caliber submachine gun. He would fight until someone was shot, then sling his weapon, pick up his medical bag, and become our doctor. Medics were always known as "Doc." Doc Gregory told me that his procedure was: stop the bleeding, administer morphine, and show concern. It worked.

Chinese activity increased with considerable patrolling and probing attacks by the enemy. We were usually used on specialized missions, but if the 24th Division commander felt the need to use us as a line unit for a period, he would. We were moved into position on the front line and dug our foxholes, coordinating our fire with units on our left and right. My assistant automatic rifle man and I had the extreme left foxhole of our company position, and a short distance to my left were positions of men from the 19th Infantry Regiment. A ridgeline ran from the front of my position to a hill opposite, which was occupied by the Chinese.

The 19th Infantry rifleman who occupied the position to my left came over for a visit as my assistant and I dug in. He was a small man, dirty and unshaven, and his eyes seemed to be looking at something far beyond. They were eyes that had seen too much and were frozen in what is frequently called "the thousand-yard stare." He was very much impressed that we were Rangers and felt gratified that we were nearby. I noticed that while his clothes and body carried the filth of living in the earth, his rifle was clean and he handled it as though it were an extension of his body.

As darkness fell, my assistant and I began to take two-hour turns on watch. It was a moonlit night. The breeze rustled bushes and limbs of trees, giving them movement and life that frequently caused me to disengage the safety on my weapon. It was difficult to stay awake, but the chill of the night gave a slight shivering motion to my body. My assistant was curled up on the opposite side of the foxhole, sleeping soundly. He began to snore loudly and repeatedly. I felt the sound could be heard in Peking. Initially I shook him but, becoming weary of this, I jammed my boot against his ribs. He would protest and go back to sleep.

As the night wore on, it once again became my turn to rest. I shook my assistant and said, "Your watch . . . are you awake?" He replied, "Yeah-yeah, I'm awake." I said, "Are you sure you're awake?" He responded, "Yeah, I'm sure." I curled up in the hole and was soon asleep.

Something heavy hit me and the sound of gunfire brought me to consciousness. Someone was on me, and my assistant was yelling. I was terrified, pushing and thrusting at what I recognized in the dark as a human form in Chinese garb. Too frightened to think of a weapon, I was just pushing and hitting out. Then I felt warm blood and could tell that the form was limp. Half in panic, half in relief, my assistant and I threw the body out of the hole. My brother Ranger kept apologizing—he had fallen asleep. Still shaking, filled with horror and anger, I cursed and kicked him. Filled with shame, he made no effort to retaliate. Neither of us slept for the remainder of the night.

When dawn came, I went to the foxhole of the soldier from the 19th Infantry. He told me that a Chinese reconnaissance patrol had come down the ridgeline. He wondered why we were not firing, but he felt it was because we Rangers planned to take these Chinese prisoner. When the lead man was standing over our foxhole, he realized we were asleep and shot the man. He was not certain, but he believed he had hit some of the other Chinese.

I explained what had happened, apologized, and thanked him profusely. He shrugged his shoulders. I could tell that his opinion of Rangers had sunk to zero. I thought of all the times I had heard Airborne soldiers mock the Infantry and call them by the derogatory terms of "straight-legs" or "legs." I would never again indulge in that practice. That little dogfaced runt with the thousand-yard stare had just saved my life.

As we were frequently exhausted from the rigors of combat, falling asleep at the wrong time was a constant threat. War is a tiring business, and the strain of combat wears on nerves and body. Some men had very close calls. On a night patrol behind enemy lines, Doc Gregory fell asleep. He awoke to find that we had moved on and he was alone in the darkness. Gregory experienced temporary terror, but got control of himself and training took over. He was able to locate the platoon before the Chinese found him. Back in our own lines, Gregory was furious with the man who should have signaled him to move on. The Ranger responded that he had and that Gregory acknowledged it. Doc then knew that he had fallen back to sleep.

With the rations was included a combination letter paper and envelope and a small pencil such as golf courses use. It was free mail. I wrote home whenever I could, but I was not a good correspondent. My dad wrote me and told me to stop using profanity, including such descriptions as "the fuckin' Chinese." He did not have a high regard for the Chinese, but felt that the words were offensive to my mother and sister. I cringe when I recall how heartless I was when writing to my mother. I told her the details of how men died. I cursed the staff officers who were living the good life in Japan. I had no factual knowledge of the staff officers in Japan or how they lived, but a vital purpose of staff officers is to give troops in combat a mystical figure to bitch about.

A prime topic of conversation was the Dutch battalion. We did not know if the story was true, but it was repeated in the manner that parents tell children: "The devil will get you if you don't behave." We were told that Chinese posing as

South Korean soldiers had walked into the center of the Dutch unit one night. They killed the commander and bayoneted Dutch troops in their sleeping bags. The Chinese had their own versions of Rangers. They were very good at what they did. When it suited them, they would dress in captured South Korean uniforms and carry captured American weapons to enter our lines. It was risky for South Korean soldiers to come near us. We took no chances. We kept our rifles at hand and pistols in our sleeping bags. My father had given me a .45-caliber automatic just prior to my leaving for Korea. I could have made good use of a shoulder holster but did not have one, so I settled for having the pistol loose in the sleeping bag. It was not a comfortable sleeping partner. During the course of a night, it would be under my jaw or in my ear. I considered trying to keep the pistol between my legs, but blowing my brains out seemed preferable to loss of sexual function, even if it was unused.

Mines and booby traps were constant threats. I was on the forward slope of a hill when an American three-quarter-ton truck on the other side ran over a mine. The explosion was horrendous and a wheel shot skyward above the hill. The driver was killed. The terrain had been fought over several times, and mines and booby traps left behind were still active. As Rangers roamed across the front, we had little knowledge of what had been put down. An American device was just as dangerous to us as one hidden by the Chinese.

The enlistments of four Rangers were expiring. They packed their duffel bags, and a jeep was brought into our reserve area to take them to the rear so they could begin the process of shipping out for home. Rudy Belluomini of San Jose, California, was one of these, and Rivera waved good-bye to him, calling out, "Say hello to the girls in San Jose for me, Rudy." Within a few days these men came back in the same jeep they had left in. Told that President Truman was extending all enlistments a year, they were going back to the front. These men were boiling with anger. None were killed, but some were later wounded.

When ordered to make a night patrol, six to ten members

of the 3d Platoon of the 8th Rangers held a form of war dance while readying weapons and equipment. E. C. Rivera, Harry Trout, and I would bellow out songs in ragged harmony while the nonsingers beat on logs or steel helmets with sticks. When we moved to the trucks or began the march forward there was little conversation. We would sit on the wooden slat seats of two-and-a-half-ton trucks and look at the man across from us, knowing it was time to get serious. Last-minute private conversations would occur in the assembly area.

On 22 April 1951, two platoons of Rangers were scheduled for individual missions. My platoon moved into an assembly area behind the 19th Infantry Regiment and, under cover of darkness, went forward to pass into no-man's-land. The sector was quiet, but there seemed to be an increasing buildup of fire to the distant east and west. As we made our final preparations, we were surprised to see a jeep with its lights on bouncing up the hill. The driver was a staff officer who risked his life to tell us to call off the mission. As he put it, "waves" of Chinese were attacking along the front.

It was the beginning of what the Chinese called their Fifth Phase Offensive. Three Chinese armies supported by reconstituted North Korean units were committed to their greatest offensive and the major battle of the Korean War. Emboldened by their early success, the Chinese political leadership made a grave miscalculation. The Chinese believed that their armies could crush United Nations forces and drive them from Korea. When the Chinese entered the war, the Americans were in a "home-by-Christmas" mood. Now the Chinese rulers had a similar attitude. The principal targets of the Chinese forces were the weaker, less-well-trained Republic of Korea (ROK) divisions. Of these, the ROK 6th Division was located in the Namdae River valley south of Kumhwa. The ROK 6th Division was on the right flank of the US 24th Infantry Division, with the US 1st Marine Division located on the other side of the Koreans. After being alerted by the staff officer, we learned that the situation in the 6th ROK area was uncertain. It appeared that the South Koreans were in retreat; this would leave a gap between the American forces that the Chinese could exploit.

We were resupplied with ammunition and cast-iron fragmentation hand grenades, which we hooked on our belts and on the webbing of our packs. It was our good fortune that we would have a last hot meal before our next mission. It was one of those hearty meals with slabs of meat and mashed potatoes. I ladled on a large amount of gravy. Lacking utensil space, I put the cherry pie on top of the potatoes. Bill Wheland, a member of my squad who had been ahead of me in the chow line, was a man of great appetite. He always wanted more food. Wheland asked the cooks for more bread. They told him there was bread on the mess truck. He climbed onto the truck, took a loaf of bread, and, with his hands laden with mess kit, bread, and weapon, jumped off. There was a cry and a commotion. Most of us came to believe later that the safety ring on a hand grenade had caught on something and pulled free. We saw Wheland struggling with his cartridge belt. He then turned away and yelled "Get back!" The grenade exploded. Wheland was hurled backward, his chest and stomach ripped open. He yelled, "Oh Christ!" Doc Gregory hurried to Wheland's side but nothing could be done. Many Rangers still kept the safety pins on their grenades relatively flat as it enabled the safety pin to be easily pulled. That probably contributed to Bill Wheland's death. The grenade that killed Wheland had also set off .30-caliber rounds at his belt. Three other Rangers were wounded in this tragedy. The food, which had looked so nourishing, was suddenly revolting. We emptied the food we had yearned for into garbage cans, cleaned our mess kits, and moved to our next assembly area.

The next day was hectic, with UN units moving about and getting hit from the flank and rear. No one had an understanding of what was happening in the 6th ROK Division area. In the afternoon the 8th Airborne Rangers received orders for a night mission. We were to advance into the area of the Korean division and provide the US 24th Infantry Division with information concerning enemy activity. We knew nothing about the location of the Chinese or North Koreans, but the indications were ominous.

Ninety of us went on the mission. In addition to our own heavy loads we carried a considerable amount of extra ammunition for our mortars and machine guns. My load included a twenty-pound Browning automatic rifle, twelve magazines of twenty rounds each, two 60mm mortar rounds, a .45-caliber pistol with extra magazines, four fragmentation grenades, rations for two days, poncho, knife, sleeping bag, entrenching tool, canteen, first-aid kit, P-38 can opener, and my faithful spoon.

Our route of march took us high into the mountains, where we could see the battle area more clearly. We climbed through the night. It was brutal. We had to pull and boost each other up steep terrain that at times bordered on the vertical. E. C. Rivera was burdened with the heavy radio in addition to his weapons and gear, and Nick Tisak and I helped him with the load. We moved as quietly as possible, but in the lower areas, others were so confident that they were unrestrained. As we continued our silent movement, we heard voices that were soon identified as Chinese. Not wanting to reveal our position, we moved off some distance while our leaders called in artillery fire on the enemy. Continuing on, we found South Korean soldiers who had been left behind when their units fled. They fell into line and were given the task of carrying some of our extra ammunition.

The next morning we reached the summit of Hill 1010. The plan was to continue to an even higher elevation, but a 1st Platoon patrol lead by M.Sgt. (master sergeant) Phil Moore found the enemy in control of the higher point. The Chinese did not know we were on Hill 1010.

It was an excellent observation point overlooking miles of the battlefront. From my position on the hill, I saw the Chinese moving boldly. They were below us in what appeared to be rivers of brown flowing south—Chinese in massive numbers moving forward to reinforce their attacking troops. American airpower was being heavily used, but the targets were five miles south of us. What we saw did not bode well for us. We were deep in enemy-controlled territory and greatly outnumbered.

The height of our observation point allowed us to use our backpack radio for intermittent communication with the 21st Infantry Regiment and the 5th Regimental Combat Team. E. C. Rivera was now our senior radio operator, and he was assisting the company commander, Captain Herbert, in sending reports. We were unaware at the time that the 6th ROK Division had not only retreated but had broken and fled some twenty-one miles. In response, the 24th Infantry Division refused (turned) its right flank and the 1st Marine Division turned its left flank to create a U-shaped defense that encompassed the former area of the 6th ROK's. To stop the Chinese attack, the British brigade and the 5th Cavalry Regiment were committed at the base of the penetration. The ninety men of the 8th Rangers were at the upper and middle portion of the U.

The retreat of the Korean soldiers forced the American 24th Division to fight on its right flank as well as its front. American forces were spread thin, with frequent gaps between units. Chinese troops took advantage of these gaps to pass through our positions and hit rear areas. Artillery, signal, and quartermaster units found themselves fighting for their lives. Throughout the area, American units were withdrawing. We had accomplished our mission of reporting enemy penetrations, strength, and movement. It was now time to leave. To wait for night could leave us so deep behind enemy lines that we would be unable to rejoin friendly forces. We would have to move by daylight. Fortunately, the Chinese were unaware that we were above them.

To rejoin the withdrawing Americans, our route from Hill 1010 had to be southwest. The ridgeline running downward in that direction was partly wooded with rock formations, occasionally giving way to barren areas that offered no concealment. The ridge was razor-backed, dropping off at sharp angles and leading down to the lesser elevation where Hill 628 would be on our right. From Hill 1010, ridges and draws led off to other hills. Coming down the narrow ridge, the valley floor would be on our right flank.

We moved with M.Sgt. Phil Moore's 1st Platoon in the lead, followed by 3d Platoon, and then the 2d. From my location at the rear of the 3d Platoon, I could see the action unfolding before and below me.

Perhaps we could have made it out without being discovered—but that was not to be. Partway down the ridgeline, 1st Platoon scouts spotted a Chinese force in the vicinity of Hill 628 preparing to attack the flank of the 24th Infantry Division. To leave them unmolested would result in serious harm to other American soldiers. A strike would disrupt their planned attack but reveal our presence. Captain Herbert ordered them taken under fire.

Their attack was spoiled, but our fire alerted the enemy to our presence and location. Chinese units on adjacent hills promptly spotted us, and a hail of fire came our way. To rejoin American forces, our only alternative was to attack southwest. The ridge was too narrow for our company or even platoons to use the tactic of one element firing while another maneuvered to right or left. Our fire and movement was based on the slope of ground. With Phil Moore leading, the 1st Platoon charged down the ridgeline while the 3d and 2d Platoons fired over their heads and at the surrounding hills. I could not see the enemy. Someone would point and yell, "They're over there," and we would fire in that direction.

Ordered to move in support of the 1st Platoon, the 3d Platoon began running down the hill with bullets zipping around us. I felt the tug of one or more bullets penetrating my pack. Running full speed, I tripped and glimpsed my sleeping bag trailing behind me like a bridal train. Distracted, I lost my footing and pitched forward, my weapon jamming into the dirt and breaking my fall. I shed my pack, staying prone, as men leaped over me. Moving again, I attempted to fire, but the bolt on my BAR slid forward with an ineffectual thud. To be without a functioning weapon in such a situation is to be useless.

Caught in the open in the midst of the firefight with the

crack of bullets going by, I removed my cartridge belt and jacket. Spreading the jacket on the ground, I took the BAR apart, placed the parts on the jacket, and cleaned them. Though a shaving brush was seldom used by men in the 1950s, it was one of the most important things we carried. We had learned that a lightly oiled, bristled shaving brush did an effective job of cleaning dirt from a weapon. My shaving brush enabled me to clean my BAR quickly. After reassembly, I test-fired the weapon, put on my jacket and cartridge belt, and began moving and firing.

My friend Len Wiggins later told me that this was a courageous act, but it was done out of desperation. Had there been cover from the enemy's fire, I would have used it. I would have gladly used another available weapon. Neither circumstance existed. I had no choice. Without the weapon I was unable to fight.

Down the trail where some cover did exist, Rangers were firing from behind rocks. The three platoons were now mixed. Men who had been seriously wounded were sprawled on the ground, while those with lesser wounds were still fighting. The medics of our three platoons were racing from wounded to wounded. Captain Herbert was down, shot through the shoulder and neck, and Lieutenant Strong had been wounded as well. I saw Master Sergeant Moore get hit in the thigh by a bullet while leading an assault down the narrow ridgeline. He was knocked from the ridge and rolled over and over down the slope, only to be stopped by some hillside obstruction. Incredibly, the sergeant immediately resumed firing. I later learned that Moore had his map case shot away while being bandaged by his platoon medic, Harold "Doc" Potter. A mortar round exploded nearby and Moore's left hand and arm were torn by numerous pieces of shrapnel, but he kept fighting.

At one spot we found large boulders beyond which were some depressions, hollowed out sometime earlier by one side or the other. To engage the enemy it was necessary to cross an open area in front of the boulders. Under heavy fire I slid across on my back, my weapon at my side. A Chinese machine gunner was working the area and traversed across me. His bullets seemed to be a hand's breadth over my nose, cracking the air and whining off the stone. He moved his fire onward, and I made a leap for an occupied depression and muscled my way in. My companion was a South Korean soldier armed with an M1 Garand rifle. Unable to converse and very busy, we looked at each other and began to fire at the enemy.

The Chinese had a strong base of fire while they attempted to maneuver against us. Most of our leaders were hit. Squad and platoon integrity had vanished, but Rangers did not shirk the fight. There was a constant roar of gunfire. My Korean companion grabbed my sleeve and began jabbering words I did not understand. He pointed at my BAR and then in the direction of a gully leading up to our position. Coming up the small ravine directly toward us was a squad of Chinese soldiers, one behind the other.

I put a fresh magazine in my weapon, took careful aim, and fired short bursts down their line. When that BAR sang, it sang a beautiful bass that was recognizable across the battlefield. The twenty rounds had the desired effect. I turned to my newfound Korean friend with a shout of exultation. He was sprawled against the back of the hole, facing skyward, a round blue-black hole in the center of his forehead. Fear seized me, and I jumped from the hole and ran to rejoin other Rangers who were attacking in the direction of Hill 628.

Lieutenant Alfred "Jack" Giacherine, the company executive officer, was the only officer still able to fight. He had come forward from the rear of the column and begun to coordinate our efforts. I saw Rivera and his radio beside Giacherine, and soon American artillery began to hammer the Chinese. We were no longer fighting as platoons or even squads. Some men were fighting in one direction while others were moving and shooting at other points of the compass. A number of us assaulted Hill 628 and drove the enemy from it. We threw their dead out of their holes and occupied them. Someone yelled to me that my friend Harry Trout was dead. A machine gun had ripped across his body. We had no time to mourn; our casualties were scattered about. Nearly one-third of the company was hit, and platoon medics were rapidly moving about, tending the wounds of man after man. I learned later that Gregory alone treated twelve men. Men who are hit hard are no longer in control of themselves. A feeling of vulnerability and dependency on others takes over. They care about what is happening to their friends and worry that they cannot assist. They wonder what will happen to them. Will they survive, will their comrades leave them? Doc Gregory was a thinking man who knew that wounded men need assurance as well as medical help. As Doc bound up the bleeding wounds of one Ranger, the man asked him, "What do I do now, Doc?" Gregory picked up the Ranger's weapon and pushed it at him. "Keep fighting," he said.

By the nature of the work, Rangers are often alone, indeed surrounded in enemy territory. We had trained to accept that, but sometimes it makes for one hell of a fight. We were in a challenging situation, with the enemy on three sides of us and the valley floor on the other. The Chinese could continue to add men to the fight—we could not. We also could not move rapidly because of our wounded men. I would learn later that Lieutenant Giacherine was making calls for assistance. Units of the 24th Infantry Division tried to link up with us, but the Chinese drove them off. Each American unit had its own battle to fight. We received a message sent by the operations officer of the 5th Regimental Combat Team and relayed through the 2d Battalion, 21st Infantry, which read, "Send message to Ranger company. Get out best way possible."

We would receive no help from friendly infantry. Looking to our right, down in the valley floor, we saw tanks remaining behind, covering the withdrawal of American forces. Giacherine wanted to link up with the tanks and picked a location in the valley where we would attempt to reach them. Rivera repeatedly tried to contact the tankers but was unsuccessful. Knowing that he would have better radio communications from higher ground, Rivera voluntarily climbed to an exposed location on top of Hill 628. Ranger

Nick Tisak, armed with a BAR, accompanied him. As the Chinese tried to shoot them off the hilltop, Tisak was hit in the leg but continued to fire.

A group of Chinese came running down the opposite slope and Tisak fired into them, dropping several and scattering the rest. One bold Chinese continued forward, diving into the corner of a small trench. Tisak fired a twenty-round magazine into the position and ended the aggressiveness of that Chinese soldier. While this firing was in progress, Rivera continued his attempt to establish radio contact. Fearing an enemy ruse, a cautious American radio operator quizzed Rivera on the occupations of famous Americans. Though furious at the name game, Rivera kept trying. When he identified Sam Snead as a golfer, his request for assistance was allowed to get through.

Lieutenant Dave Teich, platoon leader of 3d Platoon, Company C, 6th Medium Tank Battalion, volunteered to take his five tanks to a point that Giacherine believed we could reach with our wounded. While these discussions were taking place, a Chinese assault had been halted. Both sides had taken cover and were engaging one another with heavy fire. Giacherine and Rivera continued to call in artillery on the Chinese positions while Giacherine planned the route of withdrawal. On order, Rangers began to move toward the valley floor. Scouts led, followed by a security element for the wounded and those who carried them. Only men who could not walk were assisted. Some of the wounded coming off the ridgeline and Hill 628 used their hands to hold in their intestines. Captain Herbert had pushed his fingers into the wounds in his neck and shoulder to staunch the bleeding and was among those walking.

My location was far away from where the withdrawal started. Standard operating procedure in my platoon was for the automatic rifle men to cover the rear during withdrawals, which is what I was doing. Moving down Hill 628, frequently stopping or walking backward, I saw a line of Chinese coming over the top of the hill to our rear. They came fast, appearing as a dark line silhouetted against the sky. I opened fire and yelled, "BARs to the rear!" While I was shooting, Ranger Oral Baldridge came up beside me and opened fire. Soon other automatic rifle men hurried into position beside us and I heard the deep-throated roar of their weapons. To come after us the Chinese had to cross that hilltop, and this made them vulnerable. While other men took our wounded down the slope, the automatic rifle men continued to fire. Together we swept the enemy from the crest of the ridge. Each time the Chinese came rushing across the hilltop, we shot them and drove the survivors back.

A gap was now developing between those of us at the rear and the rest of the company. As I looked toward the hilltop, I saw an aircraft coming in from my right. It was a single-engine, black, gull-winged fighter-bomber—a Corsair. As the pilot swept over the top of Hill 628 he released a large napalm canister. Moments later a vast ball of flame and black smoke leaped skyward. We felt a wary joy in our small party as we again started downward. The napalm had hit the Chinese and they did not pursue us. At a bend in the trail another Ranger stopped and stepped aside while I kept moving. He was the last man off Hill 628.

We hurried onward and rejoined the rest of the company aboard the waiting tanks. Engines roared and dirt flew from under their thick treads as we sped toward American lines. We clung to any handhold we could find, scorching the soles of our boots on the tank's hot exhaust plates. The crew was under armor and could not be seen. Later I learned that when told to leave us to our own fate, Lieutenant Teich and his men had disregarded their orders and displayed uncommon valor in putting themselves at risk for us. Without the tanks we may not have made it to friendly positions. No Ranger would leave a wounded comrade. The powerful engines of the tanks roared, and we sped toward friendly units. It was a very good feeling to be back in friendly territory. Of the ninety Rangers on the mission, one-third were casualties. Among the 3d Platoon wounded who were evacuated were Lieutenant Strong, Doc Gregory, and Nick Tisak. The rest of us moved to take up defensive positions.

11

Life at the Front

Now the mission was defensive, and we were used where most needed. If a place on the line needed shoring up, we might be used there or to spearhead a counterattack. That does not imply that division rifle companies were not performing these actions. There was plenty of fighting for everyone as the Chinese sought to exploit their gains. General Van Fleet had established another defensive line, but no name was assigned to it; therefore it became known as the No Name Line.

The Chinese advance was extending their logistical supply lines and making them more vulnerable to our great airpower. War is retreating and advancing. The American withdrawal was not a rout. Coming down from a line of hills, I looked to my left and right. As far as my eyes could see, American units were pulling back, but doing so in orderly fashion. We were moving to the prepared positions of the next line. To continue their attack, the Chinese had to come into open ground. The more Chinese we had in the open, the more Chinese we could kill.

Sustained combat saps the aggressive spirit. A few men of proven courage began to seek ways to avoid patrols or cracked under the strain. While we were moving up a hill we came under a Chinese mortar attack. A veteran sergeant who had seen too much in World War II broke and came running past me in wild-eyed fright, screaming, "The mortars! The mortars!" He was finished as a combat man and was evacuated from our company.

Our Ranger company was now down to one-third of its

full strength, and soon other Rangers began to arrive. The Ranger Training Center at Fort Benning had established a training company whose mission was to provide Rangers to the units in Korea. These were fully qualified men, not those with only basic training shoved into the replacement pipeline. The men who came to us were not replacing anyone. When these Rangers joined our company, they immediately began proving their worth. Some of these men volunteered for missions again and again. One of the best was Ranger Charles "Chuck" Ouimette from Easthampton, Massachusetts, who became a close friend. Chuck's profile appeared to be carved from New England granite. His last name was of French extraction and pronounced "We met." When Chuck joined the platoon, Wild Bill Cox asked, "What's your name, soldier?" Chuck said, "Ouimette, Sergeant!" Cox snarled, "I don't give a damn if we met or not, I asked you what your name is."

Our company armorer repaired or exchanged our weapons. Ranger Chet Wolfe had that vital job, but he dislocated his shoulder in a fall and was sent to the rear to get it put back in place. That repair did not take long, but on the way back to the line the armored personnel carrier he was riding in was ambushed and Chet got shot up, and back to the hospital he went.

As we moved through a destroyed town that included a building whose exterior walls were in rubble, someone noticed a large circular safe of the type called "cannonball" standing in the middle of the debris. The safe defied efforts to open it, so firepower was brought to the task. A 57mm recoilless rifle was employed to blow the safe open. No silver or gold was found, but the safe did contain a lot of paper money. Unfortunately, it was all Korean money that was useless to us. The wind scattered it about the ruins.

When we were put into the line to shore up a weak position that was under attack, we had more firepower than a line rifle company, so we were difficult to dislodge. Chinese laundries had long been popular in the United States. During one

Chinese attack a Ranger was heard yelling above the gunfire, "Come up and get the laundry, you motherfuckers!"

Life cannot be more basic than that of an infantryman in combat. We lived in a hole in the ground, called a "foxhole," and changed our residence frequently. We dug in the earth with small shovels approximately two feet long, known as "entrenching tools." The shovel head could be rotated and locked in position to serve as a mattock. Carried on the back of the pack or on the side of the cartridge belt, the entrenching tool was a vital element of survival.

We dug into earth that had roots and rocks, and on one occasion, I dug my hole in sand. Though easier to dig, the sand would not support itself. The walls kept caving in as I shoveled. My foxhole began to resemble a bomb crater. Fortunately, the Chinese attacked another portion of the line and we were sent there, where the earth was more reliable.

The holes we dug were usually for two men, but as Rangers were wounded or killed, those of us who remained frequently found ourselves on our own and responsible for a wider area. Our foxholes varied in depth, depending on how much time we had before combat or movement to a new location where digging would begin again. I liked to dig my hole deep enough so I could stand up in it and have my elbow leaning on the ground. This gave me a comfortable firing position for my Browning automatic rifle. In defensive situations I carved a small shelf in the earth where I could lay out a line of fragmentation grenades. At one side of the bottom of the hole I dug deeper, making a sump. I had an obscure hope that, if pushed to it, I could kick an enemy grenade into the sump and cringe in the other side of the hole while the sump directed the explosive force upward. This was likely wishful thinking and fortunately not put to the test. The sump was handy for two other reasons. It could be used to drain off light rain and in emergency circumstances served as a toilet. Korea has a monsoonal climate. Living in a hole in the earth with only the sky for a roof, we were at the mercy of the eléments. Huddled under our ponchos with the rain beating on our steel helmets, we found the water rising in the bottom of our holes and the earth turning to a thick, glutinous mud beneath us. We had gallons of water coming in on us, but we would have killed for a shower. Our fatigue uniforms were soaked and mud stained and carried the ripe odor of accumulated sweat.

The steel helmet was both a boon and a curse. We would wash and shave in it, sit on it, shit in it, and scramble to retrieve it when it fell from our heads, which often happened when we were diving for cover from shrapnel. Division headquarters had a passion about soldiers wearing their steel helmet, and men were fined who got caught without it. We wore the steel helmet for daylight operations, but the soft cap with visor was used at night.

Our underwear was black with filth, and our bodies developed rashes and sores. Keeping our feet dry was always a challenge and dry socks were a treasure. If time permitted I put tree branches beneath my boots, but the mud and wet were constant companions. Still, it was better to be in a hole than in a Korean hut where rodents carried disease. No matter where we were, we encountered sickness. Some men contracted hepatitis with jaundice, others had hemorrhagic fever. We caught colds and a variety of other illnesses, but a man had to be very ill to get relief. On one occasion I had intestinal flu. I could not control my discharge. I fouled my clothing and grew constantly weaker. I was sent back to the aid station and examined by a doctor. "Yep," he said triumphantly. "You got it, and bleeding piles, too. If you ever get off the line, we'll fix you up." I don't remember even getting the traditional two aspirins!

I do remember trying to climb the back of the high hill where the 8th Rangers were dug in. I was so weak that I had to pull myself along by grasping trees and bushes. Only the resilience of youth brought me through.

We lived like animals in our holes in the earth. At times we were predators and at times we were prey. Terror was a frequent companion. When possible, we cut logs or took tree limbs to form an overhead shelter for our foxholes, and then piled earth on that. This was not to protect us from the rain of Mother Nature but from the rain of shrapnel the Chinese artillery and mortars were directing at us. Our positions would be pounded by men who knew what they were about. The earth around my hole would leap skyward in thunderous explosions. The violence of high explosives cannot be truly measured in words; suffice it to say that it hurled me about like a rag doll. I felt like the fillings in my teeth were rattling. Cringing at the bottom of the hole, I begged for my life on grounds some would have thought were irrational. "Save me, God. I've never fucked an American girl!"

I never met an atheist in a foxhole, certainly not while he was under fire. I was raised in true, religious freedom and have always been grateful that someone did not take me at age five and begin to stuff my head full of ritual and fear. No man, be he minister, priest, rabbi, or imam, knows the answers to the eternal questions. We only know what we choose to believe, and organized religions have a long history of torturing and killing those who do not share their belief. My family lived a form of Christianity that made me believe that the way Christ lived his life was enough of an example. In my belief, Christ, the Carpenter, led by example and would have scorned the rituals, gold, and costly vestments. I did not find my belief in God in churches or cathedrals or in the mouthings of another man. I found God in the great miracle of Creation, the hills, the trees, the blue sky overhead. I was a grateful part of God's miracle. I might not be any more important to God than the leaf that falls at season's end. A transient being, I, too, would someday meet my end. I believed my eternal life would be as part of nature. But I hoped death was years in the future, and so I prayed.

One Sunday afternoon my platoon was getting ready to pass through friendly lines to go out on a combat patrol. We were in an assembly area on the reverse slope of a hill that overlooked the valley we were going into. Rangers were checking weapons and equipment, and those who had finished were sprawled about. One man was reading a comic book. A chaplain came up the hill and asked if anyone would like to talk to him before we went out on the mission. We just looked at him in a silent "You talking to us?" The Ranger reading the comic book shrugged his shoulders and went back to reading. The chaplain, a good man doing his duty, got a bewildered look on his face, stared for a while, then turned and walked down the hill, shaking his head. I don't know what he thought of us, but at that moment I believe we had our minds set on killing someone and were not in the mood for praying.

The assembly area was a place of concealment located to the rear of the infantry foxholes. It was here that we made the final checks of weapons and equipment and received final instructions. When the preparations for battle had been made, we always had a time to wait before the time to kill or be killed. This was a time when men opened themselves to each other. No one said it, but we wanted to ensure that someone would remember something about us.

It was a time for revelation, opening the memories of our lives to each other. We were the boys of the Depression. The full meaning of the tragedy of that time was found in the lives of my friends. My father was a hard man, but he was sober and hardworking and took good care of his family. When I was a boy, I thought I had been deprived of much. I came to realize how fortunate I had been to have my parents alive and together to raise me. Both E. C. Rivera and Doc Gregory had lost their fathers before they were age six. I remembered that Nick Tisak told me his father had died when he was eleven. During the Depression the death of a father frequently left a young mother destitute and unable to care for her children. E. C. and Doc were raised in the disciplined atmosphere of an orphanage. I had worked hard on the farm, but my mom was always there for me. As little boys, some of my Ranger friends had to hope for visits from their mothers. Boys of age six to nine had prowled the railroad tracks collecting bits of coal dropped from the tenders of steam locomotives. The coal they gathered was critical to their families as fuel for cooking and warmth. Kids not yet in their teens sought work to buy their own clothes. I learned that many of my brother Rangers were children of hard times.

Most of them had grown up with a remarkable degree of self-sufficiency.

All of us knew that World War II had shaped our lives. The patriotism of the time was a white-hot fire that had blazed within us. Patriotism is what led us to join, but it was not what molded us. We volunteered again and again so that we might challenge and test ourselves. We were molded in stress to be men who believed they could accomplish anything.

Whatever went before, the prime motivator on the battlefield was not letting your comrades down. The unique and often temporary sharing of love, dependency, and self-sacrifice in battle is the greatest memory most combat veterans carry.

There were men in my Ranger company whom I disliked. They were my brother Rangers, but brothers can dislike each other. In combat we would fight side by side. We would risk our lives for each other during moments of battle, but when the fighting was done we went back to disliking each other. Still, we had the moments of memory when we were one.

We had efficient officers in the 8th Rangers, but when men died, the officers were frequently blamed. Men would complain that the tactics were faulty or say the officer was too aggressive or not aggressive enough. Men wanted officers to be human, but as infallible as a God. It was not fair to fault these men who were running the same or greater risk as we were, but fairness has nothing to do with mourning the death of a friend.

When we were not pulling fireman duty on the line, we worked out of reserve positions. A young lieutenant from the army historical section came to interview us about the fight near Hill 628. He did not impress us. He did not have a grasp of combat and had no understanding of the impact of terrain on battle. He wanted to know why traditional fire and movement were not used on Hill 628, and he was critical. He could not understand our inability to maneuver on what we knew was a razor-backed ridgeline, where there was no room to maneuver. All we could do was have one platoon charge while the others fired over their heads and then followed. His remarks angered men, and the interviews did not go well. I was surprised to learn that many years later this man became a famed historian.

Sometimes Korean women were available in rear areas. When war is on the land, people do what they must to survive. The story went around the company that a Korean whore had set up station in a deserted house. The men laughed, saying she was not a particularly bright whore. She was taking the money as she lay on her back servicing man after man, then putting the money above her head where she could not see it. While she was working, they reached in a window and stole the money. Some men thought that was high humor.

Some members of the 8th Rangers were going to Japan for a week of rest and recuperation. When they returned they brought cases of whiskey. Most of them returned smiling, but more weary than when they had left. One of my closest friends came back with his penis swathed in bandages and splints. I asked him how it was possible to break his cock. He was enjoying the fame and envy his exploit earned, but confided to me that it was not a break. He had a significant tear in his foreskin. The doctors wanted the area stabilized until it healed.

Whenever alcohol could be found, men drank it. Men drank anything that had an alcohol base. I had learned that alcohol and I were not good companions and I left it alone. A child could lift a drink to its lips, so I could hardly consider drinking the mark of a man. I knew from personal experience that when men got drunk, their dispositions would often change. I avoided drunken men when possible.

At times when we were refitting or filling out our ranks, some of us would be called upon to move to various areas of our division front and conduct four- to ten-man reconnaissance patrols forward of the lines. These were times that in the words of Tom Paine "tried men's souls." When a patrol returned, another patrol of rested men would be dispatched.

On one occasion we were taken to an assembly area position behind our line on a three-quarter-ton truck. We then went on patrol, and the truck driver left to bring up the men of the next patrol. We passed through our lines, went out into the night, and performed our mission. These were times of great tension and physical exertion.

Our return to the assembly area offered the promise of rest. The relief truck was late in arriving and, when it did, we saw to our anger that the men in it were drunk. We did not know what they had been drinking or for how long; it did not matter. They could not even stand on their feet. When we pulled them from the truck bed, they collapsed on the ground. We kicked and stomped on their drunken bodies, then picked up our weapons and did their patrol.

The soft cap with visor was our hat for night patrolling. We learned that back at Camp Carson, Colorado, later Ranger companies had started wearing a black beret. That was good as it would distinguish Rangers from other soldiers and paratroopers. The beret would be a worthless hat in combat. It could not keep the rain, snow, or sun off your face, but it would look distinctive when we went on pass or home leave. Proud units who have done so much to earn special recognition deserve something unique. The black beret would be a symbol of the American Ranger for fifty years. We were proud that it started in the Korean War.

The Ranger officers looked after their men and we looked after them. With Capt. Jim Herbert badly wounded, Capt. Robert Eikenberry now commanded the 8th Rangers. He was an experienced soldier, skilled in battle. He had the job of leading and caring for all of us, and it was a demanding task. In daylight he was out and about going from foxhole to foxhole, checking our ability to fire from our positions, making certain we had ammunition and water, and C rations. He had his foxhole well forward at the most likely position the enemy would attack. He positioned himself where he could best see the battle and control our fires. None of us had a complaint about digging a foxhole for him—he was busy on our behalf.

On one occasion, when several of us dug his foxhole, we had time to put an overhead cover of logs and earth on top. When night fell, the Chinese hit us with a ferocious mortar attack, explosion after explosion. One mortar round seemed to land directly on Captain Eikenberry's position. It was not wise to leave your foxhole after dark. There was too much chance of being mistaken for the enemy. During a lull in the Chinese fire, I called to the men in holes to my left and right that I was going to check on the captain. When they acknowledged, I scrambled from my hole and ran to his position, calling out to him. He made no response.

I crawled close to his hole and finally heard a sound. He was snoring! I could not believe what I was hearing. I listened again to his whistling and snorts, then dashed back to my foxhole. How could he sleep through that horror? Was he acting? I felt he had to be, but the doubt would always remain. Naturally, I told my friends and they told everyone else, embellishing it as the story went the rounds. Any story had a life of its own and grew as it lived. The 8th Rangers were very proud of their commander. The last version I heard of this story was that Captain Eikenberry was blown out of his foxhole by the force of an explosion and remained asleep.

Only the dead can be relied on for consistency. Captain Eikenberry was very much alive but causing considerable stress to E. C. Rivera, who was carrying the captain's radio. When men smoked cigarettes at night, they lit them bending over and covered by ponchos to prevent any light from showing. The cigarettes were cupped in the hand when smoking. Eikenberry paid no attention to these basic precautions. He carried a Zippo lighter that flamed like a blowtorch and opened and closed with a sound that seemingly carried for miles. We wished our captain would give up the smoking habit.

Innovation is no stranger to the battlefield. Some Ranger riflemen were firing 60mm mortar rounds as rifle grenades. Chuck Ouimette found some brass artillery shell casings, filled them with jellied gasoline, and rigged them with a blasting cap. Planted in front of our positions or along trails, they made a handy weapon. Both sides sniped at each other. The Chinese knew the range of our rifles and on occasion would run their messages back to their rear areas in our sight but out of our rifle range. The bicycle was a major means of transport to the rear-area Chinese. One messenger was a bicyclist who traveled back and forth out of rifle range. We could have made his life miserable with artillery or mortars, but he was a part of the scenery and deserved a more considerate end. I watched with professional interest as some men of my platoon dragged a .50-caliber machine gun to the top of the mountain. One of the best shots set it for single-shot fire and when the messenger was on the near side of his trip fired off a single round. Though the first shot missed, the messenger got the message and began to pedal furiously. In his excitement he fell off the bike several times, but would jump to the saddle and move his legs like pistons. He could ride that bicycle well, but not fast enough to outdistance a bullet. His career was ended. The .50-caliber machine gun made the Chinese more careful about their movements.

When in a defensive position we were careful not to fire unless we believed we had a good target. The Chinese were skilled at probing our positions, drawing fire until they could determine where our foxholes were located. Then they could plan their attack. Captain Eikenberry was a terror to any Ranger who fired his weapon without good reason.

We moved into position at the point of a ridge that led to Chinese lines and began to dig in. It was routine to have two men to a foxhole. We often dug holes in the shape of an inverted V or an L. In the event a grenade came into the hole, one of us would have some protection. Two men in a foxhole also allowed one man to rest while the other kept watch. The problem is that an infantry unit in combat loses much of its manpower to bullets and shrapnel. The frontage the unit is responsible for is too wide to permit the luxury of every foxhole having two men. As a result, battle action may mean going several days without sleep.

In this case, the platoon was stretched thin and I was exhausted and alone in my foxhole. As darkness fell I took some telephone wire and some C-ration cans with pebbles in them and rigged a trip wire to the front of my position. On the left it was tied to a small bush. I kept the wire low enough to the ground to trip anyone walking toward me in the darkness. I had a few fishhooks left from some my dad had sent me. He thought it strange that I was asking for them while in Korea, but if the fishhooks were tied to the bottom of the trip wire they could snag the clothing of an approaching enemy and make it noisy and difficult to get free.

As I finished my digging and preparations on the trip wire, daylight faded and night changed the world. A pale moon shed its ghostly light and every bush looked suspicious. It was a still night that wore on and on seemingly without end. I was at the end of my strength, desperately needing sleep. We had been issued tablets and inhaler tubes that contained a stimulant called Benzedrine, and as the waves of exhaustion swept over me I chewed these pills hoping to stay awake. How much it helped I do not know. I staggered from one side of the hole to the other and slapped my face, trying to keep my eyes open. Hour after hour passed as I fought to stay awake.

Suddenly, in the stillness, the bush moved. Heart pounding, I settled in over my BAR and waited. In my irrational mind I said, "You shake that bush again, I'm going to kill you." The bush shook and seemed to change shape. I fired a short burst and waited. There was no return fire or cry of someone hurt. I saw movement again and fired, but after several shots my BAR jammed. Now I was in trouble. Although there was no response or sign of the enemy other than movement around the bush, I was holding a weapon that would not fire. Working in the dark in a muddy foxhole, I cleared the jam and test-fired the weapon. It coughed out a few rounds and jammed again. I fixed that and fired again, only to have it jam once more.

A roar of outrage came from somewhere behind me. It was Captain Eikenberry. "If I get my hands on that dumb son-of-a-bitch that keeps firing, I'll tear his nuts off!" he bellowed. I counted my grenades and loosened their safety pins, then spent the rest of the night wide-eyed beside a weapon that would not fire.

The Chinese pulled out during the night, but I was not aware of that. I didn't know if they had run a reconnaissance patrol or if the bush's movement had been a blend of exhaustion and imagination. When sunrise came I was totally spent. I curled up in the bottom of my hole, pulled my poncho over me, and went to sleep. An object hit me in the chest, and my hands came together over something in the poncho that felt round. Coming out of sleep, rational thought was not possible. I screamed "GRENADE!" and, fighting the poncho, hurled myself from the hole. My terror was shared by two friends sitting beside my hole. They had been told that the Chinese were gone and were dozing in the morning sun when one of them inadvertently kicked a rock into my foxhole.

All war is exhausting to the foot soldier, but mountain warfare made us beasts of burden. Going south to north in Korea was one long, fighting climb carrying loads that defied imagination. Some of us used a pen to write on our soft caps, "You-call-we-haul-that's-all." A few days on some active mountaintop and we would find ourselves lacking the basic needs. Additional ammunition, water, and rations were brought to us on A-frame backpacks by South Korean laborers, called Chogi- or Chiggy-bearers. Reared in a life of labor, they could carry great weights on their backs. Water was brought in five-gallon cans from which we filled our canteens. If water was not available through our supply channels, we filled our canteens from Korean streams. When using the local water, we were trained to put a water-purification Halazone tablet into the filled canteen and shake the mixture. The water was then purported to be pure, even though it tasted like iodine.

Some men had a great fear of drinking unpurified water. On one mission, when we were carrying our wounded and trying to break contact and get back to our lines, we crossed a small stream. The Chinese were in hot pursuit, yet one

Ranger grabbed at our arms saying, "I need to fill my canteen. Anyone got a Halazone tablet?"

Hot food was a highlight in infantry life. On occasion when we were off the line, we used our oval-shaped aluminum mess kits that opened into two parts. The mess kit was accompanied by a knife, fork, and oversized spoon. Our cup was the ingenious canteen cup, designed to fit around our canteens and equipped with a fold-up handle that locked into position. The sight of meat and mashed potatoes and gravy had us slavering. On these feast days, we felt alive again. It did not matter if the cherry pie was on the mashed potatoes—they went quite well together.

When in the foxholes, on the attack, or on an extended raid, we ate when we could. The food was the army C ration, which came in a cardboard box about the size of a hardback dictionary. Opening the C ration was similar to Christmas morning. We were never certain what gift we would get. The entrée came in an olive drab can that contained some eleven ounces of spaghetti and meatballs, corned beef hash, ham and lima beans, beans and frankfurters, or sausage patties. Also in the box would be accessory cans that included a can of fruit or fruit cocktail, cocoa, crackers, and jelly. Instant coffee, salt, sugar, a cream substitute, and a plastic spoon were among the items found in a plastic packet.

We each wore a light chain around the neck that carried two metal identification discs, which became known in World War I as "dog tags." These were used to assist Graves Registration in identifying the body. For our purposes, the chain carried a can opener scarcely larger than a thumbnail. Called a P-38, the can opener was one of the most important tools in infantry life. The little P-38 could open a can lid quickly, but it was not the custom to remove the lid on the primary cans. Folded back, the can lid made a useful handle. Many times, movement of our unit or a battle meant that C rations had to be eaten cold. It was the same food but, when eaten cold, it became survival rather than satisfaction. When possible we heated our rations over cans of Sterno, holding the can over the flame by the bent lid. My favorites were spaghetti and meatballs and beans and franks. Sausage patties also rated high on my list. Sitting on my steel helmet in the mud, I would hold the can of beans and franks over the Sterno flame, spooning it until it bubbled, while occasionally reciting Shakespeare, "Double, double, toil and trouble, fire burn and cauldron bubble." If hunger forced me to eat a despised entrée, I mumbled "anxious the reeking entrails he consults."

It was a day of disaster to open a C-ration box and find a can of corned beef hash. This dull-black printed title on an olive drab can made hash of your day. Corned beef hash was impossible to trade in my platoon. I considered hash a Communist plot until I tried to get a hungry Chinese prisoner to eat it. He took one bite and spit it out.

The large spoon and the P-38 can opener were always handy. The P-38 stayed on the dog tag chain around my neck, and the spoon handle was slid down my boot top beside my leg. Most of us carried spoons in our boot tops. We always hoped that a C-ration can of peaches might come into our lives. The spoons might have a coating of dust, but a dirty thumb could wipe that dust away. People who live in holes in the ground do not concern themselves with dust.

The little can of Sterno heat was a blessing to a man standing for hours in a muddy hole. A dry pair of socks made life so much better for us. Many times I would wring the water out and dry my socks over the little flame of a can of Sterno.

Foxhole life is not conducive to good dental hygiene. Gums became sore and bleeding, fillings began to loosen, and cavities developed. Infantry war is not fought by healthy men; even those who begin in the best of physical condition soon find themselves with a host of ailments that must be endured.

In battle, close calls were routine. I never worried about the bullet or shrapnel that missed. While running down a trail, I heard a thud and saw a Chinese mortar round bury itself in the ground within five feet of me. It was a dud and did not explode, but the sight of the fins of that mortar round was an inspiration to movement. Either you were hit or you were not; close did not count. Ranger Jesse Cisneros of my squad was wearing a soft cap when a Chinese machine gunner shot it off his head. Jesse liked to poke his fingers through the bullet holes and waggle them at us.

As the struggle continued, we appreciated the extensive armament of the United States military. The Chinese had the manpower; we had the firepower. Against the waves of Chinese soldiers, we threw such an enormity of bullets, high explosives, and napalm that the hills of Korea were littered with thousands of rotting Chinese corpses. When fighting the Chinese, it is best not to be cowed by numbers. Their leaders did not hesitate to sacrifice their people. During the Communist takeover of China, they executed twenty-eight million of their own. Not even China, with its deep reservoir of manpower, could continue to sustain the losses they were experiencing in Korea. The Chinese were not a bottomless pit of manpower. The initial armies they sent to Korea were the best they had. They hurt us badly in the beginning, but by mid-1951, we had torn them apart. As the war went on, we found the quality of their fighting ability deteriorating. They began to throw untrained men into battle as cannon fodder.

Napalm was a weapon the enemy feared and we praised. It was like watching the raking of the fires of hell. Every Chinese soldier torched was one less trying to kill us. We became inured to the sight of rotting bodies. They no longer had meaning to us as fellow men. They were the enemy, the kind of enemy we liked to see. I have seen men eat rations while sitting on a body instead of in the mud. When the bodies were overripe there was a great risk of disease, and those closest to us had to be buried. At times D-handle shovels were sent forward for this purpose. I was trying to scoop a Chinese soldier into his grave when his rotting leg broke off and lay on the blade of my shovel.

Men in the infantry who were wounded and recovered did not always get sent back to their unit and sometimes had to begin anew to build family. Because of the specialized

jumped on the front of a tank, grabbed the .30-caliber machine gun, placed the muzzle against his stomach, and tried to pull the gun out of the tank. The amazed gunner on the inside of the tank caressed the trigger of the machine gun and cut the Chinese soldier in half.

We saw a Chinese infantryman run up a hill, heading for a small cave. The turret on the tank beside me began to swivel and, just as the Chinese soldier entered the cave, the 90mm gun fired and the round went into the mouth of the cave. It was superb shooting. We cheered mightily in the belief that the shell went right up the crack of the Chinaman's ass.

The British were clearing a hill on the right flank when a quad 50 gunner mistook them for the enemy and opened fire. The British quickly went over the hill. The gunner continued to fire. In a few moments a British officer came sauntering around the side of the hill. He was carrying a cerise rectangle of material called a recognition panel under his arm. The machine-gun fire being directed at him was so close, it looked like he was walking on bullets. He walked to the center of the hill, spread the colored panel on the ground, turned toward the tanks, and bowed from the waist. Then, as the fire slackened, he calmly turned and walked back around the hill.

The terrain we fought through began as hills and led to mountains with rocky outcrops and twisting roads. We ranged from woodland to rice paddies and experimented with various tactics. Someone decided to put a BAR man to the front of the formation on point as a test, and we tried that for a time. On one of these outings, when I had the point, I encountered a Chinese soldier performing the same mission for his patrol. We turned a corner on a trail and found ourselves within five yards of each other. I do not remember what he looked like. He was only a form, an enemy form. No soldier is continually alert. He may have been distracted or looking briefly to the side or was less well trained. I fired first and the bullets hammered him. I felt the thrill of the kill. I never knew a Ranger who felt remorse at the time he killed an enemy soldier. Exultation filled our hearts. To kill was to live. It was the ecstasy of survival. The Chinese soldiers must have been a reconnaissance patrol, as the remainder of them scattered. My dead man's bolt-action rifle was a Russian-made Mosin-Nagant. It is now on display at the Ranger Regiment headquarters at Fort Benning, Georgia.

The battlefield by day was a study in contrast, sometimes peaceful, a valley made for a walk in the sun, but then would come the scenes of desolation and destruction—broken bridges dumped into rivers, buildings torn apart, trees with torn limbs and trunks. The battlefield is a place where survival entails the destruction of any hiding place that may harbor the enemy.

The Chinese employed stay-behind snipers and troops armed with automatic weapons. These men were in well-concealed positions. As we moved into an assembly area, one stay-behind suddenly leaped to his feet and fired wildly. Likely terrified, he missed all of us and was quickly dispatched.

Sometimes civilians who had not fled the area tried to hide in caves or culverts. In such a circumstance civilians put themselves at great risk. Our concern was to kill before being killed, and we fired into any likely hiding place where the enemy might be. I know of no Ranger who sought to kill civilians on purpose, but none of us would enter a bunker or cave without firing into it or tossing in a grenade. Because a man is a soldier does not make his life less precious. A civilian on a battlefield must bear the risks of war.

Artillery was hitting to our front as we attacked along a railroad embankment. A Korean woman carrying a baby came from the north. The child had been hit and the mother was screaming her rage at us. I had no idea if shrapnel or bullets had caused the wounds and had no time to find out. I yelled for a medic and kept moving and firing. The sight of her desperation and anger filled me with a sense of futility and grief.

Rangers were trained for night action, but for many other soldiers the night was a time when imagination ran rampant.

The 8th Rangers infiltrated through Chinese lines and seized a hill slightly to the enemy rear, which was timed with an attack by the regiment we were with. The Chinese withdrew, and a company was sent forward to occupy our position and relieve us. As the American infantry came up the road, a Chinese sniper fired at them. In the darkness, imagination got the best of these infantrymen, who panicked and fled to the rear. Their officers and sergeants were cursing, but it took a little time to get them rounded up. We knew this unit; it was a good fighting outfit. This experience demonstrated that panic can strike any man or any unit. A unit or a man may fight with ferocity one day, flee in terror the next, and fight bravely on the third occasion.

During another operation we punched through the Chinese lines to tear up a town in their rear. Those of us in the ranks were not told the name of the town—it was not important for us to know. Something was going on there that 24th Division headquarters wanted stopped. Just after sunrise the column was delayed by enemy fire, and we Rangers were off the armored carriers, moving slowly and cautiously, trying to locate the enemy position. To reach the town, we first had to cross a hill that was wrinkled with draws and gullies, barren at the bottom and increasingly wooded as we neared the top. My squad went wide to the right, maneuvering to hit them from the flank. Weapons at the ready, leaning forward at the waist, we carefully approached the slope of the hill. I saw an open area to our front and crawled up a gully to the shelter of a tree bole, where I raised my head to look around the side of the tree. Suddenly the left side of my face was showered with splinters. A bullet had ripped into the tree bark beside my cheek. I threw myself backward into the gully just before the second shot came. My helmet rolled away and I crawled after it, my curiosity well satisfied. Our squad kept moving farther to the right to get on the Chinese flank, but in the process lost contact with the remainder of the platoon. We began to close in on the Chinese position on a wooded hillside. Still out of contact with the rest of the platoon, we continued to close, expecting to see the remainder of our people at any moment.

Suddenly the trees to our front began to disintegrate. Wanting to move on rapidly, the task force commander had decided to work the Chinese over with his quad 50s and bypass the hill. The rest of our company was informed and pulled back, but without radio communications and separated by bushy terrain, they were unaware that we were not with them.

For those of us on the hill it was sheer terror. There were thirty-two .50-caliber machine guns on that road, cutting the timber and plowing the hill with bullets. We found a small depression and huddled there, crawling under each other when possible. The roar was like an endless stream of railroad cars passing overhead and about us, crashing and grinding into wreckage. Ranger Ron Henry found a way to crawl out of the line of fire and, with great courage, took the risks inherent in signaling the machine gunners below to cease fire. Those of us who came down from the hill were furious and inclined to shoot the people who had put us in such fright. We were quickly reminded that we had some distance to go and needed everyone.

Continuing on, we met intermittent resistance. When fired on, our column would stop and Rangers would jump from the vehicles and form flank security to keep Chinese infantry from getting close to the tanks. Several of us were talking with a tank commander who was standing in his opened hatch with the upper part of his body exposed. Machine-gun bullets began to sing and whine as they bounced off the tank's hull. The tank commander dropped from view, pulling his thickly armored hatch cover closed behind him. Rangers near the tank scattered like quail, diving for the nearest cover. We had no armor plate protecting us, nothing between us and a bullet but cloth. As soon as tank turrets began to swivel in search of the Chinese gunner, he stopped shooting.

We had to cross a broad open field and, while doing so, we walked beside the tanks to protect them from hidden infantrymen. Someone spread the word that there were antipersonnel mines in the field, so we moved just behind the tanks, following in the tracks left by their treads. The Chinese took us under fire with 120mm mortars, ripping the earth apart with high explosives. We stayed as close as possible to the rear of the moving tanks, but we were helpless. I was walking in one tank track, and another Ranger was walking in the other. We exchanged glances filled with desperation and fear. Simultaneously the same expression came to our minds and to our lips. We both said, "Fuck it," gave ourselves over to fate, and felt much better. A combat infantryman who can convince himself of predestination has more peace of mind when confronting the uncertainties of combat.

The sun was hot and the physical exertion great. We had been in this attack for hours. The water in our canteens was low and we were parched with thirst. At the end of the field the tanks moved off in a sudden burst of speed. Now in the company of a quad 50 halftrack, we came to a stream and several of us laid our weapons down, knelt, and drank, cupping our hands or lapping the water like animals. I put my face in the cool water and looked up, blinking with surprise to see it suddenly spurting upward about me. It took what seemed an eternity to understand that we were under fire and caught in the open.

Picking up our weapons, we ran to the shelter of the halftrack. The quad 50 gunner, frightened and uncertain of the direction of the enemy fire, futilely spun his weapons around while bullets struck nearby. The driver started to speed up, leaving us in the open again. A Ranger thrust his rifle through the door port, held the muzzle to the driver's head, and told him to slow down. Keeping the halftrack between us and the enemy gunner's fire, we moved clear of the area.

Explosions and the whine of bullets increased as Rangers and tankers worked together. The assault on the town was one continuous roar of rifles and machine guns, punctuated by the sharp crack of the tank's main guns and the target disintegration that followed. Bunkers were sprayed with bursts of fire and grenades completed the destruction. There was earsplitting noise, then the sudden silence of success. Exhausted, we slumped where we were. Three of us were in a muddy ditch, arranged as though sitting at a card table. The space between our boots was approximately one foot square. We were checking our weapons and talking when suddenly a Chinese shell burst close by with an earthshaking explosion. A jagged piece of iron the size of a man's open hand ripped into the small open space between our feet. Our little party quickly broke up. The Chinese were on us again with the 120mm mortars. Men dashed for cover and several dived under the tanks. One Ranger came within an eyelash of being crushed as the tank under which he sought shelter moved off. The shelling stopped and I leaned against an embankment, bone tired. Another Ranger offered me a cigarette. This was the beginning of a bad habit that would last twenty years.

We were very appreciative of the men of the 6th Medium Tank Battalion. In addition to their fighting capabilities they knew how to live well. The decks of their tanks carried duffel bags full of food, water, and ammunition, while everything we had was carried on our backs. They had radios and sometimes we could listen to music. Tank engines give off a lot of heat, and the tankers knew how to use that to heat water for shaving or even to fry an egg. Some tankers had cooking utensils. Sometimes the smell of eggs and bacon would waft past my extended nostrils. One night I went over to a tank crew and watched them eat. I hoped they would share, but they didn't, even though I pressed close.

We sometimes went into action with the Rangers riding on top of the tanks. Tank commanders would begin a mission riding with their head and shoulders exposed, but when that first enemy shot came they would disappear from view as though they had their feet yanked out from under them. The hatch cover slammed shut and they were sealed off behind armor plate. A telephone in a box at the back of the tank is what we were supposed to use to communicate with them. It made us mad as hell to crouch there, trying to direct their fire with bullets singing off the tank's armor and us with nothing but cloth between us and a slug.

Rangers Hank Silka and Wallace Shaw were part of a

group of Rangers on a tank that came under Chinese fire. Silka had a yen to use the .50-caliber machine gun on top of the tank. The tank commander disappeared while Rangers tried to duck behind the tank turret. Shaw jumped to the ground as Silka looked down at him. Shaw said, "Well, that's thirty days in Tokyo." Silka could see the reddening hole through Shaw's left pant leg. He had been shot in the thigh. Hank Silka jumped toward the machine gun to begin firing, but the tank turret swiveled to put the 90mm gun in position and Silka was swept off the tank. As Silka hit the ground the tank gun fired, with the concussion stunning all of the nearby Rangers. Chuck Ouimette was knocked flat.

Ranger Sgt. George Hall was killed, shot through the chest by an enemy gunner. The bullet that killed him had spent itself and was found lodged in his jacket. A medic gave the bullet to Ranger Joe Almeida, who kept it. Hall was a Pennsylvanian from near Pittsburgh. Some years later a few of us visited his grave there and, in quiet remembrance, buried the bullet in the grave of our brother Ranger.

Patrolling forward of our lines was a constant part of our life. Len Wiggins was now squad leader, and he told me to be his point man for a squad reconnaissance patrol. We passed through our infantry in that period of dim light just before the dawn. We moved onto high ground and searched the high hills to our front, but we did not encounter living Chinese. Below us and to our right was a tiny valley, a thing of almost mystical beauty. We moved down a narrow, winding trail smoothed by the passage of generations. Near us a babbling brook hurried downward to pass near a small cluster of thatched-roof houses. It was a valley of peace and a valley of quiet, too peaceful, too quiet. Proceeding with considerable caution, I led the way down into this Korean Brigadoon. As I neared the first house, several chickens emerged from an open sliding panel.

Covered by the weapons of other Rangers, I entered the room. Though inured to the sight of death, I was not prepared for the sight before me. A Korean family, a man, a woman, and several children, were stretched out on the floor in a side-by-side manner as though sleeping. They were dead. We checked the inhabitants of the next house and they were also dead. It was obvious that none of these people had been shot. They were dead of disease. Only one person was still living, a young woman sitting upright but with head bowed in the misery of the horror that was killing her. She was wearing a light covering and the outline of her breasts showed through the cloth. I could see that she was dying. As I looked at her in helpless sorrow, another man stepped by me. He was new to our squad and had been with us only a few weeks. He put his rifle in his left hand, thrust his right hand down inside the woman's clothing, and began to fondle her breasts. Fury gripped me. I cursed him as I jammed the muzzle of my weapon against the base of his skull. I told him to get away from the woman or I would kill him. I meant my words. I was shaking with anger. He gave no argument and left. I turned away, leaving death behind me. I never had another cause for complaint against this man, but I could not be close to him.

Thus I learned that it was not only bullets and shells that killed. Disease raged across the Korean peninsula. Lacking our medical care and inoculations, the Chinese paid a particularly heavy price. They accused us of conducting germ warfare. I don't think so, but true or not, those of us who were fighting did not care how we killed each other. The "you have the honor of the first shot" style of war makes for good conversation among the stay-at-homes. Those who live in comfort, who don't know the bite of fear and the song of the bullet, don't understand that kill or be killed is the reality of the battlefield. In combat, I was satisfied to see the air force or artillery kill Chinese at long range. If we had employed germ warfare and it killed Chinese soldiers and saved American lives, I would have applauded the action.

Operating deep in the enemy rear, we saw a platoon-sized force of Chinese marching along, blissfully unaware of our presence. Rivera had the radio contact to bring in some fighter-bombers on these people. They used napalm on the Chinese. It seemed like one napalm canister skipped into the mass of them. They were burning alive, and men on the fringes were running and rolling about in a desperate attempt to put out the flames. These were people that would kill us in an instant if given the chance. The farther away from me that the Chinese were killed, the better. I did not care how they died, just so they died. We did care for their wounded.

We despised the North Koreans. Early on we had been told of American prisoners being found with their hands tied behind their backs, shot by North Koreans. Being taken prisoner is an uncertain business best avoided. Enemy soldiers who tried to use surrender as a ruse or who changed their minds were shot. I never saw a Chinese prisoner shot who had not resisted. However, I saw one master sergeant gun down three North Koreans when he did not want to spare a man to take them to the rear.

While patrolling through a deserted village I saw an ornate chest that I wanted to send home, but an infantryman on a mission can only take what he can carry with him. Looting has always been practiced by armies, including those of the United States. It played an active role in the Allied advance into Germany in World War II. Many American soldiers brought home from Europe items of value they had liberated, including money, art, and silverware. A relative who fought through Germany in the infantry told me they would shoot a German officer, and before he hit the ground our people would have his watch, wallet, and Luger. That was not the case in Korea. The enemy looted our dead, but our foe did not carry cameras or watches or rings. Save for weapons and flags, there was little booty for us to take home. No Ranger I knew was interested in collecting wooden rice bowls.

I sometimes talked with the infantrymen in the foxholes. Few were career soldiers. In Korea, I gained a great respect for the citizen-soldier. So many men come from civilian life at the call of our country. They usually provide the greatest number of junior officers and men in ranks, so they carry the greatest burden of combat. All the men in my Ranger company were regular army, but that was because we were in the army at the time the war began. Most of our Rangers did not intend to make the service a career.

It was at this early stage of my military life that I came to the conclusion that even four-star generals can make dumb mistakes. Whoever got the idea of forming independent Ranger companies in modern war was a military idiot. Initially led by captains and consisting of only 112 officers and men, we were attached to infantry divisions ranging in size from 17,000 to 20,000 men. The division operations officer (G-3) was a lieutenant colonel who had a difficult job. Busy colonels are not inclined to listen to captains, and when our captains were wounded or killed, our commander and representative was often a lieutenant until a replacement captain came in. These men were good leaders and good fighters against the enemy, but they did not have the rank to argue with the division staff. Few infantry division staff officers understood how Ranger units could be used, and they did not have time or care to learn.

Our Ranger companies should have been formed into battalions, with lieutenant colonels as commanders and staffs with the rank that would allow them to talk on a more equal basis with staff officers. These battalions should have been employed under the direction of a higher-level headquarters than an infantry division. At the higher headquarters of army or even corps level, the information and time were available to do a better job of planning Ranger missions.

As attached troops going from infantry regiment to infantry regiment, we were often forgotten about when ammunition, food, water, and equipment were needed. All of these commanders and staffs were busy men; they had a full-time job looking after their own troops. After a time we found it necessary to logistically look out for ourselves.

Getting supplies required vehicles we did not have. We were adept at raiding the Chinese rear area—now we raided the American rear area. In the rear echelons were makeshift theaters; these were hillsides with sandbags arranged in aisles and rows with a rudely constructed screen at the base of the hill. Careless drivers would park their trucks and jeeps at the back of the theater, take a sandbag seat, and immerse their attention in the film. Then we would ranger among the vehicles, take the one we wanted, and drive away. At our company command post the bumper identification of the other unit would be painted over and a fresh stencil used to identify the vehicle as belonging to the 8th Airborne Rangers. Stencils of parachute wings were also liberally applied. Using these vehicles, our people could get what we needed from supply depots. I learned many techniques of military self-sufficiency (scrounging) in Korea that would serve me well in Vietnam.

12

No Substitute for Victory

The Chinese were beaten. Our forces were now moving forward with minimal opposition. From General Van Fleet to GI Joe, we knew we could run the Chinese out of Korea. We heard a rumor that the development of tactical nuclear artillery would make their numbers meaningless. We heard that Gen. James Van Fleet had plans to make amphibious end runs behind the Chinese. Marines would spearhead the landings with infantry divisions of the army exploiting the lodgment. Our Ranger companies would be formed into a battalion and, with the 187th Airborne Regimental Combat Team, parachute inland and isolate the battlefield—we were eager to do this.

We were pulled into reserve to do a parachute jump to maintain our qualification. We could not understand why we were not parachuting into action. We learned later that General Ridgway had forbidden our company-sized units from making these drops by ourselves. He was concerned about the probability that such small forces would be surrounded and slaughtered. If the 187th was making an airborne assault, there would be a large enough force that Ranger companies could participate. We made the one practice jump, but only two of the five Ranger companies fighting in Korea would have the opportunity to make a combat jump when they jumped with the 187th.

Even though the Chinese were in retreat, the political will of America was lacking. The threats of a wider war and a Russian attack in Europe had our allies in a panic. The British and French governments wanted out and so did the

Truman administration. When MacArthur was relieved, newspapers in England cheered his relief. Seeing those who were doing their fighting being beaten, the Soviet Union proposed a truce. Talks were begun, and the Chinese sought and gained a stabilization of the lines. Now our strategy changed. Ordered to halt our advance, we were now employed in what those not on the battlefield called "limited war." War, however, is never limited for the infantryman, marine, or fighter pilot, or indeed any of those who go in harm's way. For us, war is and always will be—kill or be killed.

We made the mistake of believing the Chinese would negotiate in good faith. There should have been someone in the American State Department who knew of the philosophy of Mao Tse-tung. Mao believed that the twofold purpose of negotiations was to gain time for rebuilding and to wear the enemy down through frustration. He succeeded in both goals.

To stop our offensive while truce talks were ongoing was a mistake; the truce talks bought the Chinese the time they needed to rebuild their shattered units, reinforce, and dig in. The 8th Ranger Company had been spearheading an attack at the time the American offensive was ordered to halt. We now dug in where we were, not knowing why we were being stopped. From my position I could see a large wooded hill to our front. The hill was quiet, patrols reported it unoccupied, and it stayed that way for days.

Then in the darkness a sound came from across the way—the sound of axes ringing as trees were being cut. We could hear picks and shovels being used. Neither flares nor artillery fire stopped the work. When morning came the wooded hill had changed in appearance. The trees were gone, the timber having been used with earth to construct firing bunkers. Trenches interlocked these firing positions and barbed wire could be seen. We knew there would be mines buried to the front. By weight of numbers and absolute determination, the Chinese had turned a hill into a fortress in one night using only rudimentary tools.

We knew that many of us would die if we now tried to take that hill. Word came down that we were to be relieved and that another unit would be taking over our positions. In the selfishness of self-preservation, I felt pleased. The men who replaced us had received an order to attack the hill. Several rifle companies made the attack, which was preceded by an artillery preparation that shook the Chinese positions. To the onlooker it seemed that nothing could live on that hill, but they did. When the American infantrymen came up, they were shot to pieces. In addition to machine guns, rifles, and grenades, the Chinese used white-phosphorus shells on our men. The burns were deep, and men were in agony.

I talked to a gut-shot man lying under a tree. He was an automatic rifle man, and he was angry. He gestured toward his twenty-one-pound Browning automatic rifle and told me, "I carried this damn thing all the way from Inchon and never got to fire a shot!" The rifle units were so badly mauled that they had to be withdrawn, and we moved back into the position.

A "die-for-a-tie" attitude now prevailed. I began to despise politicians who put men in war and denied them victory. Battles would light up the night. Some nights, war would rage on the hills to our left and right, and we would be at peace. It was like having a ringside seat at Fourth of July fireworks. Then war would come to us. Parachute flares would pop and hiss, spreading a ghostly light over scarred ridges and hills. Weary men peered from holes in the earth, straining their senses, looking and listening for the dark shapes of the enemy. The distant rumble of artillery was heard, and the air would whisper death as shells passed overhead. The ground around us would leap and shudder under the violence of the enemy high explosive. Machine guns would chatter and automatic rifles emitted a rhythmic cough, the darkness split by the red tracer bullets of the Americans and the green of the Chinese. Desperation and fear mixed with determination and courage. The song of the bullet was punctuated by exploding grenades.

In the morning the American dead were taken down from

the hills. Their bodies were placed on stretchers, then covered with the olive drab poncho that once sheltered these men from rain. The poncho was not of sufficient length to fully cover the body, so the boot-covered, toes-up feet were left exposed. These boots of the infantry were often stained by water and mud, with scarred soles and heels sloped with wear. Infantry boots told a silent story of sacrifice. The previous evening this shapeless form above them had known life; ambitions and dreams, love and friendships that the silent lips had spoken of. All were now gone. Those of us who fought on would not see the weeping of a family above the yawning pit of a grave. A grassy plot, a tombstone white, visited less as years went by, occasionally guarded by a small American flag on Memorial Day, was the record of this brief life. Some of these men were scarcely known by their comrades. The memories of others would march with us throughout our lives.

In another part of Korea, men debated over the size and shape of the truce talk table and whose flag would stand the tallest. To the enemy, the truce talks were another means of continuing the war. American negotiators were forced to make concessions, not by the enemy but by our political leadership. General James Van Fleet lived in our hearts as a commander who understood that victory is the only satisfactory conclusion to war. He was overruled by President Truman and Secretary of State Acheson, whose prime concern was to get out of a war that their lack of military preparedness had brought on.

The three-year war President Harry Truman called a "police action" would cost the lives of more than 33,000 Americans. Of the armies engaged, two million soldiers died and another two million civilians died in the hell of this war. The Korean War officially would end on ground very near to where it began.

Not surprisingly, all sides claimed their goals achieved. The Chinese felt they had protected their borders. Both South and North Korea could claim they were preserved. In America, war is good for business, and economic prosperity resulted. We could claim we had shown Communism that we would fight. The Europeans felt assured that America would fight for them. The Russians knew they had driven a wedge between America and China—they achieved their goal.

However, many men who fought the Korean War had an empty feeling. We did not see it as the politicians and their loyal generals did. What was all this for? Were men to die for a tie? Our political leaders had established dangerous practices. We had allowed the enemy to operate from a safe haven, to mass forces, and strike us at will. We had turned war into a public relations game where the recruiting of allies had a direct impact on American policy. Nations that provided a battalion of eight hundred men had a powerful influence on the United States, though we were supplying hundreds of thousands of men to the battlefield. Charles de Gaulle and others have noted that nations do not have friends, they have interests. Like a new kid on the block, the interests of the United States had become making friends, and the objectives of these friends are not always best for the United States. It is not being isolationist to believe that American soldiers or those of any other army prefer to fight under their own flag. My love was for the magnificent stars and stripes of the American flag. I found no pride or will to win in United Nations blue. War by committee is stagnation.

We later came down off the hill and moved into an assembly area. The decision had been made that Ranger companies were no longer needed in this trench warfare environment. To train a Ranger was a costly and time-consuming process. It required a special effort to fill gaps in Ranger units, and assaults on hills, such as we faced, were creating the need for a significant stream of new men. No politician or general would say it publicly, but it was more cost-efficient for the men in our line infantry units to be killed.

All across the front the Ranger companies were disbanded and the men transferred to other units. There were no tunes of glory, no parades, no bands playing "So long, it's been good to know you," not even a visitor from the 24th Infantry

Division saying "Thanks." With scarcely a hiccup from the bloated belly of administration, the US Army did something to the Ranger companies that the Chinese army could not. It wiped us out. Most of us went to the 187th Airborne Regimental Combat Team in Japan, which was a good unit, but not what I had volunteered for. I determined then to leave the army when my enlistment expired.

The war continued to haunt each of us in our own way. Some men who survived battle could not survive the effect of war. Ranger Wendy Washburn had been seriously wounded and evacuated to a hospital in Japan. While recovering, he fell in love with his Japanese nurse and married her. When he wrote his parents and told them of the marriage, they told him not to come home. Wendy was despondent, but I felt it was temporary, as his nature was that of a happy person.

Wendy was corporal of the guard one night. He asked if he could borrow my .45-caliber pistol because he did not want to carry a rifle. I lent him my weapon, and he drew ammunition from the arms room. I was reading Hemingway's *The Sun Also Rises* when Wendy interrupted my pleasure, wanting to talk to me again. Now he wanted to tell me how distraught he was over his circumstance. He told me if he had it to do over again, he would not marry anyone. I wanted to read, and my responses were brief. Wendy asked me, "What would you think of someone who killed himself?" Scarcely looking up from the book, I replied, "Take more guts than I've got."

In the early hours of the following morning, Wendy sat on his footlocker, put my pistol to his head, and killed himself. Since I had lent Wendy the pistol, my company commander gave me the task of cleaning up the blood and brains of my friend. I felt a terrible guilt that I had not recognized my friend's need. I could not contemplate suicide and did not understand that someone else might find a problem insurmountable.

I returned to the United States on a ship named the *Marine Serpent*; devoid of all comfort, it was aptly named. We were caught on the fringes of a typhoon and slid sideways across the Pacific. The men played endless card games. Some were big-money poker games. I had learned my gambling lesson well and stayed away from games of chance. I played a lot of pinochle and spent many hours standing by the rail thinking. I had no close friends aboard this ship. My beloved Rangers were scattered with the winds of change, and many would leave the service. All of us felt a bitterness that this bonding of the brave had ended.

On arrival in San Francisco, I flew eastward on a Flying Tiger Airlines DC-3. The seats were of the passenger style, but otherwise the military version of this aircraft was the C-47 that I had made parachute jumps from. I expected the stewardess to cry out, "Stand in the door!" She was an arrogant woman who acted like a first sergeant. When I boarded the plane carrying the rifle of a Chinese soldier I had killed, she said, "Where you going with that thing, boy?" That was my first "Thanks for your service, soldier" from a fellow American. All the same, I took that rifle home.

I flew into the waiting arms of my mother and sister. I was home, back in familiar surroundings, and yet it was not the same. I felt somehow adrift, cut off from family and neighbors. Many of my high school friends were married and had jobs. Few people talked about the war in Korea. The war was part of the newspaper, or the radio news, or a brief report broadcast over the newest item in my parents' home. They called it television. The war seemed so far away. Get it over with and get out was the usual reaction of people I talked with. Sometimes they would ask, "What was it like?" I felt strongly about my experience, but as I talked with them, their eyes would drift past me or they would glance at their watch. "Must have been hell. Great seeing you, Bob. Gotta go."

I remembered reading that people had called Marco Polo "Marco of a million," because his experience was beyond the comprehension of his listeners. They felt he was telling a million lies. I should have known some people would not believe. They had not shared the experience. If a woman told me of childbirth, how could I truly understand her pain? After a while I stopped talking about things I needed to talk about.

I entered the clothing store where my family had shopped since I was a child. A clerk whom I knew said, "Hello, Bob. I haven't seen you around for a while. Have you been out of town?"

Some people I talked to were World War II veterans. They had their own memories to deal with. A few had an attitude that if you didn't fight in "the big one," you didn't fight. One man said, "We were soldiers then, you guys ain't nothin but a bunch of pissants." I had a feeling he was one of the millions of World War II vets who had never heard a shot fired in combat.

I asked about the friends I had known in high school, those I had enlisted with. One of my friends, who had enlisted in the air force, was now married and our paths diverged. The other airman had reenlisted. One of the two friends who had enlisted in the army with me was home. He was the man who had been in the same basic training company as I. He had called me crazy for going into the Airborne and had stayed in the line infantry. His assignment had been to the 2d Division, one of America's premier infantry divisions. The 2d Infantry Division had fought in World War I and World War II, but it lost more men in Korea than either of the world wars. My friend had been through the worst of these times. He experienced the 30 November 1950 horrible running of the gauntlet when, on the Chinese entry into the war, the 2d Infantry Division had been ambushed on the Kunuri-Sunchon road. My friend smoked incessantly, was gaunt and haggard, and hated the Chinese with a fury that was explosive. His rage at an unconcerned America was terrible to behold. He could not understand, nor could I, how a country could send its sons to war and then go back to business as usual. He was home a week and his father was saying, "When are you going to get a job?" We could talk about the shared experience, but only in anger. There was no joy in being together, so we ceased meeting. Some time later I learned that he had committed suicide.

My other friend who had joined the army had become a paratrooper and served with the 187th Airborne Regimental Combat Team. He was badly wounded, and those wounds would give him a life of pain and an early death.

I still felt the hurt from the high school sweetheart who had given me my "Dear John." I asked a young woman I met for a date, and we went out for dinner and dancing. I had plenty of couth and suave now, and what was more important . . . I became a good dancer.

Any man who is a good dancer need never lack for female companionship. I was dating a number of girls and wore a satisfied smile. The more sex I had, the less I needed it, and the easier it became to get more. I became a flowers-and-candy romantic, giving triple-orchid corsages on the first date, crooning love songs, and oozing love poetry between kisses and rumbas. William Shakespeare wrote *Romeo and Juliet* for me. Unless the woman made the initial move, the first few dates were devoted to knowing each other. I regretted all those years I had wasted thinking that sex was something that women gave as a reward. I was astounded to learn that women might just desire sex as badly as I did. Their entire existence seemed to be built around allure and attractiveness. In an age before the birth control pill, by the third date, if I was not trying to get laid, they often were.

Along the Susquehanna River, north of the city of Harrisburg, was a drive-in restaurant named the Barbeque Cottage, and not distant from that was a nightclub named the Melody Inn. The unlikely combination of pork barbecue, swing, and sex kept me sane. The drive-in restaurant with its neon lights and teenage carhops in short skirts placing the tray with my order on the partially rolled down window was a wondrous world. It was life on a different planet than the one with the foxholes of Korea.

But I was not at peace. I kept searching for something, some tie with my idealism, my belief in a valiant America. I tried to recapture boyhood dreams by hiking alone into the mountains and visiting the fields of pines. I lay on my back and looked at the blue sky that had been the stage for boyhood dreams of glory. Now there were no gallant charges replete with bugles and flying colors chasing across that sky. There were only the very real memories of war, the faces of my Ranger brothers who had died in Korea. I could hear that soft Texas drawl, "My name is Harry Trout and I'm from Childress, Texas, gateway to the Panhandle."

I walked deeper into the woods, searching for my refuge, the island of hemlock where the divided stream had bubbled so merrily among the ancient stones. The great tree that once formed the natural bridge had rotted away and now lay broken, its ends fallen to the streambed. The towering hemlocks stood like an assemblage of giants. The needles of the hemlocks formed a thick and silent carpet beneath my feet, so that only the murmur of the stream and the rustle of the breeze in the trees was heard. I had returned to my island of dreams, my place of peace. But it was changed. The cold, charred logs of a campfire violated my island. Beer cans were strewn about along with the crumpled coverings of food. My sanctuary, the temple of my God, had been soiled by the filthy hand of man. In red rage, I threw the charred logs from the island, dug a hole in the soft earth with a stick, and buried the trash. Then I sat with my head in my hands and grieved. It was no longer my private place. My island would never again be as it was.

I remembered a way-stop coming home. At Camp Custer, Michigan, we were getting discharged from the service. Most men could think only of getting that magic paper of release and paid little attention to the appearance of their uniforms. My jump boots were spit-shined, my uniform fit like a glove, and my sergeant's stripes rode proudly on my sleeves. An officer had instructed me to march these men to a distant consolidated mess for the noon meal. I stood them tall in formation and marched them off singing Jody Cadence and making them feel like a team. When I halted them in front of the mess hall, I bellowed, "A column of files from the right, column right, double time . . . march!" As they moved by me, one man turned and said, "What the hell are you getting out of the army for?"

The Army—it had disbanded my beloved Rangers and thereby hurt me deeply. To love the army is to love a false mistress, one who is frequently revealed as being untrue to the principles it mouths. Loving the army is loving a whore who will betray you again and again, but you still love her.

There is that sound of boots striking gravel in unison, the blue guidons with crossed muskets fluttering in the breeze, the campfires and the soldier songs, and, yes, the sting of battle. Battle is a time when there is a closeness between men that cannot be found elsewhere. Many men search in vain the rest of their lives for that closeness. War is the home of truth. It is found in one desperate fleeting moment when you and your comrades are eyeball to eyeball with death. When the battle ends, truth is gone on the winds of deceit. Truth is found in the battle amalgam of fear and courage, that moment, fleeting in time but lifelong in memory when you will lay down your life for a man you do not like.

The army . . . America, was there hope? Should I again put my trust in the service and my country? Would we learn from the hard lessons of Korea? Would we ever again commit men to war without an unrelenting will to be victorious? Would we ever again give the enemy safe haven, allowing them to attack while we could not attack them? Would we ever again grant a beaten enemy victory through truce talks? Surely our experience in Korea would teach us the root lesson of war. There is no substitute for victory.

VIETNAM

13

From Cold to Hot War

Heart pounding with exertion, I ran across the sunbaked rice paddy. If given time for rational thought I would have been thankful that it was not the rainy season in the Mekong Delta. I could run instead of being mired in the paddy mud that was ever-present in the monsoon. I did not have time to think rational thought. I was running for my life.

The sources of my inspiration were the whiplike sounds cracking above and around my head. I knew it wasn't whips. They were bullets. I had not heard this sound in sixteen years, but once a man has heard the song of the bullet, he remembers it for life. Infantrymen consider the sound of metal passing by their ears the greatest impetus to movement known to man.

Diving headlong up against the side of a paddy dike, I tried to determine the position of my opponent. He was not a fool. He and his comrades stayed hidden and, knowing they were outnumbered, slipped away. He had missed, and I could not locate him to get my shot. It was frustration on his part and on mine. Another day in Vietnam.

On the fifteenth of November 1967, I stood on the edge of a laterite airstrip and watched a single-engine Air America courier aircraft drop from a broiling sun and circle warily for landing.

It would be my taxi to war. That there would be differences from war as I experienced it in Korea was readily apparent. Two nights earlier I had leaned on a balcony railing of a Saigon hotel and looked out over hurrying traffic and the glare of city lights. Beyond the city was darkness, occasionally penetrated by a stream of descending light; it was the nightlight of war, tracers from machine guns fired from American troop-carrying aircraft converted to gunships called "Spookies." The sight of a city going about its business while men fought and died on its outskirts was a contradiction that gnawed at me.

It was a short flight to Tan An, the capital of Long An Province. The pilot had a large "Death Before Dishonor" tattoo on his right arm and he wore a star-sapphire ring. The combination made me keep my eye on my duffel bag. I thought about where I had been and where I was going. I was thirty-eight years old. I had tried to live my life as described in the opening lines of Sabatini's novel *Scaramouche:* "He was born with the gift of laughter and the sense that the world was mad." A war followed by personal tragedy had not stilled my laughter, but it now came to the surface through pain.

I had married a woman of quality, a model, a musician, a sportswoman. Two years after marriage she became pregnant and during that pregnancy became mentally ill. I had no experience to prepare me for this and was devastated. At times she was shrieking in fear of the terrors of her mind; at times she was like the walking dead. The wonders of sharing, of building a life and family together, the give-and-take that is the long-term relationship between man and woman were denied me. They were replaced by the constant effort to correct the uncorrectable, hope that was unfulfilled, and sadness that went to the marrow of my bones. This tragic circumstance destroyed a lovely woman and affected every aspect of my life.

Sixteen years had passed since I fought in Korea as a member of the 8th Airborne Ranger Company. Then I was an enlisted man; I now wore the gold oak leaves of a major. Commissioned a Second Lieutenant of Infantry in 1954, I had served the usual rifle company duties of platoon leader, executive officer, and rifle company commander. I had completed the basic and advanced infantry officer courses, communications officer, and trainfire instructor courses at Fort

Benning, Georgia, and earned a bachelor's degree in history by going to school nights and weekends. Somewhere I found a copy of *Red Army* magazine. On the cover was the photograph of a young Russian officer. He looked intelligent, fit, and determined. I felt that for my society to survive, I had to be smarter, tougher, and ready to go one-on-one and take him down any day of the week. I kept that photo for some years and worked for my belief.

As a result of medication and her illness, my wife would go to bed early. I threw myself into reading. Night after night I sat at the kitchen table. Spread before me was a comfortable arc of books. I studied the practice and causes of war from Sun Tzu to S.L.A. Marshall. I read Tacitus, Jomini, Clausewitz, Kipling, Machiavelli, Guderian, and Patton. I tracked the military efforts of America from the 1600s and knew the campaigns and leaders. Save for familiarity with Japan and its World War II army, the Korean War, and the writings of Mao Tse-tung, I made the same mistake as many other American officers. I did not make an in-depth study of Asia, and I did not study other languages.

The Ranger philosophy was in my blood. I began an extensive search of the history of this unique organization. The roots of the American Ranger go deep into the 1600s. I learned that Rangers were a key force in colonial times. The rangers had fought in six American wars before the United States came into being. Men who served as Rangers contributed much to our country.

Thomas Willet, the first mayor of New York City, was a Ranger. I learned that President Andrew Jackson had been a messenger boy in a Ranger unit when he was thirteen years old. President Abraham Lincoln had served briefly as a Ranger during the Black Hawk War. Lincoln had been a militia captain and left that to be a private in a Ranger unit. Not many soldiers could be credited with adding huge territories to the United States. During the Revolutionary War, the victories of Ranger George Rogers Clark gave the United States claim to the northwest. I hoped I could someday make a contribution to Ranger history.

I no longer believed that officers were gods. I met officers who were incompetents and drunks and those who were self-seekers. I met officers who were eccentrics. Wilbur Wilson was known throughout the army as an otherwise good officer who had a deep fascination for coal bins. Each World War II barracks had a coal bin beside it, and if you served under Wilson that coal bin had to be whitewashed and the coal neatly arranged. Everyone called this officer "Coal Bin Willie." There was a colonel who had command of a small post in Germany. An old cavalry officer, lean and leathery, he hated people speeding on his post. The speed limit on his turf was fifteen miles an hour, and he felt he could run that fast. If he could not catch a car, this officer would have his military police issue a summons to the driver. The sight of a colonel chasing cars made me wonder about the profession. I knew a captain who was determined to win the Medal of Honor. Fanatical in his quest, he ran ten miles a day and devoted himself entirely to preparation to win our nation's highest award. Years later I learned that he did not get the medal, but had lost both legs in Vietnam.

At one point in time all officers are liars, that point being when we write army efficiency reports on junior officers. When I wrote my first efficiency report, I rated a man as "excellent." He was a fine officer and I thought him worthy of such praise. My senior asked me if I was trying to ruin the man's career. No army officer will last long in service if he is rated "excellent." He must be "outstanding." How every officer in the army can be outstanding I never learned, but preparing officer efficiency reports was a worthy experience in creative writing.

At staff duty I had been forced to dabble at personnel and logistics, but this was brief, as my true love was operations. In Germany, eyeball to eyeball with the Russians, I found long hours of work and happiness as the S-3 (operations officer) and was later double-hatted, adding the duties of battalion executive officer of the 1st Battalion 39th Infantry (Mechanized) stationed at Worms.

I was next assigned as S-3 of the 3d Brigade 8th Infantry

Division at Mannheim. In my limited authority I tried to correct the mistakes of Korea. In the early days of the Korean War, the Chinese army slaughtered Americans because we were a roadbound army. The Chinese could march long distances over varied types of terrain. They would ambush columns of American vehicles in places where one stalled jeep could stop a convoy. Then the killing was massive.

Our army in Germany was primarily a mechanized army, with infantrymen being transported in armored personnel carriers. Anyone can be a passenger in a vehicle or in a helicopter, but a rifleman must be able to march long distances under heavy loads to be effective. I heard considerable complaining from the ranks when I got them out of the vehicles and made them move on foot. "We're mechanized infantry," they would tell me, but I had the support of my commanders, and foot movement was a significant part of our training.

I believed that citizenship incurred an obligation to serve, a view that also prevailed in Washington, D.C., as many of our young soldiers were drafted into the army. Properly led, the draftees I knew were good soldiers. The British staff college would visit my brigade while we were training at Graf. A British lieutenant colonel said to me, "We are amazed at the job you chaps do with a conscript army." We looked forward to the yearly visits of the British staff college. It was a wild week defined by a British officer as "worth a guinea a minute." American and British Airborne officers had a special bond. The counter of the bar at the officers club at Graf served as an aircraft exit door, and as the night and the drinking wore on, officers would leap on the bar and go through the motions of exiting an aircraft. The conclusion was a jump and a parachute landing fall on the floor. These exercises were loudly and profanely accompanied and critiqued in the English and American languages.

The British had success defeating the Communists in Malaya between 1948 and 1960. There were many differences between Malaya and Vietnam. Favoring the British was that Malaya was surrounded by water and British forces could go where they needed to. In Vietnam the Communists had a homeland free from ground attack and with or without permission would use the supposedly neutral countries of Laos and Cambodia as staging areas for attacks into the flanks of South Vietnam. Still there was much to be learned from those who fought this type of war. It was from the British officers who had served in Malaya that I first heard the word "infrastructure." Mao Tse-tung had written that a guerrilla is like a fish that swims in a sea of people. It requires a hospitable sea for that guerrilla to survive, and it is that shadowy group of men and women dedicated to the Communist cause that provided the food, shelter, and the intelligence that the enemy required to survive and prosper. "Eliminate the infrastructure," a British officer told me, "and you will be able to find and destroy the main force of the enemy."

While interested in information on any form of conflict I might face, it seemed most likely that we would be fighting the Soviet Union and its allies in Europe. With war one radio message or phone call away, we found ourselves working with the Germans who had been our adversary in two wars.

The Cold War was at its height. It was a time of cloak-and-dagger, a great chess game between nations. Threats and counterthreats flew. Had it not been for the fear of a nuclear holocaust, war may well have returned to German soil. A contingency plan of my mechanized infantry brigade called for us to fly into Berlin and reinforce American troops there if the Russians made threats. Had they done so, we would have been facing some twenty-two divisions of Russian and East German troops who were within striking distance of West Berlin.

Several of us flew into Berlin and were briefed on the defense plan. Anyone who needed a reason to be ready to fight had only to look at the infamous Berlin Wall. It was an outrage to humanity. When I first saw it I was consumed with anger. I felt like rushing at it and battering it with my fists. We were briefed by American officers and the German police. I was astounded to learn that the West Berlin police force could double as an infantry division. The Berlin police may have been the only police force in the world that had its own artillery. I did extensive reconnaissance of West Berlin by ground and helicopter. Flying the entire length of the Berlin Wall at a low level, I saw that it was far more than a wall some thirteen feet high. It was an open-ground killing field with rows of barbed and concertina wire, trip wires, and minefields. Tank traps blocked roads to prevent escape by vehicle. Machine-gun-equipped guard towers loomed above this scene, and heavily armed patrols moved along the track with attack dogs at their sides. Late at night, when other officers were reading or nightclubbing at Berlin hot spots, I found myself drawn to the Brandenburg Gate and to the observation tower near Check Point Charlie. Behind me was West Berlin, a vibrant city with people freely moving about. I could see over the wall into East Berlin, into streets that were dark and deserted. The East German patrols and tower guards kept constant vigil against any who would strive to be free. The searchlights of the towers licked the barbed wire and every corner of darkness was probed.

We returned to West Germany by night train, passing through Communist-controlled East Germany. The rules were that Americans on the train had to keep the window shades drawn. Why our leaders would accept such humiliation, I did not understand. When the train stopped at a station, I darkened my compartment and lifted the shade. The platform was empty save for an East German woman standing nearby. She was startled when I raised the window shade. She glanced quickly about to see if anyone was watching, then with a furtive movement slightly lifted her left hand in greeting and turned quickly away. How precious is freedom!

Germany was a very special experience, but the pride of being a part of the superb 7th Army was coming to an end. In 1965 the Vietnam drawdown began. Our forces in Germany were stripped of experienced leaders to provide manpower for the escalating war in Vietnam. It was soon the norm for a battalion to be commanded by a lieutenant colonel, with the rest of his officers newly commissioned second lieutenants. Double-hatted as a brigade executive officer and operations officer, I found my brigade staffed with lieutenants and even sergeants in positions formerly occupied by majors.

I began to lose respect for some of our military's senior leaders. We had the same mission but obviously not the same capability for performance. Still, senior generals trumpeted that "we're ready." The lives of thousands of men were at stake, yet leaders trained in the philosophy of "Duty, Honor, Country" lied about readiness. I began to look at and listen to senior leadership with greater care, to compare their statements of readiness with what I knew to be fact. I complained to friends that "some of these bastards would sell their mother to protect or enhance their careers."

14

The District

Back in the United States for a brief period at civil affairs school at Fort Gordon, Georgia, I was ordered to Vietnam, assigned to Military Assistance Command, Vietnam (MACV), and at Saigon was further assigned to Long An Province.

Long An is located to the south and west of Saigon. To the east was the Plain of Reeds and to the west was an area of difficult terrain called the Rung Sat Zone, also nicknamed the "jungle of death." Both of these areas were enemy strongholds. Attacks on Saigon coming through these areas would pass through Long An Province. In more peaceful times, Long An would have been a happy land for the Vietnamese. Fertile soil allowed for two crops a year to be grown, and it was a major exporter of two commodities essential to the Vietnamese diet: rice and the high-protein fish sauce, *nuoc mam*. To the peasant farmer, Long An was agriculturally a gift of his god. Fish and rice were plentiful, but so were bombs and bullets.

I was told by a staff officer of Advisory Team 86 at Tan An to report to the province senior advisor. As I came to attention in front of his desk, I could not suppress a smile. My new boss was my old boss. I had not seen Capt. Jim Herbert, my company commander in the 8th Airborne Rangers, since the day he was badly wounded on Hill 628 in Korea in April 1951. Now he was a colonel who would serve five tours in Vietnam. We greeted each other in army fashion. He called me by name—I called him "Sir." Colonel Herbert told me that the South Vietnamese government had formed a new district called Rach Kien. He wanted me to be the district senior advisor. One of seven districts in Long An Province, Rach Kien was located along Highway 4, some fifteen miles south of Saigon, and served as a gateway for enemy movement into that capital. Once totally under the control of the enemy, inroads had been made only through heavy fighting. The 3d Brigade of the US 9th Infantry Division furnished American troops to the area. An infantry battalion and a 105-howitzer artillery battery operated from a base camp at the primary district town, also named Rach Kien. South Vietnamese soldiers of the 47th Infantry Regiment of the 25th Infantry Division were in the district. A Vietnamese Ranger battalion often operated there, and the district troops included two companies of Regional Force troops and the ragtag militia known as Popular Force troops. An engineering unit was coming to build roads and schools for the people of the district. Colonel Herbert desired that I pay particular attention to providing assistance and security for these engineers.

We talked briefly about our time together at Fort Benning, Camp Carson, and Korea, and what we knew about men of the 8th Rangers. I then made the rounds of staff briefings and began learning about the land, the enemy, and the people I would fight for.

In Vietnam, a province bore a loose resemblance to an American state, and a district to an American county. Rach Kien district was approximately twelve kilometers east to west and eleven kilometers north to south. A four-kilometer-wide north-to-south strip in the eastern portion of the district was relatively secure, the rest belonging to whomever had the most force on the ground at the time. My district was bounded on the west and south by a river, the Song Vam Co Dong. This wide and deep river was fed by several smaller rivers that rose in Cambodia. The Song Vam Co Dong would in turn join another major river as part of the vast Mekong Delta flowing into the South China Sea. The rivers provided the enemy with avenues of approach into Long An Province. To the northeast of Rach Kien was Gia Dinh Province and Saigon—otherwise I was surrounded by sister districts. To the east was Can Giuoc, to the southeast Can Duoc, to the southwest Tan Tru, and to the northwest Ben Luc. At province meetings I made brief acquaintances with the officers who were advisors in the other districts, but we were each consumed with events in our own little world. Though some of us might share helicopter rides en route to province meetings, there was no time to visit.

The dry season lasted from November to March, then came seven months of rains. The land in Rach Kien was agriculturally flat, more than 80 percent in paddy. Rice, fish, ducks, bananas, and coconuts were the principal crops. Frequent waterways with thick banks of vegetation made for excellent concealment. Since the rivers and streams were tidal waters, many mudflats and bogs made overland movement difficult. Between 28,000 and 35,000 people lived in the district, and the population ebbed and flowed depending on combat conditions. Under wartime circumstances, census taking was unrealistic. Most of the population lived under two governments, the South Vietnamese government, when their forces occupied the ground, and the North Vietnamese government as soon as the South Vietnamese were not present.

I learned that the enemy forces were organized like the fingers of a hand. They could operate separately or together as a fist. The North Vietnamese Army (NVA) consisted of the disciplined and efficient divisions, regiments, and battalions from the north. Sometimes southerners were among them, but not often. The Viet Cong Main Force (VCMF) was usually made up of men from or planted in the south. They were often found in company- and battalion-size units under control of the Communist Central Office South Vietnam (COSVN). Viet Cong Local Force (VCLF) units were directly under the control of the enemy province or district leaders. Guerrillas were also organized into ten- to forty-man units. They were the goons who collected taxes, spread terror or sabotage, and served as bodyguards. Last, but very high on the list of my opponents, was the enemy infrastructure. This was a brotherhood of conspirators, the enemy's political and administrative groups that coordinated and supplied the Communist effort in South Vietnam. Year in and year out they had been at war. They knew their trade.

In 1954 the French were defeated by the forces of Ho Chi Minh at the battle of Dien Bien Phu. That same year Vietnam was divided along the seventeenth parallel by the United States, the Soviet Union, Britain, and France. Communists would rule in the north, and nearly a million people fled south to escape the mass executions that followed. Among them were sixty thousand or more cadre members deliberately planted to aid future Communist action. The majority of these people had been born and raised in the south. They were going home, but going home as moles. They infiltrated every aspect of life in the south and would become the informants and the shadow Communist government.

The district boundaries were not exactly the same, but the enemy had a district chief, administrators, and tax collectors, as did the South Vietnamese government. The enemy was organized at all governmental levels, from an individual hamlet to Hanoi. They sought to motivate all ages, actively recruiting among children and women as well as men. A goal was to foment hatred among the young and encourage children to join "Determined to Die" groups. "Military violence" was a slogan frequently preached. It was believed that some two thousand enemy lived permanently in Long An Province, where main-force units passed in and out. I was assured by the province intelligence officer that no North Vietnamese Army (NVA) units were in my district.

Before heading out to Rach Kien, I stopped by the arms room to draw my weapons. I was issued the old, familiar .45-caliber pistol, which felt comfortable on my hip, and an M1 carbine. The M1 carbine was not my weapon of choice. It lacked an automatic capability and was antiquated even in the Korean War. This was not a weapon to face the famed AK-47 that most of the enemy carried. The justification for the M1 carbine was that the Vietnamese district forces with whom I would be working were armed with the M1 carbine, and I would be getting ammunition from them.

The trip to Rach Kien was by helicopter in the beloved Huey that was the workhorse of Vietnam. I unfolded a map on my knee and began to study the terrain, paying particular attention when we crossed the river and I got my first sight of the district. Thick growths of palm along numerous waterways and surrounding clumps of rudimentary thatched-roof shelters defined the various hamlets. I had been told that fifty-three such small communities lay in my district. Some areas were under cultivation, but large portions of rice paddy lay fallow. It was clearly evident that a significant number of B-52 bomber strikes, called Arc Light, had hit the area. One B-52 bomber could lay a carpet of 108 bombs of the five-hundred-pound variety. They did not come as a single bomber and, working together, the explosions stretched for miles. The B-52 was a terrifying weapon and very effective if the enemy was caught in the open. They often were not, and sometimes the bombs only made holes in the earth. The ground beneath me was frequently pockmarked by bomb craters, giving it the look of a lunar landscape. Rach Kien was an area where directions could be given by saying, "Go past the burned-out house, take a left at the third bomb crater, and it's just beyond the graveyard."

We landed at the infantry battalion helipad, where I was met by a jeep and driver from my team. Driving through the infantry area, I was struck by the feeling of pride that the American troops showed. Their bunkers and tents were frequently adorned by signs that proclaimed their identity and prowess. The area was relatively quiet, as the battalion was away on an operation. Many of those who remained were airing their feet. Ringworm and infections were commonplace in the wetlands of Vietnam. Days of wading through the muck of rice paddies made the skin rot, and a malady known as immersion foot was a major problem for these troops. American units tried to give 24 hours of foot-drying for every 48 hours of paddy and stream wading. I noticed that few Vietnamese were in the American area, and American soldiers controlled the road entrance and exit to their area.

Rach Kien district town had the appearance of an oriental cowtown. The buildings were one-story structures made of clapboard or thatch. An occasional masonry effort showed as a recent addition or, if properly stuccoed, where one of the families of old wealth had lived. The dirt street was shaped like a crank handle. The grip and the dogleg right were occupied by the infantry battalion. A left turn off the dogleg took us through an open gate of two-by-six lumber and barbed wire. This portion of town appeared to be occupied by the Americans, but there was considerable Vietnamese foot traffic of all ages and dress. Numerous barefoot Vietnamese soldiers lounged in doorways, each wearing a yellow scarf around his neck. This was the Vietnamese military section of Rach Kien. Beyond that and outside the military perimeter were the marketplace and town proper. I would learn that some two thousand civilians lived in the town.

The advisor house was a single-story stucco located across the dirt street from the Vietnamese military headquarters. Waiting at the front of the house were two lieutenants and a clutch of sergeants who were members of the team. A district advisory team was intended to be eight officers and men, but its strength often varied. In addition, mobile assistance teams came from the US 9th Infantry Division. Regardless of their paper chain of command, they worked under the direction of the district senior advisor (DSA). These teams, commanded by a lieutenant and consisting of five men, were armed like American troops, with M-16 rifles and M-79 grenade launchers. They provided training to Vietnamese Regional and Popular Force troops. I had one such team located in my northernmost town of Trach An.

Lieutenant Mike Primont, the intelligence officer, told me that a captain would be assigned as team executive officer and that an operations sergeant and medic were also due. The sergeants who occupied the latter two positions were completing their tours and would soon be leaving. Two interpreters were with the team. The first, whose name was Ho Voung, spoke passable English. The second, Interpreter Lang, had a unique manner of combining English words and phrases. Days after a translation I would wonder what he meant. The language wall was a major problem with the advisory effort in Vietnam. Not many Americans, myself included, became proficient in the language. Vietnamese was not a language that Americans would find useful in most parts of the world, so we did not study it. Usually it was the Vietnamese who had to learn English. The interpreters who finished the forty-seven-week course were very helpful, though nuance was often missed in the conversation. Second Interpreter Lang was the product of a twelve-week course. His English was unique unto himself.

Lieutenant Primont took me on a tour of the advisor house. Originally too small for American needs, the house had been enlarged by pouring concrete slabs in the front and rear and screening in those areas. The front porch became a living room/bedroom combination. A few lawn chairs vied for space with two double-tiered metal cots. The rear slab was the kitchen and contained an electric refrigerator without electricity, cabinets, a sink, and a small offshoot room rigged for a shower. The house proper allowed room for the team radio, which was the standard infantry portable radio known as a PRC-25. The radio had been set up on an army "field" table and connected to a long antenna that vastly improved the distance over which the team could communicate. In addition to containing the radio, the center portion of the house was given over to a sleeping area. Several two-tiered steel army cots were placed against the wall. Living space was tight, but the area was neat. All cots were made up and the floor was clean. A 1.5-kilowatt generator provided limited power when it worked, and a hundred-gallon water tank mounted on a small tower provided water for the shower and sink. Behind the screened-in kitchen was a three-holer latrine with a sawed-off fifty-gallon drum under each hole. I was told that each week one of the men would drag out the drums, pour gasoline on the feces, and burn it off. Burning shit is a miserable job, one that offends both dignity and sense of smell. Who would burn the shit became an early problem to be solved. The officers did not do it, and the men obviously resented what they considered as having been dumped on them.

War is misery, and nothing is gained by making it more so. I was glad to see that the men had looked to improving their lives. Less pleasing were the security arrangements. The house offered no fighting positions or protection from mortar or ground attack. We had no plan to call mortar or artillery fires in support of an attack on the village or coordination with the American infantry. Radio frequencies had not been exchanged with the American units, and landline (telephone) communications were not established. I was told by my team that the primary Rach Kien District military units consisted of the 555 and 627 Regional Force (RF) Companies; these were province troops stationed at the district level. They were supposed to be the muscle that would back up the platoons of Popular Force (PF) militia, who were to defend the villages and hamlets. When I inspected 555 Regional Force Company, I was appalled. Too young to have been with Washington at Valley Forge, I had never seen such a ragtag, often shoeless rabble in arms. These men were beyond poor; they were destitute. They lived with their hungry families where they could, were ill trained, and carried antiquated weapons. No one seemed to care about their welfare, and these were to be the troops I would go into battle with.

Rounding out this discouraging quasi-military assortment were the white-shirted National Police, which Americans called "white mice," and the tiger-stripe uniformed soldiers of the Provincial Reconnaissance Unit (PRU). The latter were paid by the US Central Intelligence Agency. I only had one squad of ten men, but they would prove to be worth a company of Regional Force soldiers to me. PRU members were recruited with more care, and many had had relatives killed by the enemy. These men were excellent scouts and had the best fighting reputation. According to my team, none of these district forces were engaging in operations against the enemy. There were no Vietnamese forces permanently in the outlying hamlets. Primont related that the Vietnamese leadership felt district forces were needed to guard Rach Kien town, and that South Vietnamese and American battalions should go in search of the enemy.

The most significant surprise was the sight of a refrigerator and a brand-new American house trailer sitting next to the advisor house. My men told me that both were meant for my civilian assistant. "But he won't come out here," said a sergeant, "so they are going to take it back to Province." A refrigerator in hand is worth any number on requisition. I had no intention of giving up the refrigerator. I told Primont not to return the trailer and to have its wheels taken off and lost.

At the rear of the trailer was a brackish pond about thirty feet across; beyond that the paddies stretched away to a line of palms about eight hundred meters distant. A few strands of barbed wire were implanted behind the house, and the Vietnamese had some poorly constructed bunkers. The Vietnamese bunker line ran in a perimeter around the district military and administrative complex, except where it fronted with the American infantry. Taking no chances, the Americans had bunkers around their perimeter, including facing where we were located with the South Vietnamese. The Vietnamese preparations for defense looked scarcely better than the nonexistent effort of their advisors.

There seemed to be no incentive to be prepared for enemy action. When I questioned this, I was told that the district had recently been established and there had been no effort by the enemy to attack it. There was a feeling of security due to the presence of the American infantry, but the sight of the infantry bunkers facing our position told me their intentions were to protect themselves. I was informed that 70 bags of cement and 236 pieces of sheet metal roofing were available as construction material; these had been sent down for the Vietnamese, but we had no sand for the cement and no housing on which to put the roofing. No lumber was to be had, and no one had requested sandbags. American units were able to get what they needed, but no other construction material was available to the advisors. I gave orders not to turn the material over to the Vietnamese.

Returning to the advisor house, I was introduced to a Vietnamese woman carrying an armful of folded fatigue uniforms. The men called her Ba, which is Vietnamese for Mrs. Her husband had been killed in action, leaving her with two small children. The men each paid Ba in Vietnamese piasters, with a going rate of exchange of 118 piasters, or "P's" (as they were called by Americans), to the US dollar. For the equivalent of two American dollars per man, per month, Ba washed the clothes, made the bunks, and kept the house clean. Her once attractive face was lined and worn from the hard times of her life. She bowed her head and said, "*Chao Thieu Ta* . . . Hello, Major.*"

I was anxious to meet my Vietnamese counterpart. However, it was nearing noontime and, in the great heat of day, the Vietnamese were observing siesta and their offices were closed. The small generator was not functioning, and lunch was an unrecognizable Vietnamese dish prepared by Ba. Fortunately it was accompanied by rice. The men told me that advisors were expected to eat the same food as the Vietnamese. I felt it was enough that men put their lives on the line for the United States. They should not be asked to sacrifice their stomachs.

With time on my hands, I walked to the American compound to pay a courtesy call on the infantry battalion and artillery battery commanders. The battalion was of the 39th Infantry, a regiment that I had served with both as an enlisted man and as a commissioned officer. Their unofficial motto from World War II was A-A-A-0, which I remember as meaning "anytime-anyplace-anyhow-bar nothing."

The battalion was returning from an operation, and the air was filled with helicopters and their unique beating sound. Laughter came from the battalion operations center. A radio call that was clearly from the enemy wanted to know what time the helicopters would depart in the morning. A staff officer told me the battalion commander was Lt. Col. Don Schroder. Since I knew Schroder would be busy for some time, I told his rear-area staff that I would return and continued on to the artillery area.

The artillery unit was a 105mm howitzer battery. The men had just finished eating in a mess tent, and some of them were beginning to unload ammunition from trucks. The wooden boxes appeared to be about three feet long and twelve to sixteen inches wide. In addition to wood, they contained nails and hinges, and the rounds were wrapped in plastic. When the boxes were unloaded, they were placed in a stack to one side. A dapper-looking Vietnamese lieutenant wearing the yellow scarf of the 555 Regional Force Company stood by with a hopeful look in his eye. When he came closer, one of the American sergeants snarled at him and he slunk away.

"That little bastard's name is Antoine," said the captain, who was battery commander. "His family has political clout, so he gets away with a lot of crooked crap. He's a drug supplier and runs the whores. When I first got here, he offered to help unload the ammunition. He had his men dump my ammo on the ground and they ran off with the boxes." Obviously these empty ammunition boxes had value to the Vietnamese. The battery commander informed me that ammo boxes were valuable because wood that could be used for building material was not available in Rach Kien.

The artillery battery commander was friendly and offered me an American lunch, which I gratefully accepted. I arranged to exchange radio frequencies with him and run a landline so we would have telephone communications. We also discussed development of artillery concentrations that I could call on if needed. Even with the sides rolled up, the tent was stifling and perspiration darkened our fatigue jackets. The battery commander mentioned that he wanted to build a screened-in mess hall for his men. He had all the material except roofing. I leaped at the opportunity. Within a few minutes we had come to an agreement. I would supply the roofing he needed. The advisors would be allowed to eat American food at his mess hall. If the ammo boxes were important to the Vietnamese, they were important to me. The battery commander had a constant supply and agreed to supply me with ammo boxes that were excess to his needs.

At the infantry area I talked with several members of the battalion staff. This battalion of the 9th Infantry Division had a much larger area of operations than my district, and their men had more experience than I at fighting this type of war. I wanted to listen to some of the lessons they had learned. They related tricks employed by the enemy, such as putting a dummy soldier or soldiers out in the open. Concealed nearby would be sufficient firepower to shoot down any troop carrier or gunship helicopters that responded to the bait. They talked of not using a .45-caliber automatic pistol when searching tunnels. The noise of firing left men deaf. A .38-caliber revolver with a silencer was better. They argued the advantages of a point team rather than a point man at the head of a column and recommended shotguns and M-79 grenade launchers to complement the M-16 rifle. Since I had only WWII carbines and a .45, some of the recommendations could only be mentally filed for future consideration.

While we were talking, the radios began blaring traffic about an action in my district. An American scout dog team was being employed, and the enemy had killed the dog. Without hesitation the handler tried to help his canine friend and he, too, was killed. The two lay close together, the man's hand resting on his dog. Faces were grim as we listened to this action run its course.

I met with the battalion commander, Lt. Col. Don Schroder, and a friendship ensued. He was a superb soldier on a second tour in Vietnam. Again, frequencies and landline communications were discussed. We talked of mortar and artillery concentrations and of my need to know of his patrol activity. As district senior advisor I was responsible for coordinating the artillery fires in my area. Don said the Americans had good reason to be careful about letting the

Vietnamese have knowledge of American plans. Vietnamese security was not to be relied upon. As district advisor, I had to know the who, the where, and the why of bodies of troops moving about the district. We sought ways to compromise, primarily by my keeping the knowledge of what the Americans were doing to myself. I would tell Don if I saw a possible conflict. I had nosed about the battalion area, and the sight of some bales of sandbags gladdened my heart. Don Schroder agreed to supply me with a goodly quantity of sandbags and the loan of some shovels. In turn, he asked that I do what I could to control the venereal disease (VD) rate. A soldier whose thoughts are on his pus-dripping penis is of little use to his unit. The men needed sex, and Rach Kien had a plethora of whores. I had not expected to become an expert on prostitution, but it looked like it would go with the job of being district senior advisor.

15

Counterparts

Back at the advisor house, I told the team about the food arrangements and that construction materials were available. I instructed them to get the sandbags from battalion and swap material with the artillery. The afternoon had worn on, and it was time to meet my counterpart, Maj. Phan Van Dong, and his military assistant, a Captain Ngi. I was told by interpreter Ho Voung that Major Dong did not speak English.

A common language is the principal bridge of understanding. I was aware that in my dealings with my counterpart, I did not have that bridge. We had a difference in language, beliefs, and practice, yet the relationship we established would in large part spell success or failure in this district.

Accompanied by my No. 1 interpreter, Ho Voung, I set out to meet my counterpart. It was only fifty meters to the white masonry building with green roof and trim that served as district headquarters, yet a world apart. A throng of suppliants gathered outside waiting to seek assistance from their government. The dirt yard contained a number of yellow-scarved members of the 555 Regional Force Company and the tiger-striped uniforms of the PRU. The door was guarded by several white-shirted National Police.

The interior of the building was open to the small breeze. Several male clerks were interviewing those in line. The clerks were displaying the universal smug superiority of those who occupy low-level governmental positions and wield their limited authority with a heavy hand. A number of

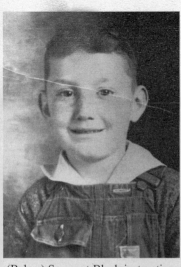

A very young Ranger,
indeed. The author at age six.
(Author's collection)

(Below) Sergeant Black instructing a young recruit on fieldstripping
an M1 Garand rifle. The M1, the premier rifle of the U.S. infantry in
WWII, would remain in service throughout the Korean War and even
saw limited use in Vietnam. (U.S. Army photo)

Exiting an aircraft on a training jump. Soldiers wore a main chute and a reserve chute. Some Ranger jumps were made from such low altitudes that there would have been no time to deploy the second parachute. (U.S. Army photo)

The fifth week of jump training. The aircraft in the picture are C-119s, known as Boxcars for their distinctive blocky shape and twin tail booms. (U.S. Army photo)

The author in Korea in 1951. In the foreground is the U.S. Army BAR (Browning automatic rifle), a weapon first introduced in World War II. The weapon closest to the author is a captured Russian-made Degtyarev DP light machine gun. (Author's collection)

A typical Airborne Ranger Company during the Korean War, with its personnel and support weapons and equipment displayed. Some of the weapons include 3.5-inch rocket launchers, .30-caliber machine guns, 60mm mortars, and 57mm recoilless rifles. (U.S. Army photo)

Ranger E. C. Rivera looking a bit more like a pirate than a Ranger. He's holding a Thompson .45-caliber machine gun. (Photo courtesy Ranger Nick Tisak)

Men of the 8th Airborne Rangers sit exhausted amid their gear after coming back from a physically and emotionally draining night operation. Moving silently through Chinese positions in the dark put a considerable strain on even the toughest soldier, Rangers included. (Photo courtesy Ranger Nick Tisak)

The author with SFC Leonard "Len" Wiggins, holding a captured North Korean flag. (Author's collection)

Which way is the enemy? The author striking a dramatic pose with an M1 Carbine with bayonet attached. (Author's collection)

Maj. Robert Black as a military advisor in Vietnam, in Rach Kien Province, 1967. (Author's collection)

Nothing really changes. Returning from a patrol, this time in Rach Kien, Vietnam, 1967. Author with M.Sgt. Ed Surbaugh behind him. (Author's collection)

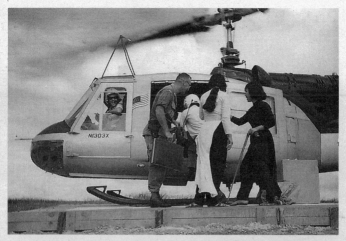

In a show of one-upmanship, Major Black prepares to board an Air America Huey while being attended by two of Major Dong's secretaries. (Author's collection)

Col. Robert Black being inducted into the Ranger Hall of Fame in July 1995, while the next generation of Rangers looks on. It is interesting to note that the Rangers still wear the black beret at this point. (Author's collection)

After a long and successful military career the author began a new career as a travel writer. Here he is looking very much like the early Americans who ranged out across the land in search of challenge and adventure. (Author's collection)

attractive Vietnamese female secretaries roamed about. Long black hair plummeted down their backs over the brightly colored *ao dai*, a gauzelike outer garment with a black, satin pajama bottom. Long-sleeved and close fitting, the garment separated at the waist into panels that extended front and rear to the ground. Their footwear consisted of a rubberized version of the Japanese geta, a clog with the thong between the big toe and the first companion. The women had dirty feet, but few men are concerned about that.

I was met by Dai Ui (Captain) Ngi, a lean, short Vietnamese officer dressed in a neatly pressed fatigue uniform. He was carrying a copy of *Time* magazine. His English was surprisingly good as he welcomed me. He reported that the district chief was busy but would see me soon. I felt this was gamesmanship and told Ngi that I was busy and would see the district chief at another time. Ngi hurried off and quickly returned with a tall, hawkfaced, neatly uniformed officer who ushered me into his office. Captain Ngi and Voung accompanied us.

Major Dong was friendly but businesslike. His attitude was that of a gracious landlord entertaining an important tenant. A secretary brought tea, and I listened as Voung translated Dong's description of the district. Standing in front of a map board, Dong spoke of how the district was organized. His finger ran over a blue line some two thousand meters to the west of Rach Kien town; this was a stream of some significance, and I inquired about it. Voung spoke the name in Vietnamese and added that in English the name meant "river of ants." Voung said that over the years of war, many men had died along that body of water. Much of the district was not under effective government control. I learned that there was no school in the district above the level of an American fourth grade. The district had no Vietnamese doctors and only one midwife to care for a population Major Dong estimated at thirty thousand. Dong's conversation stressed administrative aspects and the importance of my task in helping the people improve their quality of life by securing American supplies so desperately needed.

I acknowledged the need for assistance but noted that there seemed not to have been an opportunity for his military units to take offensive action against the enemy. I related the importance of initiating combat patrols, ambushes, and search missions to reduce and then take away the Viet Cong influence in the outlying areas.

Orientals are masters at concealing their thoughts, but I could see a slight change in his face as Dong reiterated his emphasis on the administrative aspects. He restated his view that the task of fighting the enemy was primarily the responsibility of the South Vietnamese and American combat units. I countered by saying that Americans were fighting and dying in Vietnam and that no one knew Rach Kien better than those men who had lived here most or all of their lives. I told him that Americans expected every Vietnamese to seek ways to defeat the enemy and bring the war to a satisfactory end.

Voung indicated that the interview was at an end, but I was not yet finished. In a friendly, smiling manner, I told Major Dong that I was proud to be working with him and that all American money, material, and assistance that came into Rach Kien District would come through me. I added that I would give his requests for assistance the same high degree of consideration that I knew he would give my suggestions. Major Dong replied that he would appreciate it if I would share my ideas on military operations with Captain Ngi and, as soon as ammunition was furnished from Province, we would begin some military activity against the enemy.

The meeting ended and I returned to the advisor house. Team members were unloading a truckload of 105-howitzer ammunition boxes and stacking tools and bales of sandbags. I went to the back of the house to determine the best location for a bunker, a location that would give us a fighting position and some protection from enemy mortar fire. We finished the day by going with the Artillery to an American dinner. We then lit Coleman lanterns and had a team meeting. I outlined the responsibilities for the next day. The nightly meeting to review accomplishments and plan the following day became standard operating procedure (SOP).

For me to move into the crowded house would cause a ripple effect as men were displaced according to rank. I moved into the trailer. It was filthy but had the potential of high living. The thought crossed and recrossed my mind that a mortar round would go through that roof like steel through hot butter. I very much wanted to do something about that.

The next two weeks were filled with continuous intense activity. We filled ammo boxes and sandbags with paddy mud from the pond and built a bunker at the rear of the advisor house. I was able to get a few spare pieces of pierced steel planking from the infantry and used these to roof the bunker, topping that with mud-filled sandbags. At the screened-in front and rear of the house we built chest-high sandbag walls.

Furniture was moved out of the trailer and space made for the other officers to sleep there, which allowed more living space in the house for other ranks. We built upon our relationship with the Artillery. Their cooks were very appreciative of the roofing for the new mess hall they were building, and they gave us eggs, bacon, ham, cheese, coffee, and juice. One of the lieutenants had some experience in culinary arts and began to teach Ba how to make eggs and omelets. Within a week she was turning out breakfast to order and we were living the good life.

From our breakfast table we had the less than inspiring sight of the latrine that served the Vietnamese district headquarters. The latrine was a large box built high on stilts above the paddies; those who used it walked up a plank and squatted over an opening in the floor. Their head and shoulders were visible, as was whatever fell to the paddy beneath. Watching people defecate is on a par with a low-grade situation comedy. It made for idle breakfast conversation such as, "It looks like Major Dong is bound up again" or "Has she still got the runs?" The rainy season would not begin until April and the heat was oppressive, soaring to well over one hundred degrees Fahrenheit. The stench from the

Vietnamese outhouse hung in the air like a blanket. The insects came in clouds, but the Vietnamese made no effort to
remove, burn, or cover the feces.

I was sympathetic to the complaint of the enlisted men
about burning our shit. Everyone understood the need for us
to maintain sanitation. The men reasoned that all of us were
crapping and all should share in the burn detail. The men
were prepared to take care of their own waste, but not that of
the officers. It was a problem of perception. One sergeant
told me, "Sir, it is enough we have to take it from officers,
but we should not have to burn their shit."

I took a turn at the detail to set the example for the other
officers. It was a disgusting task. I dragged the sawed-off,
fifty-five-gallon drums away from the latrine while swarms
of feces-laden flies buzzed about me. Gasoline is a dangerous explosive. I had no desire to be blown up in a blast of
turds, so I carefully measured in a quantity of gasoline and
threw on a lighted match. Like an erupting volcano, a dense
column of black smoke shot skyward. The wind changed
quickly and I was engulfed in an odious cloud. I heard muf-
fled laughter from the house and knew that the men were enjoying themselves immensely. I had come up through the
ranks. I remembered all those days and nights when I had
done kitchen police, ash and trash, and night fireman, all of
the necessary but disgusting work of a soldier slave. I had
done more pearl diving in urinals and toilet bowls than these
men, and had not become an officer to burn shit. There had
to be a better way.

Soldiers like to complain. It makes a man feel a part of
events. In building the bunker and improving house security,
I felt that the better protection was so obvious that it required
no explanation—I was wrong. The work was heavy lifting in
the hot sun, and soon men began to question the need for the
labor. They said there had only been one motar attack, a few
rounds that went wide of the target. I told the men that in my
experience Asian mortar men could put a mortar round in
your hip pocket, and that it was likely the mortar crew had

been testing the range for future use. I capped my explanation by telling them to "Shut the hell up and get to work." Being good soldiers, they understood that best.

I was far from satisfied. We now had a decent fighting position and some protection, but only if we survived to make it to the bunker. We were vulnerable to mortar rounds penetrating our roofs. We were separated from the Vietnamese we were supposed to be advising.

I came from an aggressive, competitive culture. "Don't just sit there, get up and do something" is the American way. The Vietnamese officers and men I encountered in Rach Kien were products of their quiet culture. A sense of urgency was not a part of their makeup. Their philosophy that "tomorrow is as good as today, we'll do it then" had me burning with impatience. The advantage I had with my Vietnamese troops in 555 Company was that they were local men, born and raised in Rach Kien or surrounding districts. They knew the people and the terrain better than any American ever would. They knew the trails and who should or should not be at any hamlet. This knowledge was not being used because the Vietnamese commanders and the men knew they were weak. The Regional Force companies and Popular Force platoons in Rach Kien were light infantry bordering on weightlessness. Whatever military thought was in their heads was defensive. I hoped to change that by improving their training, weapons, and equipment and getting them accustomed to go in search of the enemy.

On paper, advisors did not command or exercise operational control or responsibility. Fortunately, Captain Ngi and I shared respect, and a friendship was formed between two very different men seeking the same goal. Where possible I tried to make my comments in private and when in front of his men was careful about stepping on his pride. It was unjust that Ngi was politically an outcast as he had courage, determination, and was a skilled warrior. He always listened and followed as well as he led. Most of the time we worked well together.

On occasion, men with the local VC would rally to the

government side. From one such rallier, Dong learned that a Viet Cong official was believed to be holed up in a house some four kilometers east of Rach Kien town. Ngi received a good description of the house and surroundings. While we made our plans to go after this VC, the informant was held under close confinement, allowing no communication with anyone else.

Taking only the experienced PRU, Ngi and I and our radio operators moved out shortly after midnight. To prevent someone reporting our movement, we left town moving south. We traveled well beyond the inhabited area before we switched direction to the east. Ngi provided a few men on our trail in the event we were followed. A pale moon gave us enough visibility to choose our route, and among our men were locals who knew the area well. We maintained radio silence, having radios with us only for emergency or after-action use. It was routine for the artillery to fire night missions or some harassing and interdictory (H&I) fire in the free-fire zones. Every effort was made to continue those things that the enemy could expect. I had carefully gone over our route with the artillery and plotted where and when H&I fires might be made. I had coordinated our patrol time and route with any others being run by Americans. Ngi had done the same with the South Vietnamese. We checked equipment and weapons and had the PRU men jump up and down to be certain nothing rattled or made sounds that would betray our movement.

Ghosting through the night, I felt my blood pulsing, anticipating the high adventure of the hunt. I was searching for one man, a man far more important to the war than some frightened draftee hustled down the Ho Chi Minh Trail into American firepower. This was the personal war against the enemy infrastructure. The informant told Ngi that the official had grown overconfident and did not have a guerrilla bodyguard with him. We would get into position to strike at first light. I remembered the words from verse 17, chapter 24 of Job: "For the morning is to them even as the shadow of death: If one know them, they are in the terrors of the shadow of death."

The PRU soldier in front of us whispered something to Ngi. He signaled to me that we were close to our objective. Moving carefully, we took up positions that allowed us to cover all sides of the house. We then waited for the soft light of dawn. With the coming of light, the occupants of the house began to move about. An elderly man and woman, a younger woman, and several children were present, among which was a girl approximately eight to ten years old. I looked at Ngi, questioning if the old man was our target. He made a negative sign, so we waited.

As the sun grew stronger, a wave of disappointment swept over me. I could see the same expression on Ngi's face. At length, seeing nothing suspicious, we came into the open and Ngi engaged the family in conversation while the troops searched the house. The family members were obviously frightened, but disclaimed any knowledge of our man. Both Ngi and I went inside and made a search of our own, in particular looking for any sign of a hiding place or tunnel in the floor. We found nothing. Houses in the outlying area had paddy-mud bunkers with narrow openings in which families often slept to protect themselves as best they could from artillery fire. A PRU had crawled in with a drawn pistol and checked to make certain nothing was within.

Nothing was found and we prepared to leave. The little girl was standing with her back to her family and made a gesture with her hand that both Ngi and I saw. She was holding her hand in front of her chest but pointing toward the ground. Ngi and I had the same thought as we looked at each other. Ngi said something loudly to the PRU and we began to move away. We were talking as men would when there is no thought of action. Once out of sight of the house, Ngi ordered most of the PRU to continue on and continue talking. Taking three men, Ngi and I circled wide, returned, and, using foliage for concealment, crawled near to the house.

Again we waited. After a time a middle-aged and physically fit man dressed in black pajamalike peasant garb came out into the morning sun. Our carbines went up. I flipped off the safety and drew a bead on his stomach. Ngi shouted, calling on the man to surrender. The Viet Cong official stood for a moment, frozen by the sound of Ngi's voice, and then ran. I tracked his movement and fired, hearing the sounds of the PRU carbines and Ngi's revolver blend with my shots. Dust spurted at his feet, but other slugs were tearing into his body from several weapons. I believed, but could not be certain, that my shots were striking home. The VC leader was flung to the ground by the force of the bullets.

Dead before he hit the ground, he lay in that peculiar position that I had seen before and would see again, that of a dead man attempting to run. With his body before them, the family was quick to talk. They pointed out the cleverly concealed hiding place. This was not a tunnel in the floor, but a space behind a false wall. I had looked at that wall as had the others; it was so cleverly done that I understood why he required no bodyguard. His security lay in concealment. The older members of the family were now in terror, as they expected reprisal. Ngi talked to them sharply. He was convinced that they were just another family caught in the middle of a war and trying to survive. We left them alone. I did not mention the little girl until we left. It was best to keep her action unknown to others. I would have preferred a prisoner that could have led us to others, but this VC had made his choice.

Thrilled by the first success, I went back to work. To do my job, I had to know the land that I was responsible for. From my first day in Rach Kien, I established a policy of calling for a helicopter from Province and flying over Rach Kien District. I tried to make these reconnaissance flights at least twice a week. We did not have the opportunity to get the OH-23 light observation helicopters. I later learned that it was best we did not have the OH-23, as the enemy knew them to be scout aircraft. My reconnaissance flights were in the UH-l, the beloved Hueys, and I seldom had the same pilot and copilot. I joked with them, saying that if my pilot was a major with a wife and three children, he preferred to fly at 1,500 feet and resisted my efforts to go lower. A first lieutenant with a wife and no children liked to cruise at 1,000 feet. If I flew with a twenty-year-old warrant officer with no attachments, the flight was down on the deck, zooming around palm trees, allowing me a view not much different than if I had been on the ground.

At that altitude I could locate bunker construction. Enemy bunkers were usually about four-by-six-by-four feet in size with overhead cover, sometimes two feet thick. They were well camouflaged, mutually supporting, and usually had connecting trenches. Difficult to spot, it was not effective to attempt destroying them from our helicopter. On those occasions when I located bunkers, I passed the information to both the Vietnamese and the Americans. When possible, I took Captain Ngi and a member of my team, rotating these so that all team members would have an understanding of our area.

The aerial recons were an exciting time. In Rach Kien the enemy rarely fired at aircraft flying at fifteen hundred feet or higher. Sometimes we were shot at while at a low level. When flying a few feet off the ground, we approached the enemy so fast that they were unable to react in time. To fire at us and miss was a mistake on their part, because it would earn them some artillery, with their location also being passed along to our big brothers in American infantry. I began to pinpoint the areas where district forces should go and where enemy assembly areas and potential ambush were likely.

A critical part of these flights was to locate landing zones for our helicopters. These were required to be close to the objective, but not so close that an ambush could be set in an unsecured landing zone. There could be no dead falls, camouflaged pits dug to snare an unsuspecting pilot, or impediments to landing. I had to consider the season, as downdraft from the helicopter blades would kick up blinding clouds of dust in the dry season and water and mud in the rainy months. Also under consideration was how far those of us making the landing had to move to cover and the best route to the objective. No doubt, enemy eyes were watching our aircraft. Lingering too long in one area betrayed interest, and an ambush might be waiting on the next trip. By covering the district again and again from the air, I came to know all parts of my territorial responsibility from both high and low levels.

Captain Ngi was with me on a flight when we spotted a sampan attempting to conceal itself along a riverbank in a free-fire zone. I felt certain this was enemy movement. One man was visible on deck. I pointed at the sampan and looked at Ngi for verification. Ngi said, "VC." I instructed the pilot to have his door gunner engage with his M-60 machine gun. The gunner opened fire and could easily have walked his tracer bullets into the target, but he did not. I could not understand such poor marksmanship. The crew chief and I yelled at the gunner while I opened fire with my carbine. The machine gunner was obviously rattled. His shots kicked up water but did not strike the sampan. Only when the man on the boat dove overboard did the gunner bring his weapon to bear on the sampan and sink it. That was all very noble, but he had just left a killer or potential killer of Americans alive. The pilot understood that he had a crewman whose poor marksmanship or sensibility could cost him and his crew their lives. I did not have to say anymore, but just listened to the colorful language of the pilot.

I was a member of a conventional army, an army that had been built to meet the Soviet threat in Europe. There were two wars in Vietnam. One was a conventional war against the enemy main force. Our army did quite well against it. The enemy did not beat the American army on the battlefield. The second war in Vietnam was the unconventional war. We were not prepared to fight in this manner and learned our lessons too late to be successful.

In most cases the enemy in Rach Kien was content to lie low during the day and practice a night war. During the day, US and Vietnamese government sweeps usually kept them out of sight, but at night two men with rifles can overawe or terrorize an unarmed village. Strangers in a foreign land, we could deal with those who chose to slug it out toe-to-toe; each time the enemy tried that he was bloodied. I had to develop a new mental process for this war. The peasant working the paddies with his water buffalo might be the Viet Cong district chief. The driver of a three-wheeled Lambretta bringing produce to market might be the Viet Cong tax collector, and a pretty secretary working Major Dong's office might be a Viet Cong mistress who lures South Vietnamese officials and army officers to ambush and death.

The enemy infrastructure made it possible for northern forces to operate effectively in the south. They preached nationalism, helped the people where possible, taxed them heavily, and tolerated no resistance. They ruthlessly killed any civilian who stood in their way. They used fear to enhance their other activities. I did not possess the sledgehammer power that American or even South Vietnamese battalions had, but the infrastructure was best met by the rapierlike thrust of the ambush and the raid where this was within our means. I felt the situation called for Ranger tactics. I hoped we could build a small group of hunters from among our Vietnamese. I had confidence in the PRU and began to watch the training of 555 Regional Force Company, looking for men who would go beyond what was required of them.

Ngi was a good man, a good officer. I grew to love him as my brother. He had been a district chief, but angered a powerful politician. Downgraded to assistant and denied promotion, his authority was greatly limited. He tolerated my constant badgering and followed the Asian principle of "face." Though sometimes angry with me, he held himself under control. On one occasion, when he could take my badgering no longer, he cried out at me, "You are here for one year, and I have been fighting this war for twenty years!" I replied that I was certain he had seen much combat, but we were doing little and must do our part to keep applying pressure on the enemy.

I had lunch with officers of the infantry battalion and listened to them talk about the Long Range Patrol teams. Since the 1700s the regular army establishment had had a love-hate relationship with Ranger units. Useful in war, they were soon disbanded in peace. Conventional generals in command complained that Ranger units take off the best men, or they are prima donnas, or contend that a well-trained line unit can do it better. Yet in war after war the call soon goes out for men who volunteer to do the Ranger mission.

There were no Ranger units in the active army when the United States entered the war in Vietnam. Many of the aggressive volunteers who would have been Rangers were serving in Special Forces, an organization that many in and out of the military confuse with Rangers. The Special Forces concept was rooted in the OSS experience of World War II. They recruited exceptional volunteers and trained them in languages, weapons, demolitions, communications, and other skills. These men would then by parachute or other means enter a Communist-occupied country and provide training and logistical support to those who were trying to overthrow the occupying force. If NATO and the Warsaw Pact nations had gone to war, Special Forces would have been employed in many Russian-occupied countries in Europe.

War happened in Vietnam, and the Special Forces concept seemed the ideal way to support the South Vietnamese without making a large investment of American troops. President John Kennedy liked the Special Forces approach and for a time they were looked upon as a cure-all. This presidential favor had the lamps burning late in the Pentagon. Special Forces did not have a long history, so the army ignored these differences in mission and historical truth. To promote them to the public the Army wrongly gave Special Forces the history, lineage, and battle honors of the World War II Ranger battalions and Korean War Airborne Ranger companies. Special Forces were not Rangers; they had their own valid mission and their own pride. This ill-advised action meant that any Ranger unit formed for Vietnam would not have a

Ranger history, and when Ranger units came back on active duty the army would resort to historical fiction to make a history and lineage fit.

Though the name Ranger was found only at a Fort Benning, Georgia, course of instruction, the need for Ranger activities was always there. In Vietnam, small teams of volunteers were formed called Long Range Reconnaissance Patrol (LRRP). Their missions frequently expanded beyond reconnaissance, and they became known as Long Range Patrol (LRP).* These men performed traditional Ranger missions, including reconnaissance and combat patrols, ambushes and raids. Their companies were usually under the control of a Division commander. Company E of the 50th Infantry (LRP) was with the 9th Infantry Division in my area.

The men of the Long Range Patrols who were later justly called Rangers were a breed apart. They were men who volunteered for this hazardous duty after they came into Vietnam. As such they did not have the opportunity to attend the Ranger course at Fort Benning, Georgia, but they were every bit as much Rangers as the men of World War II and Korea. The army does not take men out of overseas combat to send them to school in the United States and then send them back to the same job they left. Trained in Vietnam, with action against the enemy as their school, these brave men operated in small teams of six to twelve men throughout Vietnam. They were masters of reconnaissance and ambush techniques.

*That these men were Rangers was demonstrated in 1969 when the army decided to name them so. One day a man was called an LRP by the army; the next day the same man doing the same mission was called a Ranger. One of the injustices of Ranger history is that these men are not authorized to wear the Ranger tab. The army justification is that Ranger School existed during the Vietnam War. This ignores the fact that the men volunteered and fought in Vietnam and were given no opportunity to return to the United States for training. In the 1960s the men of the World War II 5307th Composite Unit (Provisional), called "Merrill's Marauders" by a newspaperman trying to promote himself and them, were sent Ranger tabs by the army to hand out at a reunion. The army defended that by saying there was no Ranger school in World War II, so men of the 5307th CPU had no chance to attend.

Though organized in companies, they operated in small teams and were led by junior sergeants.

In the 9th Infantry Division area, Rangers of the Long Range Patrol often worked in conjunction with Navy SEALs along the many rivers and streams of the Mekong Delta. They were inserted into their target areas by assault boats, Boston Whalers, Navy patrol boats, and helicopters. I was eager to try waterborne operations and proposed a joint American/Vietnamese operation along the Song Vam Co Dong, making our landing along the eastern part of Rach Kien District.

Each day I spent time with Major Dong, Captain Ngi, and the people who surrounded them. The Vietnamese military headquarters staff included various military ranks and civilians. The secretary, Kim-Anh, was a beautiful girl, finely boned and clear-featured. Her raven black hair cascaded down over a sky-blue *ao dai* to her waist. At the desk beside her was a Vietnamese *trung si*, the equivalent of a US staff sergeant. His name was Kinh, and he was a handsome young man, hardworking, friendly, and loyal. It was obvious that these two were deeply in love. I mentioned to Captain Ngi that we might have a wedding to attend. Ngi told me that the match was impossible. Kim-Anh was of a much higher caste than Sergeant Kinh. She would marry someone her family had selected. It seemed to me that this relationship looked too hot to be cooled, and I watched it as a friend to both of these young people.

Bad things could happen without warning in Vietnam. While making my rounds of the town, a sniper, whose location I could not pinpoint, fired one round that was close to being a head shot. The slug was at eye level and tore into the woodwork of a building I was passing. I moved with dispatch to get where I could return fire, but there was no second shot. Captain Ngi and I and some PRU made a sweep of the area but found no sign. I wondered if it came from one of our Regional or Popular Force troops. Some Vietnamese did switch from side to side, and one could never be certain when that would occur.

In the heat of the afternoon, several jeeps with pedestal-mounted M-60 machine guns and three-quarter-ton trucks with heavily armed soldiers rolled to a stop in front of the advisor house. They were the advance party of the engineer detachment led by a determined major. The Vietnamese had previously decided the location of the engineer area. In Rach Kien town, the advisor house was directly across the street from the Vietnamese military headquarters. Across the street from Major Dong's administrative center was a vacant lot. The engineers would be quartered in that open space. We were all located in an area approximately eighty yards square. I felt that this was a tempting target, but understood the Vietnamese refusal to relocate from established positions. Nothing else appeared to be better, and they were trying to run a civil government and convince the people that they were in control.

The engineer major was aggressive and soon had his men setting up tents in the open space. He told me that the engineers were there to build schools and roads and provide a better life for the people. To accomplish this, they required laborers and job site security. In previous discussions with Major Dong we had worked out a plan to provide a Regional Force platoon as security at each job site. Most of the young men of the district were in the service, but there were many women who were accustomed to hard labor and anxious to earn money. Finding laborers would not be a problem.

I related to the engineer major that I had little confidence in 555 Regional Force Company and recommended that his men keep their weapons at hand. I told him that the enemy would try to prevent the engineers from providing assistance to the Vietnamese people. The Communists seldom bothered a corrupt government official or an inefficient operation. They allowed the people to grow to hate them. The enemy attempted to coerce or kill any honest man or woman in the South Vietnamese government or anyone helping or influencing the people in a way that threatened Communist efforts.

Terror was a major weapon of the enemy, and they were skilled at using it. When targeting a teacher or government official, they would often send letters telling the individual to cease support of the government and do as the Communists instructed, or die. They meant their warnings and often pronounced formal death sentences. Recently an honest district chief had been assassinated by Communist gunmen in a district north of Rach Kien. The enemy had also succeeded in killing several teachers in that area. Several of our own civilian leaders in the district had had narrow escapes.

Many brave South Vietnamese lived under the shadow of these threats, but there was no way to ascertain, until it was too late, who had knuckled under. I recommended that if the engineers' trucks had been loaded by Vietnamese, the major's men should be careful when removing the cargo. Sometimes the enemy would wedge a grenade with the safety pin pulled among the boxes on a truck. When the boxes were unloaded, the grenade's handle would be released and the grenade would explode.

I was also concerned about the engineers being put in tents instead of bunkered sleeping quarters. To have men in tents, I told the major, was an invitation to the VC to attack and that his men should have protection. The engineer major reacted as though this showed cowardice. His sneering response was "We're not afraid of Charlie. We came down here to build, not hide in bunkers."

The major departed in the direction of Saigon, leaving a captain as detachment commander. American engineers are a marvel of efficiency. Sizable tents known as general purpose mediums sprouted from the hard-packed soil. The tents boasted wooden floors, canvas cots, and large lockers for stowage. They circled this area with barbed wire and placed some machine guns in position. I checked the guns and found one situated to fire into the district chief's house and another into the artillery battery.

As a young Ranger, I'd watched our sergeants and officers get down in position behind every weapon and check the field of fire. Many soldiers drop into a position without thinking of their ability to fight from that spot. They may have a stone wall, a tree, or a rise in the ground directly to their front, but they just do not think. With the cooperation of the engineers, I got their perimeter tied in with the rest of the defense.

A strange thing happened to many of us who worked directly with the Vietnamese as advisors. We lived in a middle world. Scrounging was a way of life. We were not privileged to enjoy the many benefits of the American supply system, and most of our contacts were with the Vietnamese. We certainly were not Vietnamese and had difficulty grasping their culture and practices; however, we did not feel part of the American team. After a while we began to talk about "the Americans" as though we were not part of either society. A conversation might include "Well, the goddamn Americans have run another patrol south of town without telling us, and the dumb-ass Vietnamese from 555 blundered into them."

Given the sudden growth and size of the American effort in Vietnam, it is unlikely we could have properly prepared the large numbers of advisors that were used. I felt that my brief preparation at civil affairs school had been inadequate to the task. As a student in that school I wrote a paper on the impact of railroads on improving life in this developing nation. I never saw a railroad in Vietnam and doubt if one in my area would have survived a week. If I had known more of the culture and especially the language of Vietnam, I would have been more effective.

It takes some knowing to understand a people, many of whom believe they are descended from the coupling of a dragon and an angel. The Vietnamese were deeply attached to their families and the place of their birth. Many Vietnamese men on both sides fought because of an order by a respected family member. It was their duty to follow their family elders. The Vietnamese family is much larger than the American family and worthy of a Gilbert and Sullivan theme, "All of his sisters and his cousins and his aunts." The young relate to the old with respect, and homage is paid to ancestors. The man is the authority figure and the female takes a secondary role, but each have their responsibilities. They were frequently shy, yet quick to smile. No people can be lumped into a single description. I met good Vietnamese and bad, heroes and cowards. In that regard they were much like Americans, and like those Americans who served in Vietnam, the South Vietnamese people deserved better. Corruption hamstrung the South Vietnamese government, bullying and favoritism that sapped the strength of patriotism. On the surface it seemed that the Communists were nationalists, more caring and closer to the people, but it was a ruse. They wanted more than the people's money—they wanted the body and soul under total domination.

I often talked with Ngi about the differences of the South and North Vietnamese. He had a higher regard for those in the North. "Life is too easy in the South," he would say. Food was abundant and, in his view, the weather was pleasant. People were easygoing in the South. In the North, life was hard and cold. Ngi thought that hard life made a better soldier. Life in Rach Kien was an example of Kipling's "East is east and west is west and never the twain shall meet." Vietnamese business practices were often frustrating. I would say to Dong or Ngi, "We are going to do this. Right?" They would reply, "Yes," but it would never happen. In time I came to realize that they did not want the embarrassment of an argument. When they said "Yes," they simply meant "We hear you."

What a telephone was to people back home, the radio was to us in Vietnam. We soon had two-base-station PRC-25 radios with long antennae that were our lifelines of communication. We operated on one frequency for communications within the team when we were conducting our own operations and another frequency for constant contact with Province and the other districts.

Each of the districts had a randomly selected radio call sign that would change periodically and was published in Signal Operating Instructions (SOI). Province might be "Smash Mouth," and each district had a number. Rach Kien would be "Smash Mouth 14." All commanders had the number 6, and staff officers would be 1-personnel, 2-intelligence, 3-operations, 4-logistics. We usually omitted the preceding words and went with numbers; thus, my call sign was 146. If I called the province senior advisor, I would call for Smash Mouth Six and, once communication was established, address him as "Six." I frequently wondered who in the Signal Corps had the job of inventing these combinations. Call signs could be dramatic such as "Power Hawk," or embarrassing such as "Sweet Hips," and at times confusing. One advisor told me he was having a night radio conversation with a gunship whose pilot said, "This is Black Knight." The advisor could not resist saying, "Yes, it is, probably gonna rain."

The joint American/Vietnamese supply system had me baffled. Near Saigon, I had seen supply depots bursting with material that we needed, but the system did not deliver the material to Rach Kien District. We submitted endless requisitions for the district through the Vietnamese supply system. We asked for construction materials, weapons, uniforms, equipment, and ammunition, but little came of it. Each item had to be fought for. This often required a trip to Province, where the Vietnamese discussed their differences with each other politely and the Americans yelled and cursed about these supply frustrations. While stationed in Germany, I was accustomed to saying to the S-4 (logistics officer), "This is what I need," and he got it. In Germany, as long as the requests were reasonable, they were fulfilled. For an advisor in Vietnam to go up against the supply system was like punching a pillow.

In the Vietnam War we had an organization called USAID, the United States Agency for International Development. Another district advisor described it as a system in which the United States government gave the Vietnamese government money to buy matériel from the United States that would make American contractors wealthy and provide many jobs. It also enabled the United States to build a considerable self-serving bureaucracy to administer the program, while the Vietnamese benefited through many opportunities for graft and theft. Meanwhile, in Vietnam, we advisors would do without the material we needed to pursue the war effort and improve the life of the people.

How accurate the description was, I could not tell, but I was not getting the material we needed. I was only a small cog in this great wheel. If I could not work in, beat, or even understand this system, I had to develop my own. I was at the sites where the projects were to be done and the local battle was to be fought. I stressed that as the senior American on the ground, any US material and money for Rach Kien District should come through me. Then it would be my job to see that American taxpayers (of which I was one) received their money's worth in winning the war and helping the people in Rach Kien.

War is waste, but the military should not abuse the taxpayer. I was present when a colonel told a lieutenant to fly a helicopter to Saigon in order to pick up an item the colonel wanted from the PX. That was bad enough, but when the lieutenant said the only helicopter available that day was a large cargo-carrying Chinook and mentioned the cost, the colonel replied, "I don't care what it costs."

Each day I walked the Vietnamese, advisor, and engineer perimeters and down through the town of Rach Kien. I varied the time and route to preclude easy ambush, but felt it was important to be out and seen by the people whom I was there to help. Captain Ngi and I would talk of the military situation. I would stop by district headquarters and wave to Major Dong. He was usually buried behind a pile of documents and would raise his hands in mild frustration. I would pantomime my commiseration and continue on. I had a deep-seated concern that while I was walking the town, my enemy counterpart was walking the hamlets and meeting the people in the countryside.

The engineers were at work on a five-room elementary school that would be the pride of Rach Kien. The youngsters were presently crowded into a Buddhist temple, so ancient that the venerable Buddha himself had probably worked on the construction. The engineers were delighted to be working. They told me that they had been constructing a golf course near Saigon and were greatly angered by that. They wanted to do something positive for the Vietnamese people and this was their chance. The engineers were a proud bunch who kept their weapons handy and talked about giving the VC hell if they were bothered. The women laborers were working out well and showed promise of learning concrete finishing and basic carpentry.

Beyond the engineering area was the billeting area of 555 Regional Force Company. This was commanded by the *trung ui* (lieutenant) called Antoine, about whom the artillery battery commander had told me. Antoine spoke some English and attempted to cozy up to me, but he was a shifty little rat and I kept him at arm's length. I knew he was behind most of the illicit activity in the district and also knew that his political connections protected him. Whatever profits he was making were not reaching his troops.

The Regional and Popular Force troops were the bottom of the barrel. The RFs were paid the equivalent of nineteen US dollars a month, on which they could not prosper but only barely exist. They were poor men, yet some were good soldiers. We called the company medic *bac-si*, meaning doctor. He was about four feet, nine inches tall and worked very hard at his trade. I saw him practice placing a head bandage on a snot-nosed scabious urchin who was urinating in the dust. Antoine paid little attention to his men or their training, and I complained about him to both the Americans and Vietnamese.

Passing through the barbed wire gate, I walked into the town of Rach Kien. Houses and open-front shops lined the dirt street. A fifty-meter walk took me past the National Police station to the center of town. Here the street greatly widened and divided, flowing on each side of a long one-story building that was a roof on supports. This was the marketplace, the largest building in town, and, like the market Socrates knew in ancient Athens, was the gathering place and news exchange of the community. It was a farmers market. Each morning it thronged with people bringing their ducks, fish, and produce to exchange or sell. Here, the long carrying pole came into use, supporting wicker baskets. Selling was done from the concrete floor, where vendors squatted beside their merchandise. As there were no tables, chairs, or display cases, sellers placed their products on broad leaves or pieces of newspaper on the ground and haggled with prospective purchasers. Women, old men, and young boys were the buyers and sellers who came in from the outlying areas. Men of military age were conspicuous in their absence, either recruited or conscripted by one side or the other. Sanitation was nonexistent at the market. The lettuce frequently showed the feces used for fertilizer. The meat, cut up and left exposed to dirt and dust, was usually covered with a swarm of flies. Occasionally the vendor might seek to brush them away, but that was seldom and futile. These people had lived this life for centuries, and with diseases long since reduced or conquered in other parts of the world. It was part of my mission to find ways to make their lives healthier while giving them an opportunity for freedom.

Beyond the market, the town ended in an iron bridge that spanned a stream that flowed southwest to connect with the River of Ants. The name "River of Ants" fascinated me. It was discussed by the Vietnamese as though it were Caesar's Rubicon. I was anxious to go there. My thoughts returned to the scene at the bridge. Young boys swam and dived from the bridge while old men worked on their fishnets. Beyond the bridge, the houses looked deserted and the road little used. This was no-man's-land. Captain Ngi had warned me that I could not walk there alone without risking getting shot. I intended to change that.

The children frolicked about me, drawing themselves up tight and standing stiffly while they rendered a mock salute. They were captivated by the fact that I had hair on my bare arms. Few Vietnamese were cursed with this barbaric affliction. The children were like children anywhere. Playing, happiness, and bullying each other formed the core of their desires.

Turning left along the water's edge, I moved along the path

that formed the town side of the stream; this was the whore area. It was usual to see several American soldiers running away. Forewarned of my approach by a child lookout, they exited this off-limits area at high speed. I always went through the motion of checking each building so that I could truthfully tell American officers that I was doing what I could to keep the VD rate down. Major Dong and Captain Ngi could not understand the American approach to sex. Born under French rule, they assured me that the French never made a problem of sex. The French arranged for supervised houses where soldiers could fulfill their needs and women could ply their trade under medically supervised conditions. Dong made no secret that he thought American attitudes about sex were unenforceable. While promising support, he made little effort to drive out the whores. When he could no longer tolerate my complaints, he would have the police close down a house and temporarily move it, but do nothing when it reopened. It was possible that Dong and local officials were profiting from prostitution.

I was not in Vietnam to teach morals. I could see the lieutenant, named Antoine, taking his ease among the women, often surrounded by three or four of them. Sometimes the women were bitter when I interfered with their livelihood, and they would spout a stream of invective at me. Some laughed, and some tried to take me to their pads. Many of them kept tin pans of water by their mats. When they finished a trick, they would splash water on their genital orifices. It was from this practice that I began to call the area "Tin Pan Alley."

Close by Tin Pan Alley at the edge of the stream was the favorite laundry spot for village housewives and their daughters. The women would squat for hours scrubbing clothes in the slow-moving water, pounding the cloth with rocks in the oriental fashion. They kept a lively conversation going while they worked. When the older women looked toward Tin Pan Alley, their faces often registered disgust. Many of the young girls would look with envy. The prostitutes were dressed in clothes that these girls could only dream about. The whores had plenty of rice and tea, and other women laundered their clothes.

Most days, when I walked through the wash area, I would be approached by a barefooted girl in her preteens in black pajama-type bottoms and a frayed white-cotton blouse. This little *co* (miss) was a special person, a girl whose goal was to be a high-income prostitute. She worked hard to learn English and could not understand that men thought of her as a baby sister instead of a sex object. She knew value and understood that in a land without lumber, the 105-howitzer ammunition box was a valuable commodity. Our conversations began with pleasantries and ended with propositions:

"Chao thieu ta." (Hello, Major).

"Chao co." (Hello, Miss).

"You want make love me?"

"You baby."

"Me no baby!"

She would place her damp hands under her young breasts and push upward. "You like?" she would ask.

To spare her feelings, I would pat my pockets and say, "Have no money."

"Thieu ta," her child's face bright and shining. "You give me ten ammo boxes, I love you too much."

The discussion would be broken off by a sharp cry from her mother, who would send her back to the wash line, but her lips usually formed the words "Ten ammo boxes." I learned that she propositioned other Americans in the same way. I do not recall her true name. Everyone called this little miss with big dreams "Ten Ammo Boxes."

Beyond the wash area was the white-painted dispensary. It was formerly the private home of a wealthy family, but they were executed by the Viet Cong in 1964 when the Communists had control of the district. Some of the townspeople, who had nowhere else to go, remained in the district and suffered or prospered according to their support of the Communist government. Other people fled to Saigon and returned only when American power had destroyed the major enemy forces. A great number of the Vietnamese had col-

COL. ROBERT W. BLACK

laborated with the Communists, just as many now collaborated with the South Vietnamese government. Unless the collaboration had been blatant, resulting in the death of a relative, residents were wary of discussing who had supported the Communists. One never knew when circumstances might change again.

The midwife and my team medic worked together to help the people of the district. One large room in the dispensary had been converted to a ward. The remainder consisted of an office, an operating room, and a small room used by the midwife for her bedroom and kitchen. The ward was filled with female patients, mostly in late pregnancy or recovering from childbirth. Some were recovering from shrapnel wounds. The heavy shutters were kept open during the day, allowing the sunlight to offset the peeling dark green paint on the walls. The female patients lay on rice mats, hands resting on swollen bellies, or guiding eager young mouths to filled breasts.

To a Vietnamese, pain and suffering was life as it had been lived for centuries. To a twentieth-century American, the medical situation was intolerable. What American could imagine thirty thousand people without a single doctor to look after them? The accidents of life and war and the illnesses of our species produced a stream of desperate people needing help, yet there was so little available. People bore pain with a stoicism that was remarkable. Americans helped when and where they could. Army medical personnel worked wonders with outreach programs to the Vietnamese while accomplishing their own mission of providing care for our troops. The infantry battalion surgeon had a weekly medcap (Medical Civilian Action Program), when he would treat Vietnamese civilians, but his primary duty was to our soldiers. Their needs had to come first.

I told my team medic to make a wish list and let his imagination run wild. I did not yet know how we were to solve our medical difficulties, but the first step in the problem-solving process was to identify the problem. In this case, it was lack of basic medicines.

After the dispensary, I would visit the artillery battery to have a cup of coffee. Here, I would inquire about what was happening in the war and in the States. I then went to the infantry battalion, stopping by the tactical operations center (TOC). They usually left for work early, their helicopters sweeping into land on the road north of town. With a fast pickup, company by company, the battalion went off to fight. They were good infantry. The battalion tactical operations center was the rear-area nerve center, a place of squawking radios and acetate-covered maps with grease-pencil markings of troop positions and objectives. Both the Artillery and Infantry knew me as a beggar, always with my hand out asking for a battery for the radio or a dozen eggs. When I left them, my final stop of the morning would be to count my ammo boxes and make certain none had been stolen by the Vietnamese.

In our battalion of the 39th Infantry, the Reconnaissance Platoon was charged with going out each morning to clear the roadblocks from the dirt tracks that connected us north and west to other districts and the rest of the country. Dubbed the "Roadrunners," these men daily made their rounds in jeeps mounting M-60 machine guns and 106mm recoilless rifles. Ambush was an ever-present threat. Aggressive action was the only suitable action when ambushed. A violent response and getting out of the kill zone were critical.

In Rach Kien the VC seldom built their earthen roadblocks completely across the road. Rounding up local farmers to do the digging at night, they would construct mounds of paddy mud three-quarters of the way across the road. A short distance away, they would duplicate the action from the opposite side of the road. A Vietnamese Lambretta could usually maneuver through the roadblock in the same manner that a skier in downhill racing negotiates the gates. It was not so easy for a larger vehicle, such as an American two-and-a-half-ton truck. The technique was designed to hinder military movement while allowing smaller Vietnamese civilian vehicles to pass.

The Roadrunners had the task of clearing away these crude

obstacles. They did this carefully, as booby traps were frequently employed. While clearing a roadblock, one of the Roadrunners found a note and returned it to the battalion intelligence officer, who had it translated by a reformed VC member of a group called "Kit Carson" or Tiger Scouts. The note was from a farmer who said he was tired of working all day to pay taxes to both the government and the VC and being dragged away at night by the VC to pile up mud roadblocks. He expressed the opinion that he was not built for a twenty-four-hour-a-day operation. Since the government was not leaving, he wished we would remove the three VC who were making his life miserable. The VC were staying at the house of Tran Van Nguyen. Naturally there was no signature, and someone in the battalion dubbed the writer "the Phantom."

Responding quickly and carefully in the event of ambush, the battalion sent a heavily armed night patrol and staked out the house only to find it occupied by a toothless old man who shit himself when suddenly beset upon by a horde of hairy American warriors.

A few days later another note was found, and this time it was brought to me for district military translation. The Phantom was a direct man who wrote that the wrong Tran Van Nguyen had been visited. He wrote the equivalent of doubting that we could find our asses with both hands, but the three VC were still at the same location. The problem was that the Vietnamese working for the battalion did not have a good knowledge of individuals in the district, as did my local soldiers. That night I accompanied Captain Ngi and a PRU scout to guide a team of Americans to the correct house. These men may have been part of the Long An Province CRIP (Combined Recon and Intelligence Platoon) force, a very select group of volunteer hunters. Whoever they were, they knew their business and made quick work of the enemy. I did not have to fire a shot. For a while there were no roadblocks. Though they were resumed later, we did not have another note from the Phantom. Either the Viet

Cong chose to harass someone else or they learned who had talked and killed him.

Two new and much-needed men joined the team. Captain Ray Byers would be the executive officer. Slender in body and with a quick and active mind, Ray was on his second tour in Vietnam, having previously served with the 101st Airborne. Sergeant Ed Surbaugh was a powerful man, solid and dependable. He was the senior noncommissioned officer and the steady-hand, experienced enlisted man leader that is an invaluable asset to any military unit.

Ray had been around Saigon more than I and had an understanding of the many supply depots in the area. I decided to send him and another team member on a scrounge trip to test the waters of generosity. Ray took our team jeep and borrowed a two-and-a-half-ton truck and driver from the battalion. The initial trip was a modified success. Ray was turned away from some places, but others had been kind, giving us bales of sandbags, barbed wire, some food, and surprisingly another radio. Most important, Ray had uncovered the possibilities that lay in these depots. He found that what these supply people needed were war trophies. They wanted something they could show to the folks at home, including enemy weapons, flags, and helmets. The supply people had made it clear that they were willing to trade, so the possibilities were there if we could come up with the product. Carbine ammunition was now on hand, and Captain Ngi and I were looking forward to action.

We had run the landlines and had telephone communication with Artillery and the Infantry, but we had only sufficient telephone wire to run one line to each. Experience in Korea had taught me that two separate lines are best, as a single line may be cut by shell fire. A radio antenna was set up at the bunker and a phone line run there. Communications must always be considered open to intercept by the enemy. Americans have a tendency to be careless with communications, and the enemy gained much by intercepting and breaking into both our telephone and radio communications.

Enemy intercept units routinely monitored our communication nets. Some Americans found English-speaking voices on the telephone asking the number of men in the bunker and the location of bunkers as hot food had been prepared and was to be delivered. A radio ruse used by the enemy was to break in on the same radio frequency when American artillery or air was being used. "Cease fire, cease fire, you are hitting friendly forces," the voice would say. We used authentication codes, and when challenged to give the correct authentication response the enemy went silent.

My Vietnamese perimeter defense had much in common with a sieve. I was concerned that we needed to be better prepared and talked at length to Dong and Ngi about improving our bunkers and firing pits. Even a good defense faced a lot of challenges from the enemy. We were in a town where civilians had to move about to do their daily work. I had no doubt that among them were informants who could accurately report our positions. The enemy was very adept at making well-planned attacks. They had a highly motivated force of sappers believed to have been drawn from a North Vietnamese parachute regiment. These men were well trained in the use of explosives. They wore very little clothing when attacking, as clothing snags and creates noise. The sappers specialized in blowing holes in the wire or knocking out key bunkers to allow the attacking force to close with the defenders. I went to sleep each night knowing that if they attacked, they could go through our perimeter in the manner Gen. George Patton described as "like shit through a goose."

I had one consolation that many districts did not—an American infantry battalion at my back. While that helped somewhat, it also meant that my people would be overrun or caught in a crossfire. You can die as quickly from friendly fire as from the enemy's. Much needed to be done to help the people. The engineers had specific missions, but they could only begin to fulfill the district's needs. During the dry season, drinking water was always in short supply. Water had to be trucked into the village or carried long distances. I had to find the Americans who had the knowledge and equipment to dig a well through saltwater to the freshwater beneath. We needed to convince farmers to plant the new miracle rice. We could establish fishponds and put a system into the production of bananas. Even if we could get the material to do all of this, we needed to be teachers. Many Vietnamese in Rach Kien lived in poorer housing than American farm animals. Electricity was power to accomplish, yet we lived in a world of oil lamps. To improve the quality of life for the Vietnamese, we needed to supply and teach. It is futile to tell a man "Here is the material—do it yourself " if he does not know how to use the material.

During one of our daily meetings we decided to throw a Christmas party for the children of the district. All of us wrote to our friends and relatives in the United States, asking them to send bags of individually wrapped candy that we could pass out to these fun-loving children.

I knew the Viet Cong had a parallel structure of government to ours, and I spent much time trying to develop ways to identify these people and kill them. Assassination and ambush were prime weapons in their arsenal. I meant to do unto them what they sought to do unto us. They were great diggers, and used techniques in Rach Kien where they could enter a tunnel underwater and come up into breathing, sleeping, or fighting positions. They frequently concealed sharpened bamboo stakes, called "punji," beside the trails. When Americans came into the area, the enemy would open fire on the trail and Americans diving for cover would be impaled. This often resulted in retaliation on the area, including the destruction of any houses from which the enemy would fire. That, in turn, angered the local people, which is exactly what the Communists wanted.

A Communist sniper tried to harass the engineers while they were at work. The Regional Force Platoon provided close-in security, but the random shot could not be protected against. Whoever was doing this was obviously not a skilled enemy marksman, but someone seeking to disturb and distract. I took the team out on a hunt for the sniper, but whoever it was never hit anyone and vanished after a few shots.

Hunting men in the broiling heat was stripping pounds from my body. My weight would drop thirty pounds in the first six months in Vietnam.

Several kilometers from Rach Kien town was a mud fort that was the base of operations for an Army of the Republic of Vietnam (ARVN) infantry battalion of the 47th Regiment of their 25th Infantry Division. The fort spoke volumes about this war. These troops protected themselves. Out in the hamlets the people were left exposed to the control of the enemy. The only time the government controlled the outlying areas was when forces passed through on operational sweeps. The enemy would vanish, only to reemerge when our side was gone. The South Vietnamese government felt it did not have the manpower to put troops everywhere.

It seemed to me that rather than have a battalion stationed together in a mud fort, it would have served a better purpose to have a Vietnamese ARVN platoon in each hamlet with a rapid reaction force of Americans. Both Vietnamese and Americans used a policy of moving from base camps to search for enemy units and destroy them. We could not be everywhere at the same time, but protecting the towns and cities and searching for enemy units was not enough. The hamlets and the countryside were visited but not protected. The enemy vanished at our coming and reappeared upon our departure. Informers were ruthlessly dealt with, so a wall of silence and lies met our questions. I do not know why so much territory was left without government troops on the ground. It may have been the inability of the Vietnamese to logistically support scattered elements or a fear that they could not be reinforced in time. The enemy could mass forces quickly and was adept at picking off isolated units.

I did not have enough warriors to fight big battles or control much terrain. I very much wanted to hunt down and kill the local infrastructure that supported units of the North Vietnamese Army. Without the support of the infrastructure, units from North Vietnam would be without guides and logistical support. Sometimes I observed bunkers from the air, yet sources of information suddenly dried up as though they were smothered. I was now convinced that enemy regular force units were in Rach Kien, and they could exist only with the support of the Communist infrastructure.

A dirt track some thirty-five hundred meters long extended between Rach Kien town and the fortified community of Me Ly in the southern part of the district, the location of 627 Regional Force Company. Accompanied by No. 1 interpreter Voung, some team members, and a Vietnamese escort, I made an unannounced visit. What I saw was encouraging. The 627 was under the command of an experienced captain. His company occupied a star-shaped mud fort and he had done all that could be expected with the limited material available. This was a religious community of the Buddhist sect called Hoa Hao. I was told that the North Vietnamese had executed the religious leader of the Hoa Hao. True or not, these people hated the Communists with great passion. This company was more prepared to fight than was 555.

After returning to Rach Kien, I met with Major Dong and Captain Ngi. I told them of my visit to 627 and my thoughts that this unit was far advanced of 555 in capability. Ngi assured me that a training program was having results. We now started to send out small night ambush patrols from the Regional Forces, which I hoped would soon make contact. We had so much to do that the days seemed like minutes. From conversations with other advisors, I learned that some felt it was best not to initiate new efforts. One man told me to do only what was required and get home healthy. I could not accept his advice. I might be proved wrong, but I would not be proved lazy.

At night, time had to be set aside for reports. The hamlet evaluation survey (HES) was the most significant Vietnamese district advisor report of many that was required to be forwarded to higher headquarters. It was a hamlet-by-hamlet evaluation of progress requiring detailed information that, in my view, would have been difficult to get in the United States, let alone Vietnam. Written reports are a vital part of control, but they are too often weighty with extraneous detail and become a burden rather than an asset. In Vietnam, some reports generated were essentially tools for the generals to tell the politicians so that they could tell the American people that we were making great progress. I had no confidence in HES because the true situation in most hamlets was unknown. People would naturally tell us what we wanted to hear when we passed through. They spoke whatever the man who had the gun wanted them to say. I sought to counteract by giving lower ratings of security. I was distrustful of HES. I was not surprised when more experienced district advisors said they were creative.

16

Life in Rach Kien

I was doing paperwork when a frantic rapping on the trailer door told me there was trouble. A team member told me that Captain Ngi had received a radio message from an ambush team they had sent out. En route to their position, they had been ambushed by the Viet Cong and several men were wounded. Captain Ngi was taking out a reaction force. I gave instructions as to who would go with me, and I told Captain Byers to let the Infantry and Artillery know we were moving south and to request the artillery to put a howitzer tube pointing south and a radio on our frequency.

I joined Ngi and asked if he had anyone on the ambush team who could adjust artillery. Ngi said he did not, and that contact had been broken and our ambush force was laying low waiting for help to come. My team members joined me and we stood in the darkness of the street, letting our eyes adjust themselves to the night. Men of the 555 Regional Force Company were hurriedly coming out of their houses. Team members asked questions, which I could barely hear, and I suddenly realized that, although we were standing in front of the advisor house, we were talking in whispers. When I pointed out how ludicrous this was, we had a good laugh on ourselves.

I had learned the fighting trade in the 8th Airborne Rangers. The philosophy of the tactics and of the will to win of the American Ranger was the core of my being. Rangers knew how to move at night. Slings on weapons were taped down, dog tags taped to prevent their clinking together, and canteens filled to preclude a sloshing noise. Everything possible was

212

done to ensure that the movement could be done with stealth. I required my team to take these precautionary steps, but as we began moving in the darkness, the sound of the Vietnamese troops' weapons, ammunition, and other equipment rattling and clanking together sounded like a junkyard sliding down-hill.

What I had experienced with the PRU was far different than with this Regional Force unit. I told Ngi that we should stop and correct the men, but he replied that there was not sufficient time. Barbed-wire obstacles had to be pulled aside as we left the town, and the Regional Force soldiers talked loudly and excitedly. When I asked Ngi what they were talking about, he replied that they were telling each other, "Watch the wire." Although I was angered by the noise, I could not suppress a smile in the darkness. Wire traps and trips men. Be it fence, barbed, or communication wire, it is an enemy of silent movement at night. What "Peace be with you" is to the clergy, or "I was in the neighborhood" is to the salesman, "Watch the wire" is to the infantryman. Dong and Ngi employed trip wires on part of our perimeter. I asked Dong to use a Ranger trick of hanging shorter pieces of heavy cord from the main wire. Fishhooks would be attached to the cord. Freeing oneself from fishhooks is extremely difficult, and the effectiveness of the trip wire as an early warning device would be increased. Dong liked the idea but believed that village children would steal the fishhooks.

We moved swiftly and noisily, and as we crossed the bridge, a pale moon slid from behind a cloud and bathed us in ghostly light. I could see the seldom-used dirt road stretching away, somewhat elevated and exposed. I expected that we would leave the road and travel cross-country. It is impossible for an enemy to cover all cross-country routes, so he will concentrate on places most likely to be used by the unwary. Roads are killing zones. One of the most dangerous of military operations is to go to the relief of an ambushed force. The route of relieving forces is often where additional and perhaps larger enemy forces are lying in wait for the unwary hurrying to succor their comrades.

To my surprise and disgust, we continued on the road. Ngi told me he had to reach his men. My hope was that the enemy would mistake us for a herd of water buffalo. All of us dived for cover at a burst of gunfire, but it soon ended and was followed by a babble of Vietnamese. Voung, my interpreter, told me we had found our ambush party. Several Vietnamese turned on flashlights and clustered around the located men, chattering in excitement. Voung related that our people had been establishing their ambush when they ran into a Viet Cong force, which they believed was establishing its own ambush. Our men said they killed many of the enemy. I felt if that statement was true, the VC must have laughed themselves to death.

The moon disappeared and we headed for home in darkness. The Vietnamese talked rapidly and loudly among themselves in the manner of a group of friends out for a Sunday stroll in the park. It was not long before one of them turned on a transistor radio. I began to understand how hard this job was going to be.

A few minutes before midnight, the first mortar round struck. The round entered through the canvas top of a general purpose medium tent of the engineer task force, killing and maiming men within. "Incoming! Incoming!" yelled my team member on radio watch, who followed our procedures to notify Province that we were under attack. He then disconnected, took the radio, his weapon, and a spare battery, and ran for the bunker. We advisors had rehearsed our moves and it went well. I had asked them to be prepared to move quickly, and as a personal measure I did not go to sleep until my clothing and equipment were situated for rapid response. While explosions continued, we arrived in the security of the bunker. It was not long before a number of engineers crowded in with us. They were shaken, knowing that a number of their unprotected men had been hit. We heard another explosion as a round hit beside the house, where we kept our two vehicles.

From the bunker, we tried to establish communication with the district Vietnamese, Province, the infantry battalion, and the Artillery. We reached Province and the Artillery but not the Infantry or district Vietnamese. My belief was that as far as the Infantry was concerned, we advisors were often afterthoughts and our calls would frequently go unanswered. I did not know what caused the lack of communication with the Vietnamese, but felt it was a language problem. We fired flares over the paddies to the west to see if a ground attack was coming in. Nothing was moving, so it was likely they intended only to hammer us with mortar fire. Another engineer squeezed into the overcrowded bunker, yelling that their medic was hit and they needed help. Men standing outside were pressing to get into the small enclosure of the advisor bunker.

I took the team medic and ran across the street to the Vietnamese headquarters as another explosion hit the engineer compound. Unlike the tents of the engineers, the roof and sides of this building offered some protection from shrapnel. More of the engineers had taken shelter here, and the medic began to treat the wounded who had been brought in. The interior of the building was dimly lit by a lantern and candles. Many of the engineers were in their underwear and some had their weapons with them. I was told by Ngi that the RF outposts were reporting no sign of ground attack. In his long experience the VC would fire a few rounds, then pack up and go before counterfire could be directed against them. I had experience with mortars and understood the technique. We had a saying that a good gunner could put ten mortar rounds in the air before the first one hit and be home having coffee before the reaction came. On this occasion the attack had been unrelenting—nearly fifty rounds struck home. It was the first serious attack on Rach Kien District. Confident that we were not aware of their location of fire, they were no doubt enjoying the pasting they were giving us. Nothing was hitting in the infantry, artillery, or town area. They knew the target they had in the tents of the engineers and hit them hard. As the advisors and Vietnamese military headquarters were close by, we took a considerable number of rounds as well, but we were prepared.

The team medic came to tell me that he had a patient in serious condition. The engineer's lower abdomen had been ripped by shrapnel. I stepped closer to the medic's lantern and bent over the man. He was young and husky with a thick mat of black body hair. His T-shirt was pulled up and the remainder of his body was nude. Two engineers were holding him down as he struggled to see what had happened to his body.

The team medic took me aside and related that the man needed prompt attention. He said that recently announced helicopter medical evacuation procedures were that evacuation would be not accomplished while under fire. The enemy had no mercy on medical personnel and would not hold their fire for a medical evacuation. I was not aware of that aspect of evacuation policy and felt a sense of guilt that I had not familiarized myself with procedures. I had no confidence in our Vietnamese perimeter, and even if I could bring in a dustoff (medical evacuation helicopter), I knew they would need a secure place to land. The man began to moan and cry out. I turned back to him. "Oh, please, please," he moaned, "somebody help me." I knelt beside him and motioned them to hold the lantern close. His stomach had been ripped and his intestines bulged. I had no medical knowledge beyond rudimentary first aid. "Please help me," the man pleaded with me. "I don't want to die."

I asked for a report from the engineer commander. He related that men were dead, and he had a number of wounded. The man with the stomach wound was the most seriously wounded. Another explosion told me that the enemy was not finished firing. I felt that for the man to have a chance, he must be moved to the infantry battalion surgeon. After telling the medic to do what he could to make the man ready for movement, I ran across the street to the bunker in an attempt to call for help.

I made a radio call to Province to plead for a dustoff at the infantry battalion helipad. They did not talk procedures, but said they would try. I called the infantry battalion on their primary frequency and then tried the alternate. In both cases I had no response. I surmised that they had made a routine change of frequencies and, as advisors were far down on their list of concerns, someone had neglected to tell us. The phone did not work; the line was cut by a mortar round or some Vietnamese had chosen the worst possible time to steal the wire. I finally made radio contact with the artillery and requested them to relay to the infantry that I would be bringing a seriously wounded man into their perimeter. While I was making this call, I noticed that the explosions had stopped. I had no way of knowing if they would begin to mortar us again—we needed to work fast.

One of the many things that make me proud to be an American is the effort we put forth to save a fellow soldier. When they understood my request, there was no shortage of volunteers. One team member brought the team jeep to the front of the Vietnamese military headquarters. Engineers and the medic put the wounded man on a litter, placing it on the back of the jeep. They stood by the side of the litter, steadying it. We were in the blackness of night, about to attempt to enter the US perimeter at a time when fingers would lie heavy on the triggers of weapons. As a Ranger in Korea, my unit had frequently made night reentry into friendly lines. It is a hazardous time. I instructed the driver to start the engine and turn on his lights. I walked in front of the jeep in order to be in the beam of light and clearly visible to the infantry on their perimeter. Their barbed-wire gate was closed, but we moved forward as I called to them. While they were opening the gate, the medic told me the man was dead. I told the driver to turn our vehicle around. I returned to the radio and canceled the request for the medevac from Province.

As suddenly as it began, the attack ended. It was the first of forty-seven mortar and rocket attacks on Rach Kien town that I would experience during my time there. Feeling the awful emptiness of frustration, I returned to my trailer. Sitting on the bunk, I tried to think of the mistakes I had made and how I could correct them. I had not done a good job on communications readiness, nor did I have a thorough knowledge of medical evacuation procedures. There was no consolation in saying that a medevac would not have arrived in time. It is a terrible experience to have a man dying before your eyes, calling on you to save his life, and being unable to do so. I was glad we had built our bunker; it may well have saved my life and that of my team. But our bunker was separate from the Vietnamese military, the people we were supposed to be working with.

I did not have the authority to order the Vietnamese military out of their own area, but I crossed the street and asked Captain Ngi to not allow any civilians into the military complex until the damage had been repaired. He had already given these instructions. It was important to do everything possible to deny the enemy information on the accuracy of their attack. At morning light we looked about at the damage with a masochistic curiosity. The enemy fire had been accurate, with the engineer area hardest hit. Fortunately, in the advisor area we had not taken any roof hits, but the torn sandbags were proof that our preparations had paid off. We set about making repairs. The jeep had a shattered windshield and shrapnel holes in the hood but was functioning well. The recommendation was made to me that we not repair the jeep. A battle-scarred vehicle would draw attention at a supply depot and reinforce our authenticity as good sources for war trophies.

It did not take long in Vietnam to learn that while Napoleon had said, "God is on the side of the big battalions," advisors were on their own. As I suspected, the infantry had made a routine change of radio frequency and someone had not deemed it important for us to be informed. The phone wire had been disconnected. Don Schroder corrected this attitude with alacrity. I decided to take no chances and made it a part of our team duties to have daily communication checks by radio and landline. As usual, the battalion was heading out on an operation and the air was filled with helicopters. Lying on a battalion field table was a flyer about a

USO show that would be coming to the battalion. It included the photo of a blonde who had a chest that was alpine. Since there was little chance that any advisors would get near her, I wondered if it would be possible to get a USO show specifically for the advisors. Would it be possible to get such a round-eyed beauty in the advisor house, perhaps in an up-close and intimate show? I decided to give it a try.

None of us knew the source of the enemy fire. It could have come from anywhere in a 360-degree circle. But there was a technique I wanted to try. When a mortar round lands, it comes in on an angle, digs into the earth, and, when exploding, has a tendency to kick the dirt from the hole and send earth and most of its shrapnel forward and to the sides. It often leaves the mark of its entry on the back side of the hole, sometimes in the form of a small trench approximately one-quarter-inch deep. Using my compass, I shot an azimuth on this trench, looking from the front side over the rear of the hole. I repeated this with every mortar shell hole I could find; this gave me the direction the enemy had fired from. It was from the west, to the rear of the advisor house.

Judging from the size of the holes, the weapons were likely Russian or Chinese 82mm mortars. The maximum range of the weapon was 3,000 meters and it had a listed rate of fire of 25 rounds per minute. I could see across the open paddy for some 2,000 meters. It was unlikely they would expose their gunners in that space, and given their superb accuracy, they were not firing at maximum range. They were firing on the line I had established and from a position 2,000 to 2,800 meters to the west. Men have a tendency to stay with what works. I felt that since they had not been hurt, the enemy would continue to use the location from which they had zeroed in on us. But 800 meters is still a significantly large area. I had to develop a plan that would cover that distance with American fire. I passed my findings on to the infantry battalion and artillery battery.

The dead and wounded engineers had been evacuated. Others went back to work on the school, leaving a squad to clean up the area and remove the bloody clothing and bedding. Their commander was faced with his initial experience at cataloging the personal effects of the dead and preparing letters of condolence to the families. The engineers also sent a message to their battalion commander near Saigon; he was en route to Rach Kien with materials to build bunkers.

I made my morning rounds, putting on a happy face for the villagers and stopping by the Vietnamese military headquarters, where the two young lovers were gazing at each other with soulful eyes. Captain Ngi and I drank tea and discussed the attack. I told him of my idea to place a bunker on top of his headquarters building. I felt we needed better observation and fields of fire. Ngi agreed that the idea had merit but told me he must remain on the ground floor in order to be promptly available to Major Dong. I did not see that as a problem. We were close enough in the event of trouble, yet the possibility of losing all the leadership to one mortar round would be forestalled.

I asked Ngi if he had any Viet Cong or North Vietnamese flags or weapons available. He was taken aback at the question, wondering if I was questioning his loyalty. I explained that we had the opportunity to trade these items for supplies that would be of great help to the district. I suggested that a seamstress be found who could make enemy flags. Believing that I was joking, he began to laugh. I told him about our critical need for water, electricity, and housing, for adequate weapons and ammunition, and the belief that we could get material in exchange for war trophies. When he realized that I was in earnest, he sobered and said he would talk to Major Dong.

I had arranged with Province to take a helicopter reconnaissance over the district that afternoon and invited Ngi to accompany me. I planned to scout the entire district, but without revealing my intent to observe the line of fire that I believed the enemy had used. I watched training of 555 Regional Force Company. They were doing better, but their commander, Antoine, was worthless. Ngi and I started to plan several missions to outlying hamlets.

As I returned to the advisor house, I noticed that foot, motorbike, and the three-wheeled Lambretta traffic had resumed. Little damage from the attack was visible. A hole in a roof had been covered with canvas. My jeep was covered with some items of clothing as though drying in the sun. The townspeople knew the police would be watching to see if anyone was showing interest in the damage. People did not stop and talk with each other but hurried along the street, anxious not to call attention to themselves.

With the exception of a sergeant on radio watch, the team was asleep. The thin metal roof of my trailer was an inviting target, but I was too exhausted to care. I decided to get some rest, but had barely turned in when the trailer began to shake. I dressed and went outside to see the street crowded with vehicles and GIs. A bulldozer had just been unloaded outside my trailer and was clanking its way along the street. The column of trucks and heavy equipment transporters stretched around the corner in the infantry area and out of sight. Men were using forklifts to unload stacks of lumber and construction materials. The raucous sound of chain saws filled the air. I had never seen an engineer battalion of the American army at work, and the sight was astounding. One small group stood apart like an island in the surf. They wore steel helmets and flak jackets, and all carried .45-caliber pistols in regulation holsters. The advisors did not possess flak jackets, and the first use of steel helmets was during the mortar attack. The black leaf painted on a steel helmet and the air of authority told me that this was the engineer battalion commander and his staff. Feeling underdressed in soft cap and fatigues, I joined the group and was introduced by the engineer detachment commander.

The battalion commander's stern air of authority was replaced by a genuine look of appreciation. "We know you told our man to give our people protection," he said. "We did not listen to you and men are dead because of it. I need twenty-four hours of uninterrupted work. Any suggestions?" I suggested that he disperse his transport vehicles, putting some in the infantry and artillery areas with guards. I would arrange for artillery harassing and interdictory fire about the district for the night and would get the Vietnamese to be as active as possible in providing laborers and sending out patrols.

Thanking me, the engineer said, "Anything you want, Major. If it's within my power, you will have it." I promptly responded with my desire to have the advisor house and trailer fortified against mortar attacks and that I would appreciate larger water tanks and the plumbing hooked up in the trailer. Further, I would like to have sufficient generator capacity to keep electricity going in the advisor house and trailer and the Vietnamese military headquarters, and that I would prepare a list of other matériel that would help us do our job. I don't think this officer expected such a rush of requests, but his word was his bond. Scarcely able to contain my joy, I watched the amazing ability of American engineers with awe.

I talked with Captain Ngi and walked up to the artillery and infantry areas to keep my promises. The 39th Infantry had already left for work, but they had some mortars that could put out a few rounds during the night, and the artillery agreed to do the same. Harassing and interdictory fires are means of disrupting enemy plans. We may not know where the enemy is, but random artillery rounds fired during the night can help in keeping his head down. Both American units had looked at the engineer train with hungry eyes. I was in the position of a man who has a beautiful girlfriend. You want your friends to know about her, but not to know too much.

When I returned to the engineer area, structures were already taking shape. A stakeout team would do its work, then a tractor-mounted posthole digger bored holes for the six-by-six supporting timbers. The soil was quickly filled around the timbers and mechanically tamped. The sidewalls and tops were of two-by-eight boards. Doorways and firing slits had been allowed for. Next came crews with sandbags and the pierced steel planking (PSP) used for aircraft runways. The sides of the structures were packed three sandbags wide. On top of the two-inch planking were two layers of sandbags, a layer of PSP, and two more layers of sandbags. The engineers were so efficient that one of my sergeants said, "Damn it, those Americans are really good!" Once again we had to remind ourselves that we were Americans—having the engineers close by helped.

I was not surprised that the night was quiet. The North Vietnamese, including those who were cadre for the Viet Cong, were seldom given to making impromptu attacks. They knew well that when they showed themselves they would be hammered by American power. Enemy strength lay in meticulous planning and reconnaissance, sudden strikes, and quick withdrawals to the safe areas that the United States government allowed them. Mao Tse-tung had written that he learned the art of guerrilla war from his mother. She never attacked her husband directly, as he had too much strength. When she wanted her way, she came at him from the flank, nibbling at him until he gave way. The enemy knew and used this strategy well, but it would not have worked without the cooperation of the American political leadership. The American military could have crushed North Vietnam in rapid time, but it was not North Vietnam that worried American politicians—it was China and the Soviet Union. Just as in Korea, American politicians put us into a war. Then they were afraid it would expand. As a result the enemy was given the advantage.

We were hit with another mortar attack, this time from both sides. The infantry battalion was firing its 81mm mortars over our heads in response to the enemy and began dropping short rounds. I could not tell the explosion of a Chinese or Russian mortar from that of an American, but this time a dud round protruding from the earth had US markings, and the direction of impact told its source. It turned out that the mortar men had a bad lot of ammunition. Most of it had exploded around us, but we were under cover. We walked softly until the battalion sent an explosive ordnance demolition team to destroy the dud.

I was advised by Province staff that visits from senior

officers and congressional groups were expected soon and I should be prepared to brief. By the time anyone is a field grade officer in the United States Army, personal briefing techniques have been developed. I had the engineers make a briefing cabinet of plywood with sliding panels. Each panel had a map or chart tacked to it that gave information on the team and our district. I practiced a few times and, when unannounced visitors arrived, seated them on folding chairs in front of the cabinet and showed them chart after chart, discussing each aspect of Rach Kien District. The briefings went well, but some American civilian observers had a tendency to hang on, asking questions such as, "Have you visited every family in your district?" "Why don't you just build a high school?" "Why don't you do something to get a doctor for these people?" They may have been trying, but they just didn't understand Vietnam.

17

Doctor Zhivago

Enemy forces were building up in Long An Province. The province intelligence officer informed district senior advisors that more than a thousand men of the enemy main force from the 2d Independent Battalion, the K-3 and Phu Loi Battalions, and the 265th and 506th Battalions had now joined the local guerrillas and district companies. He continued to say that no units of the North Vietnamese Army were in Rach Kien.

The enemy became bolder, and in Rach Kien we were frequently hit with mortar and rocket fire. The violence of high explosive, the awe-inspiring power of it, shook the soul; we respected it, but we were now prepared. During an attack, initial shock was followed by a scurry of activity as men dove for their bunkers. I had some of the advisors remain in the house to make a prompt report of the attack and keep an eye out on the flat paddy land to the west. The rest of us ran across the street to join the Vietnamese military command post. It was a brief run in the open but seemed an eternity.

Attacks came by day and night. In the late hours of darkness, one attack began with a mortar round landing on the roof of my trailer. Had it not been for the protective cover constructed by the engineers, I would likely have died. The concussion shook me like a rag doll but, thanks to the engineers, the heavy beams, pierced steel planking, and sandbags took the shock.

On one attack, a mortar round exploded next to the house. Shrapnel tore holes in my briefing cabinet. When I would pull out a map or chart, the jagged tears were better than a thousand words. Sooner or later during a congressional or straphanger visit, someone would ask, "How did those holes get in the charts?" I had several large and wicked-looking pieces of shrapnel close to hand and would pass them around, describing them as the result of a recent mortar attack. Without exception the group would find a sudden need to move to the next place.

One of my team was caught in the open and wounded. He was evacuated by helicopter; I knew he would not be returning. He had been a new man and was not well known by the team members. We knew he was married, and we had his home address in the United States. As we inventoried his belongings for shipment home, we found a collection of a dozen or so photos of a very attractive woman in the nude. She was posed in a variety of sexual positions. My men gathered around and studied the photographs at some length. I assumed that the pictures were of his wife and should be sent home. I was quickly cautioned that if the photographs were not of this man's wife, I would be destroying the marriage of a man who shed blood for his country. Knowing what my men were about, I then proposed that the pictures be destroyed. This caused great alarm. There was always a chance that he might recover from his wounds and come back to us. He would then want his pictures. This comradely affection touched my heart, so I told them I would keep the photos in a safe place by my bunk. They did not think that was worthy of an officer. Finally I relented and entrusted the photos to their care.

Captain Ngi came to visit and give me a Mauser Karabiner 98K bolt-action rifle. The rifle had a date of 1942 and the Nazi swastika thereon. I would see a number of these in the months to come. What stories they could have told! Probably the weapons had been carried by German soldiers on the Eastern Front during World War II. When they were killed or captured by the Russians, their weapons had been part of a shipment sent to the Communists in China or North Vietnam. Major Dong had approved the enemy flag project, and Ngi showed me some VC flags that were new and clean. I asked Ngi to put a few bullet holes in them, muddy them up a bit, and sprinkle some chicken blood on them. He left with a smile on his face and was soon back with some authentic-looking war trophies. Captain Byers set out to borrow a two-and-a-half-ton truck and began making plans for a scrounging trip to the supply dumps near Saigon.

One Viet Cong (VC) flag sufficed to get us three "sundry packs." These were cardboard boxes about two feet square that contained cigarettes, candy, writing paper, canned fruit, toilet paper, and a host of other items that made life better. The candy was preserved. We continued to save all the candy we collected for a big party for the children. They were like kids anywhere, so fun-loving and devoted to play. It was enjoyable to hear them recite their lessons or sing in unison as they were led by young female teachers dressed in colorful *ao dais*.

When we had sufficient candy for the party, I felt like Santa Claus. It was pure pleasure to do something nice for the children. We advisors stood before the boxes and bags of candy on tables, while several hundred little people waited in lines to come forth and receive their treat. At first everything proceeded smoothly and there were smiles everywhere. But they were children and they were impatient. They began to break ranks and surround us, clutching at us for their treat.

What started as a rivulet became a raging tide of youth. They stormed and overwhelmed us until we finally had no choice but to break free and let them struggle for the candy. The resultant scene was ugly to the extreme. What had begun with the best intentions was a disaster that pleased no one. I was deeply ashamed when Major Dong and Captain Ngi told me in soft but firm tones that they did not appreciate Americans making beggars out of Vietnamese children. I would never again give a Vietnamese or foreign child candy, gum, or money unless a service was performed.

With the help of the engineers we now had the material to begin helping the Vietnamese improve their quality of life.

We secured more ammunition boxes from the artillery and some sand and lime from the engineers. Our first project was to build housing that would end the overcrowded and pitiful living conditions of the 555 Regional Force Company and Provincial Reconnaissance Units. Sitting around our kitchen table, we designed a prefabricated house from the slats of an ammunition box built over a concrete floor and roofed with our remaining tin.

After consulting with Dong and Ngi about need and design, we placed the project in the capable hands of Lt. Mike Primont, with the advisors providing the material and initial supervision. I felt it was important that the Vietnamese be involved from the beginning, with the Vietnamese providing the labor and running the entire operation as soon as possible. We used the cement from Province with lime and sand from the engineers to make a concrete pad for the floor. The two-by-fours used for framing were part of my wish list from the engineer battalion commander. The 105-howitzer ammunition boxes came from the artillery and contained within them the siding, nails, hinges, and plastic that completed the sidewalls, doors, and shutters. The slanted tin roofing topped a single-story dwelling that was approximately ten by ten feet. It was a single room with board walls and plastic-covered gaps between them. There was no glass in the windows and the floor was concrete. For the first time these people had some space and a place to call their own. They had neighbors on the other side of the board wall, but it was more privacy than they were accustomed to. The project was a great success with the Vietnamese.

Teaching our Vietnamese the concept of mass production began with the old system of speaking pidgin English slowly and very loud, "TAKEE BOARD, NAILEE-NAILEE, SAME SAME." This, accompanied by a hairy American waving a claw hammer in the air, left the Vietnamese looking concerned. We soon switched to Ho Voung, who explained the process, and the Vietnamese went to work.

We standardized the walls and framing so that different

crews could specialize and we could have an assembly line operation. The housing area was at the southern end of town, and we called it "Primont Village" in honor of Mike.

In conversation with Ngi and the battalion intelligence officer, I learned that the enemy had both a quota and an incentive system to kill us. Each hamlet and each unit had a quota. For example, each hamlet was expected to kill one or two of the local government. Each VC company was charged with killing a platoon of Americans or two platoons of South Vietnamese. They were told that if they achieved this quota, they would be awarded the designation of "good" company.

Sanitation was improving in the marketplace. Part of my wish list to the engineer battalion commander had been for window screening. Using this scrap lumber from engineer projects and hinges from ammunition boxes, we framed out screened display cases for the meat. Now vendors could provide better protection from the swarms of flies. But I had difficulty convincing them to do so. They were accustomed to flies crawling across the meat and did not believe that change was necessary. In the 1500s, Niccolo Machiavelli, in his classic work *The Prince*, wrote that "Nothing is more difficult to accomplish than to change an existing structure." Western sanitation was beyond the knowledge of these people, and many thought it unnecessary. At length, I pressured Major Dong into issuing a decree that the sanitary procedures would be observed.

I had to make my own adjustments. The problem of who would burn the outhouse waste had gone beyond discontent. The enlisted men and officers were angry at one another because of it. While I sympathized with the men, I would not order an officer to burn shit. I cannot say that I studied this problem from every angle. I took a topside view of it, knowing that shit by nature and tradition flows downward. A prime item on my wish list to the engineer battalion commander was that he instruct his people to install plastic soil pipe from the trailer toilet to the pond at its rear. Now the officers no longer used the same latrine as the enlisted men.

The men were burning only their own waste and their bitching had lost steam.

I was very proud of my solution until the day I walked by the pond and saw Ba washing our clothes while stools could be plainly seen in the water. I had noticed that my fatigues had an unusual aroma, but the sun was so hot that after any activity the jacket was usually black with sweat and stunk of perspiration. I told Voung to pass along to Ba that it would be better if the clothes were washed in the flowing river. That was a long carry for Ba, and I suspect that she did most of the washing when I was out on an operation so she could do as she pleased.

I was told by team members when I entered the district that places existed which were too dangerous for us to take district troops. Nicknames were often given to especially dangerous areas. I recall "the Testicles" and "the Rat's Nest." Wars are not won by giving the enemy safe haven. I intended to accustom our local forces to the belief that this was their land, and that they needed to think that they could go anywhere within it and make that belief stick. We were running operations now. Three to four times a week, 555 Regional Force Company, Popular Force units, the PRUs, and advisors would go out on search missions. On occasion the 627 Regional Force Company would sweep toward us or establish an ambush, where we would seek to drive into the VC in a hammer-and-anvil tactic. The missions were both daylight and night. The training and experience I had as an American Ranger stood me in good stead. Little by little we improved noise discipline, and our shooting was better in 555 Regional Force Company and the Popular Force platoons. The housing efforts had helped morale.

Ngi and I were trying to hunt down a squad of local guerrillas who served as bodyguards for the Communist infrastructure. They also helped collect taxes for the VC, did propaganda, recruited, and assumed terror and assassination missions. With some intelligence that they were going from hamlet to hamlet in the southern part of the district, we decided to attempt to ambush them. Taking a select group of

PRUs and members of 555 Regional Force Company, about forty men in all, we moved out of Rach Kien at about 0130 hours, avoiding the road and traveling quietly cross-country. The training was paying off. Our men were better prepared and I felt they had learned patrol discipline.

A PRU scout led the way. He, like many of the men on the mission, was from the area and skillfully led us through the blackness in what would have been a tedious trek for Americans unfamiliar with the area. After a time we halted, and Ngi and I were signaled forward. As the moon slid from behind thick clouds, I could see the outline of a hut to our front and beyond that a trail. I was aware that trail ran across the southern portion of the district. Ngi whispered briefly to several men, and they went forward into the hut. As no sound came from within, I went forward, expecting to find it empty. It was not. A woman with a small child was within. They were both frightened but remained quiet. Ngi whispered questions to the woman and returned to me with an air of satisfaction. Though the guerrillas did not pass on their rounds every night, if they did come they would likely move just before dawn, and at that time they usually came from the west. Their eastward movements were done on random days and usually just after dark. They did not have a set routine, but there was a sufficient pattern to give us hope.

We took the chance and arranged our men in an L-shaped ambush. Those on the long axis had concealment and an open field of fire across rice paddies. Those on the short axis were concealed and given firm direction on fire discipline. They would fire directly down the trail, while those off to the side on the long axis would hit the enemy from the flank. We sent a few men down the trail to take care of the point man or men we intended to let pass. Everyone was cautioned to allow these people to pass and wait for the larger group and Ngi's shot before firing. I was keenly aware that our ambush was old-fashioned. (The Americans had claymores, command-detonated mines that could send 750 steel ball bearings across a 60-degree arc low to the ground. A marvelous weapon for an ambush, they were not in our

Vietnamese supply system and we had no luck trying to get them by trade.)

Ngi and I waited in the hut with several PRU. The woman sat quietly in a far corner with her child. The PRU poked their rifle barrels through the thatch wall and made openings through which we could cover the trail. We waited for hours, anxiously watching the ribbon of trail. Sometimes my head would nod and I would suddenly jerk awake. I heard Ngi briefly snoring. The PRU were taking turns on watch. The woman and child now slept. Finally I could see the coming of light and with it came the taste of disappointment. Objects could now be distinguished, and I felt that though full light had not come, the enemy would likely not pass before us.

Suddenly a slight sound came from one of the PRU. Ngi and I peered through the slits in the wall and saw an armed man cautiously approaching us. A thrill of exhilaration went through me. This was the scout, the point man. If we permitted him to pass, the men down the trail would take care of him. The main body of the guerrillas would be walking into our fire.

The VC point man had walked by the hut when there was a burst of gunfire. Barely able to contain our fury, Ngi and I ran from the hut. Fire now came toward us from down the trail and the men in our ambush were firing in that direction—it was not long in duration. It was soon obvious that the enemy had made their escape.

Both Ngi and I knew we had botched the ambush. Fire discipline had not been maintained. We had one dead VC to show for the night's work. I knew that someone had fired early, but not why they did it. Ngi was angry. He was difficult to understand, but I gathered that one of the 555 men had a genuine case of hatred for the man who had come down the trail. When he recognized him, his only thought was to kill.

The government had an amnesty program for those who left the VC and rallied to the government cause. This program was called *chieu hoi,* and a man who rallied was known as a *hoi chan*. Many came over to the government cause for good, and some of these were effective fighters. Some used the program as a Viet Cong form of rest and relaxation (R&R), going back to the enemy when they were well fed and rested. The man we killed was one of these, so he was especially despised. The troops slung his body on a carrying pole and brought him back to Rach Kien town. This was the first kill by 555 Regional Force Company, and they were very proud. They propped his body on display in the marketplace and stuck cigarettes up his nostrils.

I was presented with the AK-47 rifle of our late and unlamented VC, and I drove up to Saigon with Ray Byers to watch him work. Soldiers knew that they could not take an automatic rifle home. They wanted rifles or carbines. We had to find easier prey. Many highly paid civilians were working for the construction organization known as Pacific Architects & Engineers. Ray took me to a hotel patio restaurant, where we had a pleasant lunch, with the AK-47 propped against the table. We could see the weapon being admired by a civilian at a nearby table. As we lingered over coffee, he summoned up the nerve to approach us. Ray was eloquent in his description of the mythical action in which the weapon was secured and rattled off its many salient features faster than the weapon could fire. I had the feeling he was soon going to say that it had belonged to his mother and begin to cry! He sold the weapon to the civilian for a goodly sum of military scrip, and the man dug frantically through his pockets before coming up with the purchase price. As we started to move away, the man called after us, "Say, I can take this weapon home, can't I?" Ray responded, "See your local provost marshal," and we made a hasty withdrawal.

Captain Ray Byers was working miracles. Making the rounds of the Saigon supply dumps, he traded the Mauser for a host of materials, and the district-made flags were moving well. We received more radios and batteries, paint and brushes, M-16 rifles, and ammunition for the advisors and Captain Ngi. Ray brought home food that allowed us to be self-sufficient and dine with the artillery only when we wanted to eat out. Once he came home with a case of steaks and we had a cookout. When he couldn't trade for material he often sold the flags for money, which we used to purchase items not available elsewhere.

We bought three sets of medical tools and birthing aids, our purpose being to improve medicine in the district. Our midwife and team medic were teaching basic medicine classes, and the infantry battalion surgeon was helping when possible. All the sights of a Third World country were still visible; the clubfoot, the goiter, and festering wounds were a daily sight in Rach Kien. We were making small progress, but it was progress.

We also used the money to employ Vietnamese carpenters on district projects that I wanted done but did not want to go through Major Dong to accomplish. For the Vietnamese, a simple project took reams of paperwork and weeks of waiting. We were there to help, not to do it for them, but I could not afford the time to show oriental patience. I had a gut feeling it was wrong for an advisor to do this, but I wanted progress. Right or wrong in technique, we got it done. The four carpenters we hired looked to be in their eighties. They were white-bearded patriarchs, so ancient that they appeared biblical. For advisor purposes I named them Matthew, Mark, Luke, and John.

Captain Ngi had assured me that these men were craftsmen, and he was correct. They used the most simple tools but could work wonders in wood. My affection for these seniors was deeply felt. They favored my attention. I had the feeling that at night they told their families about the special relationship they enjoyed with us. Each Friday we had a ritual inspection when I would examine their work and their tools. Some minor concern had to be expressed during the inspection. "Was the edge of this adz chipped?" "Was that rust on the side of this auger?" These were serious matters, and they would gather around Voung, talking with animation to assure me that all was well. I had them repairing doors and making furniture for the troops' families. They were old men so proud to be doing something constructive. Payday was a spiritual experience; they stood in line, bowed, and cupped their hands together to receive their piasters.

Lumber was difficult to find. The engineers tired of my constant begging. I thought of the green-wooded hills of Pennsylvania and of my father, who never cut a tree without planting two. In the flat paddy lands of Rach Kien, usable lumber was a precious material and its lack a constant source of concern. On one occasion Ray Byers brought lumber back from Saigon and we stacked it adjacent to the advisor house. By morning it had vanished, stolen by Vietnamese. I was gripped with fury and told Major Dong and Captain Ngi that they would get no help from any American until the lumber was returned. I shut down all cooperation for a week while we tested wills. It stretched our relations to the breaking point, but, board by board, the lumber was returned.

We continued searching for the enemy, reaching out to keep them on the defensive. Each military operation was a learning experience. I pushed the Vietnamese to initiate operations that would take us to different areas of the district. I felt it was crucial to establish the government presence in outlying areas. The south and west were hotbeds of enemy activity. Sometimes when I would point to an area on the map as a likely objective, Major Dong and Captain Ngi would indicate that we were not ready to go there.

I had come to the conclusion that the war in Vietnam was similar to a time in history when nobles grew so powerful that they waged private wars that national leadership could not control. Especially during night operations it was difficult to tell which force you might encounter. The Americans came and went as suited them in Rach Kien, as did the South Vietnamese army. On one night mission we found ourselves in a firefight with a Vietnamese Ranger battalion that we did not even know was in the district. I complained bitterly about this loose cannon conduct. As district senior advisor, I had the responsibility of coordinating fires in Rach Kien between American and Vietnamese forces operating there. Like Cassandra crying her warnings from the walls of Troy,

I was ignored. There was no trust. Americans were not about to tell the Vietnamese what they were doing, as they had on early operations; those operations had been compromised. When Americans had to tell the Vietnamese about a planned operation, they would frequently use a false name for it. If they told the Vietnamese that the plan was named Operation Eagle, in reality it would be Operation Tiger to the Americans. False operations plans were sometimes issued for Eagle, while at the same time that identical plan was being executed elsewhere as Tiger. Most of the time I persuaded the Americans to tell me what they were doing in Rach Kien by agreeing not to pass it on to the Vietnamese. I was sometimes asked to pass information to the Vietnamese that I knew was false. Dong and Ngi would tell me if they knew what the South Vietnamese army (ARVN) was up to, and I sorted it out as best I could, asking people not to fire unobserved artillery until they cleared it with the advisors.

Coordination of when and where artillery was firing was critical, as both friend and foe knew that lack of this information was an invitation to death. We varied the time of operations, sometimes hitting at dawn, other times at midday or just after darkness. The Rangers have known for centuries that to survive in war, never, never establish a predictable routine.

Despite my misgivings, the situation was falling into place. I started to feel as though I had a grip on my job as district senior advisor (DSA). As I was grinning to myself, Captain Byers said jokingly, "Look at him. A few months ago he didn't know what a DSA wuz, and now he are one."

I thought about how much my life was like that of the American Ranger of the seventeenth and eighteenth centuries. Most of them were builders as well as warriors, creating while protecting, giving people an opportunity for a better life. What a wonderful challenge I faced to be more than just someone trying to kill. I was helping a community come alive while fighting off the savages. Few people ever understood what American advisors did in that regard, and few people cared when I tried to explain. One media visitor to Rach Kien said, "I want to see bodies." I wanted to see a community grow and prosper and be safe. For me, the opportunity to be both protector and builder made Vietnam the best year of my life.

Our night movement was improving. We went forth in darkness, traveling cross-country until reaching the ambush position that we hoped would bring contact with the enemy. We were always in position at the time of day when sufficient light provided visibility for a man moving cross-country, but when it was too dark for him to be seen at any great distance. This period is known as before morning nautical twilight, or BMNT. It precedes the dawn, that time defined by the Muslim as when one is able to distinguish a white thread from a black. BMNT is a favorite time of ambush and attack. It is a time of wetness as earth and vegetation are touched by dew, a quiet, lonely, and very private time. Our force consisted of some forty handpicked men. Many had reason to hate the VC, as they had lost relatives to them. We would frequently use a cross-shaped ambush, with the horizontal line covering a trail or road. Coming from any direction, the enemy could be taken under fire from both front and flanks.

The ambush was a tactic both sides practiced with frequency. Patient reconnaissance was the key to many successes by the enemy. They would bide their time, knowing that man is a creature of habit and routine. To do the same thing over and over again in Vietnam was an invitation to ambush. Americans had a variety of ambush procedures. One that worked well was the false extraction. When troops were in an area and then flown out, an ambush force would stay behind in a concealed position. The same number of helicopters that brought the troops in would arrive to take them out. Troops would be dispersed among them, and the rapid extraction process would occur. Sometimes the enemy would come back to search the area, as Americans had a tendency to leave equipment behind. The VC also reasoned that the evacuated area was now the safest place to be. They learned the hard way that they were wrong. At times, the

American stay-behind force would not reveal themselves by firing. When they saw the enemy, they would radio for an L-19 spotter aircraft to come overhead. The concealed Americans on the ground would actually direct the artillery fire that killed the VC on the ground, but to the enemy it appeared as though the fire was being controlled from the air. They had no idea Americans were concealed nearby.

In this chess game of war the enemy was equally skilled. When Americans would establish outlying fire support bases for operations and then evacuate them, the enemy reasoned that at some time the Americans might grow lazy and return to the same spot. The enemy would lay mines in the area, which might lie for months until the time American helicopters began to land.

Some American units made use of centuries-old words of Ranger wisdom that stemmed from the French and Indian War. About 1757, then-captain Robert Rogers of the Rangers was given the task of taking a body of men, primarily British regulars, and transforming it into a Ranger unit. To assist in their training, Rogers put on paper twenty-eight rules for survival and success on the frontier. He did not originate these thoughts. They were the hard lessons of the frontier passed down from father to son. Some of the rules had previously been written out. Rogers did not always follow the rules that he set down, and when he did not, his men paid a heavy price. Still, Robert Rogers put the words to paper and they have been useful ever since.

The rules included: making certain you and your equipment are ready for battle, security on the march, taking a different route home than the one you went out on; before leaving an encampment, look for a sign that the enemy had been scouting your position, and if you are being trailed (as Americans in Vietnam often were), circle back and ambush those coming behind.

We were all aware that the sight of helicopters landing was a tip-off to enemy observers. Sometimes false landings would be made. These might be covered by smoke-laying helicopters. To prevent frequent takeoffs and landings, troops would occasionally be sent out with rations for two or three days. They could then move overland without the helicopter being seen, yet the helicopters were available to hurry troops to the scene when action developed.

During daylight, American infantry units would sometimes occupy a well-concealed defensive perimeter and rest the men. After darkness, numerous ambush forces would be sent out. All units would be positioned so that mutual support could be rendered.

American units would sometimes stay in a suspect area for seventy-two hours, the reasoning being that VC hiding in tunnels would need to come out for food and water. For enemy tunnels hurriedly dug, the system worked, but their tunnels were often well stocked.

Many areas we operated in were full of streams and marshes with heavy thickets of vegetation. The enemy was adept at concealment in and under water. Concussion grenades were helpful in this regard. I was told that American forces who had the fuel would sometimes pour gasoline on the surface of slow-moving water; when it had spread, they would touch it off with a match. That worked well if the ambush was set on the lower end to greet the VC when they came out.

I remained in contact with the advisor house by radio. In the advisor house we had two PRC-25 radios on an army field table. These radios were attached to a tall, pole-mounted antenna rigged beside the house. The long antenna greatly increased their range of reception. Each house radio was equipped with external speakers that allowed everyone in the room to hear the transmission and hand mikes with push-to-talk switches for transmission. One of the house radios was on the Long An Province net, which allowed communication between the districts and province headquarters. The second radio was used for advisors conducting operations. Telephones to the infantry and artillery rounded out our communications, and our communications check system was working. I always informed both the infantry and artillery of our movements. I had a great respect for American firepower. It was called friendly fire. Having been caught under the firepower of quad 50s mounted on halftracks in Korea, I knew it was not friendly when coming at me.

The night operation always turned into a daytime sweep. We would visit hamlets, and Captain Ngi would talk to the old men, women, and children who remained. I had the feeling they wished both sides would go away. Their thatch houses with dirt floors showed an existence few Americans at home would understand. Within the hut, thick layers of mud had been packed into what appeared to be a beehive oven with a tunnel entrance, which was their protection from the shrapnel of artillery fire. Their fear was American artillery, since they lived in areas frequented by the enemy. They were patient and hardworking people. Ngi was trying to help them, and our advisor medic would treat any problems that he could. We recognized, however, that when we were out of sight the VC would surface again.

Vietnamese intelligence had learned about a buildup of VC recruiting and resupply in the south and west of the district. Night sampan traffic was increasing on the river. Friendlies did not travel the river at night. On several occasions helicopter gunships, which specialized in night operations, swooped in and picked me up to serve as guide. Night flying was not my element, but I did enough of it to be able to identify the key waterways and know the likely hiding places along them. We would fly these waterways engaging enemy boat traffic. This was high adventure, exciting missions in which we whirled along at low level through the darkness, then suddenly a target would be to our front. Down we would dive, our radio transmissions punctuated by the rattle of machine-gun fire and the *whoosh* of rockets. On one flight we attacked a string of sampans. As they were torn apart by our fire, a sampan loaded with ammunition or explosives blew up with such a thunderous blast that it was heard in the advisor house. Death was on the water that night, administered with the efficiency of a well-oiled machine. I admired the cool professionalism of these young pilots. This was all in a night's work for them; their voices were calm and unruffled.

We varied our tactics from raid, to ambush, to sweeping an area or doing a cordon-and-search. Surprise and speed were the keys to the latter technique. We sought to surround an area before the inhabitants were aware of what was happening. The inner cordon was backed up by an outer cordon in case anyone slipped through. Search and interrogation teams would work the cordoned-off area looking for arms, ammunition, explosives, documents, or enemy personnel. Then the locals usually got a pep talk from Captain Ngi.

The enemy hid both weapons and food supplies. In some areas of the country, anthills were used for this purpose. Rice caches were frequently used, and Americans learned to look for gatherings of birds. The birds often used their natural instincts to locate caches of rice.

While most of our operations were on foot, at least once a week we would be able to secure helicopters and fly to a more distant part of the district. I was particularly fond of helicopter operations. I would rise early, turn on the radio beside my bed, and, while shaving, listen to the jovial cry of "Good morning, Vietnam!" Then came the adventures of the mythical creature "Chickenman." Some songs that were played would stay with me as a memory of Vietnam, in particular the Fifth Dimension version of "Up, Up and Away." I will always associate it with the roar of helicopters. I would go outside on the street where the troops would be lined up ready to board. The command and control (C&C) ship would swoop in, picking up Captain Ngi, myself, and selected members of the team. We would lift off and, as I gazed down, I would see the troops running for the gaggle (the line of helicopters) as they touched down. We flew toward the objective area, sometimes taking a roundabout route, hoping to confuse the enemy as to our intent. As we approached, the gunships would put down suppressive fire to our flanks and, on occasion, a smoke screen would be laid. The first time I saw helicopters laying smoke I thought they had been hit by enemy fire. Smoke was also used by American ground forces. However, its most effective use was from the helicopter.

Sometimes the landing zone would be hot and enemy tracers would spray past the aircraft. Most of the time we arrived in an envelope of noise, the helicopters barely, if at all, touching the surface of the earth. We jumped out and ran to establish a perimeter. Just as quickly as they came, the helicopters were gone. Where all had been noise, only silence remained. We would then move in search of the enemy. They could go to ground fast, and more than once I would briefly see men running. We had time for few if any shots, and they would disappear. For many men who went in search of the enemy in Vietnam, the sudden transition from the noise of a helicopter insertion to the eerie quiet after they departed would be a lasting memory.

The enemy was very effective at propaganda. They would round up the people of a hamlet and bring them together in an area bedecked with North Vietnamese, Chinese, and Russian flags. There they would entertain and preach to the people with what were called "proselytizing" teams. Usually this was done at night. Sometimes they would leave the Communist flags flying in a hamlet in the hope that we would fire on them. If we did, innocent people might be killed or their property destroyed, turning the people against us.

Ngi had word that a proselytizing team was active in a western hamlet. We took the PRU and some handpicked members of 555 RF Company and proceeded overland by a roundabout route. No one was working the paddies, so we felt that the locals had been dragooned for a meeting, which was very bold to do in daylight. The enemy liked to demonstrate their immunity from our actions, and sometimes it brought them to grief. The flags were out and the speaking in progress when we appeared on the scene. We had to be careful whom we shot. We settled for those who ran. Ngi spent a long time questioning people and took a couple into custody. On this occasion the enemy flags were authentic. Though homemade, they were very profitable for the district. The sale of these flags paid for more improvements in the village market. I brought home a set of Chinese, Russian, and North Vietnamese flags.

At the district level the enemy forces usually dressed in the simple clothes of the peasant farmer, what appeared to be black pajamas or shorts. Their sandals were made of old tires with supporting straps from inner tubes. Like many other techniques of the enemy, their footwear was simple but effective. They could put their sandals on backward and leave tracks that, to the inexperienced eye, appeared to be going in the opposite direction from their actual route. They lived off the land and ate from a squad pot, using one end of chopsticks. They were foot-mobile but accustomed to hardship and long marches. They recognized that getting support from the local population was vital to their survival. Where possible, they helped plant or harvest the rice and treated the people well. When the people disobeyed, they killed.

The underground havens that the enemy built were marvels of construction. Sometimes Americans and South Vietnamese used tear gas to drive them from these tunnels. The enemy began to stock gas masks in the tunnels, and some of their troops carried them. Another district advisor told me that the VC in his area tried to use captured tear gas on his Regional and Popular Force troops, but they did not allow for the wind and the gas blew back on them.

When we had contact, a body count was required from on high. Our political leadership in the United States was eager to show progress in the war to the American public. The higher numbers of enemy reported as killed, the stronger their claim. On the ground in Vietnam, this translated into tired men pushing themselves through an adverse land that was often mined and booby-trapped. When the rains came and the paddies filled with water, the exhaustion was agony. Some officers believed that all orders must be followed to the letter. That belief brought ruin to Germany in World War II. I had seen the lives of many men wasted by politicians during the Korean War and had no intention of being part of that in Vietnam. I wanted to kill the enemy and preserve my men. I made estimates of enemy casualties and radioed them in as fact. The technique later became known in computer language as "Garbage in, garbage out." In later years, when

I was reviewing American combat reports from Vietnam, I was disgusted to see the time and energy that went into telling politicians the "kill ratio."

War is destruction and pain. On one operation we landed behind the covering fire of the gunships. The sound of the helicopters faded into the distance and we were left in silence. Then the sound of a man crying in distress came to us. He was a *trung nong*, a farmer, a poor simple peasant whose life and that of his family depended on planting and harvesting. His water buffalo had been machine-gunned. As deprived as his life had been, it was now much worse. I had no way of knowing if a bored gunner had killed the beast for the mere experience of it or if it was an accident of war. It was a small tragedy in the war in Vietnam, but very large to that man trying to survive. Captain Ngi related that the farmer would be paid for the loss of his animal, but I knew that even if true, it would not be enough. Whatever that farmer's political persuasion had been prior to this incident, I knew that the VC now had a willing supporter.

We were receiving news reports about discontent from the college campuses and some radio and television commentators in the United States. It angered us, as it gave support to the enemy. I had my own questions about the war in Vietnam. Remembering how the United States had turned away from victory in Korea, I wondered why we were making the same mistake in Vietnam. In Vietnam we all knew that the American military could roll over North Vietnam in quick time, but our political leadership would not allow us to go after the enemy homeland. To achieve victory we needed to crush North Vietnam. But the politicians were afraid of Chinese entry and a widening war, so they sent men to the slaughter while the enemy had a safe haven from our ground force attack in North Vietnam, Laos, and Cambodia. Comics frequently use the old joke about military intelligence being a contradiction in terms. But the ultimate stupidity in war is found in the civilian leadership. Why do they put men in a war they are not prepared to win?

I do not accept the philosophy "Theirs not to reason why,

theirs but to do and die." Most Americans will fight valiantly for a good reason, but we are not cattle to be herded to the slaughter. In my view the major fault of the war in Vietnam was the indecisive leadership in Washington, D.C.

District advisors had limited call on troop-carrying helicopters, and in most cases we walked home. Returning from any operation was the opportunity to shed rifle and pistol and the harness with its weight of ammunition, grenades, and two canteens that most of us carried in the intense heat of the Delta. During the Korean War a man was expected to preserve water. To do a twenty-mile march and come back with a full canteen was something to be proud of. By the time of Vietnam the medical people understood the importance of replacing body fluids. In the heat of South Vietnam, the fatigue jacket would blacken with perspiration and glisten with crystallized salt. Rolling up our trouser legs and stripping off our boots and socks, we would air our feet, treat ourselves to a drink, and discuss the events of the operation while looking forward to a shower.

We faced a skilled and experienced enemy. In most cases he knew his strengths and weaknesses. His encampments were always difficult to find and inaccessible. To hunt them, we had to go deep into the muck and thick vegetation. There are more than two thousand species of the tropical evergreens we call palm. Though many varieties grow in Vietnam, American soldiers in the Delta identified with one species. The *nipa fruticans* or nipa palm is a short-truncal tree that thrives in the brackish water on the Mekong. Its featherlike leaves extend to a distance of twenty feet. For those of us who were south of Saigon, all vegetation was frequently described as nipa, whether it was palm, mangrove, or bamboo.

We struggled through the water and mud of rice paddies, streams, and bogs, sometimes sinking waist-deep in the thick, dark mud. It was a clinging, cloying mud that held men close and sucked them down. The hungry, bottomless mud drained our strength. Crossing one such rice paddy was an ordeal—crossing many was torture. In the paddies the lightweight Vietnamese had the advantage. They seemed to speed across the surface like water spiders. Often when we heavier Americans became mired, we had to be pulled out by hand or rope. Sometimes we would lie gasping against a paddy dike. I did not think about it at the time, but when we came back from a hunt in this water world and did not have contact, we referred to it as a "dry hole." In the monsoon season from April to October there was nothing dry about Rach Kien District. Weapons had to be frequently cleaned and test-fired. Mildew and rot permeated food and clothing. The humidity beat upon us, body fat fell away, and we were lean and inured to hardship.

If I had been born in another land and been a soldier, I would not want to fight the Americans. People who fight America have a tendency to die in large numbers. We fight wars of matériel with utter disregard for cost. A three-man enemy patrol might find a million dollars' worth of artillery shells being fired at them. Most American commanders will expend matériel knowing that our logistical system is the best in the world. There are good soldiers in other armies, men who are inured to hardship and dedicated, but soldiers of other countries are not backed with the system of matériel support that we enjoy. Some armies write off men in difficulty, but that is not the way of the American army. Units occasionally get isolated and wiped out, but every effort is made to rescue any American who is trapped.

The support improves with each war. I often thought of how helpful it would have been to call in helicopter gunship support when in trouble in the Korean War. In Vietnam, I was often supported by pencil-thin Cobra gunships, slim and deadly as the snake for which they are named. The Cobra could fire 800 rounds per minute in searching fire and a phenomenal 4,000 rounds a minute in attack fire. The rate of fire was so fast that it sounded like a piece of paper being ripped. Punctuating this stream was the *whoomp!* of exploding 2.5-inch rockets followed by cascades of black mud and the lush green of foliage.

One time we were getting automatic weapons fire from

our front, and gunships came in response to my call. I was grateful to have the Cobras overhead. The gunships would fly directly over our heads or between us and the enemy. They were very careful not to put the gunner in position where he would be shooting friendly troops. They often made a teardrop or U-shaped descent to get into firing position. When they came in, they could give support fifty meters in front. A Cobra pilot came in low and worked over an area in front of me, effectively silencing the enemy fire. The pilot called me on the radio and asked, "How did you like that?" I made the flippant response, "It's close enough for government work." He had just put his life on the line, and let me know he did not appreciate my humor. I apologized. It is not good practice to make gunship people angry.

18

The River of Ants

I had returned from an operation and was beginning to relax when a burst of gunfire erupted from the town. It was the distinctive sound of a carbine firing, and I felt it was probably some trooper letting off steam. After a time another shot was followed by heavier fire. I put my jacket and boots on, and as I finished, my interpreter Voung came running into the house, panting from exertion. He told me that a member of the PRU had returned from the operation to find a policeman having sex with his wife. The policeman had made a hasty retreat to the police station. The PRU thought it over for a short time and then shot his wife, killing her. Along with his buddies, he had now taken position opposite the police station; the PRU and the police were firing at each other.

I told Voung that Major Dong would handle the problem. He informed me that Dong was at a meeting in Province, Captain Ngi had borrowed my jeep to take some supplies to Trach An, and Antoine could not be found. It was now my responsibility to keep them from killing one other. I told Voung to walk clear of the line of fire but stay close enough that I could call him if needed. I then began what seemed like a very long walk down the dirt street of Rach Kien. This had to be stopped, but I was not pleased to be the man taking action. My only advantage was that I had truly worked to help these people and they knew it. I had shared the danger of operations with them. I believed that they trusted me and would obey my orders. Although I thought this, I was not certain of it. I felt fear and exhilaration and a sense that the entire scene was ludicrous. It was like being the marshal of a western town, walking down the dusty street to restore order. I had the feeling that I was outside myself and observing the actions of someone else.

The PRU were using an A-6 machine gun to work over the police station, and chips of masonry were flying off the building. Fortunately they jammed the weapon. Trying to appear as though on my daily stroll, I continued walking until I stood between the opposing forces. I heard the click as the machine gun was primed and felt a weakness in my knees. The moments seemed like an eternity, but neither side fired. When I called to Voung, he came quickly to my side. I instructed him to tell them that I was an elderly man, and this gunfire was disturbing my sleep. I assured them that whatever the problem was, Major Dong or Captain Ngi would ensure that justice would be done. I instructed them that the PRU should return to their area, and both sides must stay apart until the situation was resolved. When they obeyed me, I felt both surprise and great relief.

Some team members discussed the accuracy of the shooting. It developed that the PRU had put seven carbine slugs in his wife's belly. One man thought that was good shooting until informed by Voung that the range was about two feet. Some jokes were made about whether I looked more like John Wayne walking down that street or the cowboy comic, Andy Devine. I was ready to kill Antoine, with his tailored fatigue uniform, pencil-line mustache, and cigarette holder. He wore Vietnamese parachute wings, but I doubted he had ever jumped on anything but one of his women. When I found him I told him he was a piece of shit, and a few other English-language profanities that he understood. He was not pleased. In his culture I lost face by showing rage. At the moment I did not care about his culture—I wanted his hide.

We completed our falcon's nest, a bunker, and an observation tower perched high atop the Vietnamese military headquarters. When the timbers, sandbags, and ammo box walls were in place, a standoff chicken-wire fence was constructed in front of the tower. The Russians had passed their

RPG-7 rocket launcher to the North Vietnamese; it had a range of five hundred meters and its round could penetrate twelve and a half inches of armor. Such a weapon would have made short work of our tower. Experience had taught Americans that if the nose cone touched several strands of wire before it hit the target, the fuse might be shorted out and the round become a dud. We had no way to test this theory but sincerely hoped it was valid.

In mid-January 1968 we learned that the North Koreans had seized the US intelligence ship *Pueblo*. I had trouble understanding how a US Navy ship could be taken without a fight. This did not fit with our navy tradition. I thought our country would not tolerate this action and that North Korea would promptly return the men and ship or pay dearly. Nothing happened, and we came to the conclusion that men of the American military were expendable. The general feeling was that, with the exception of a man's family, people might mumble but no one at home really gave a damn. The homefolk were long on oratory but short on action. The United States home front would not look after its own—that was not the case on the battlefield, where Americans frequently risked and many lost their lives trying to save those they did not know.

Our quality of life was improving. The mail helicopter now came in daily. Province supplied a projector and we began to get American films. An exchange of movies could be counted on at least three times a week. I would sign for a movie until it was flown to the next district. My monthly shopping list to the engineer battalion commander included a request for a four-by-eight-foot sheet of three-quarter-inch plywood. We painted the plywood white and mounted it on poles across the street from our front porch. The engineers built a tall wooden platform to support the projector, and a sergeant of the team served as projectionist from inside the screened-in front porch. The advisors, engineer officers, and Captain Ngi would sit inside the porch on folding chairs. Rank has its privileges, and my chair was set atop a table to allow maximum viewing. It worked well unless I inadvertently moved the chair and fell off the table, which brought howls of amusement unless the film had the men in the grip of emotion. Then uncomplimentary remarks came from the safety of the darkness. The young engineers usually showed up in shower slippers and jungle fatigue trousers. They wore flak jackets over bare chests, carried steel helmets, and consumed vast quantities of beer. They threw the cans in the street or, if they did not like the film, at the screen, which began to take on a pockmarked appearance. On the orders of their commander they returned the next morning and cleaned the street.

On movie night the engineers would bring their beer and remove a number of our sandbags to make temporary seats outside for themselves. The Vietnamese military and their families would flock to the scene. Most of the Vietnamese could not understand English. But they liked the films and soon understood that all Americans lived in mansions with servants and had swimming pools, big cars, and airplanes at our beck and call. The audience was close to cover and needed to be, as the enemy frequently dropped mortar shells on us. When these attacks occurred, beer cans went flying as men and women scattered to gain the nearest protection.

I have never watched the classic film *The Sound of Music* in its entirety. On the night we were to view it, I took my elevated position and looked forward to an evening of enjoyment. The film rolled and the airborne camera soared over alpine mountains and valleys to settle on Julie Andrews from whose talented lips came forth the words "The hills are alive with the sound of . . ." Just at that moment the first mortar round hit in a thunderous explosion. The streets of Rach Kien were alive with explosions. This may be the only occasion that Ms. Andrews gave her stellar performance without an audience. After the attack, the still-running film was stopped, rewound, and run again, but I did not see it. I was visiting the artillery and trying to work out my revenge. A week later I did see the film *Doctor Zhivago,* and it became the bane of my life as an advisor.

I wanted to kill those enemy gunners, but nothing seemed

to work—patrols could not find them. We would set an ambush only to come up empty. Harassing and interdictory fires did not stop them, nor did night gunship flights. They picked the time when they wanted to hit us. A day or even a week might pass before they would shell us, or they might strike an hour after the first attack, hoping to catch us in the open. I studied each attack with my compass in hand and came to the conclusion that they were becoming careless and firing from the same general location each time. To prevent them from knowing my calculations, we always included a number of other areas in whatever firing response we made.

While we had only a single battery of 105mm howitzers in Rach Kien, many other artillery pieces could also reach into the district, including more 105s and the increasingly larger 155mm and 8-inch howitzers and 175mm guns. Considerable firepower was available if I could catch it at a time when it was not in use elsewhere. With the assistance of the battery commander, I worked out a series of labeled grids along the azimuth from which the enemy was firing and within the reasonable range. I named these alphabetically: Alpha, Bravo, Charlie. The theory was, when the enemy fired it would trigger a response from all the friendly artillery within range. We would fire what is known as a "time on target." This is surprise fire, with all weapons of all artillery batteries within range delivering their rounds to explode at the same time over the same rectangular grid. The gunners would fire a variable time fuse so the explosions would be airbursts, since the mortar crews would not have overhead cover. They usually fired and ran. We would fire one grid, then the second and the third, hoping to hit them before they could get away.

I called for this several times but our artillery was always busy. Finally the night arrived when our gunners were not engaged. As the enemy began to shell us, I called for our artillery. We could hear the rumble of the guns and see the flashes of explosions in the area I wanted covered. A week went by without additional mortar attacks, and then a second week. At the end of the third week they resumed, but with a difference. This group was learning the trade and was not as accurate. A town is a fixed target, and they would soon become reasonably accurate gunners, but I knew this was not the same mortar crew. Months later I learned that an ARVN regiment had picked up a number of wounded VC. One man, whose legs had to be amputated, said they were shelling Rach Kien District when suddenly everything exploded. The VC were never again so careless as to continually fire from the same location. From then on, they moved about. We were a large target and they could hit us, but their constant movement hindered their accuracy.

A great commotion ruffled the Vietnamese ranks. Word had filtered up the Vietnamese chain of command that Captain Ngi and Major Dong had been seen with Viet Cong flags. Both were deeply concerned that they would be considered traitors. I made a trip to province headquarters and talked with both the Americans and Vietnamese. I hated to reveal the success of our flagmaking factory, but we arrived at an understanding that, while unorthodox, we had a good thing going.

We took turns on radio watch and, in the small hours of the night that soldiers call oh-dark-thirty, I had a radio call from the province staff duty officer, who wanted to know how many people in my district had "pinkeye." I did not even know how many people I had in my district; they moved in and out and I had visitors from the north. In some parts of my district, my own Vietnamese did not feel that we had enough district forces to enter. My problem was compounded by the fact that I did not know what pinkeye was and had no intention of waking my hardworking medic to find out. I replied in candor, "I don't know." I was informed that I had to know, as this was an important report that required an immediate answer for people all the way up the line. I asked the officer what pinkeye was—he did not know. I told him I would call him back shortly and signed off on his weary complaint that he needed the information pronto. I went out in the kitchen and made a sandwich and some coffee, came back to the radio, called him, and said, "Three hundred seventy-two." He said, "Roger. Out."

Radio call signs were changed at intervals to make enemy intercept more difficult. I wondered who dreamed up call signs. The province call sign might be Hairless Joe or Honey Flower. It was incongruous to pick up a hand mike and say, "This is Sweet Moonbeam 146. Where the hell is our mail?" In Korea, when those of us in the 8th Rangers were up to our hips in Chinese, our radio call sign was Old Rose. I recalled my buddy E. C. Rivera on the radio, saying, "If we don't get those tanks, Old Rose is gonna be No Rose."

Two things were evident about the war in Vietnam. Improved communications and the helicopter had changed the battlefield. Commanders were on the scene in their own chariots, and at times it would have been better if they had stayed at home. A company commander fighting a battle would likely have his battalion commander flying overhead. Above him would be the brigade commander, and above him the division commander and who knows what else above him. On occasion these VIPs would stack up over an objective area like early arrivals at a football game. Of course this alerted the enemy. Ugly rumors went around that American communications were so good, people in Washington, D.C., could interfere with the conduct of a ground operation. On one occasion I was in the advisor house listening by radio to Don Schroder employing his battalion in a ground action. It was a masterful performance. He was like the conductor of a symphony. He employed artillery and air and used maneuver as he crushed the enemy. Throughout the action he was subjected to constant harping from commanders who had their own helicopters over the scene. Much of what was said was of no assistance to him and fell in the category of "horseshit and gun smoke." He managed his troops, the enemy, and his commanders with consummate skill. The culmination came when someone on the ground reported killing an enemy officer and having the officer's pistol. A senior officer landed and took the pistol from the man who captured it.

Don Schroder and I would have dinner or a cup of coffee together from time to time. He was a man who loved life and adventure. He was fed up with our no-win policy in Vietnam, and at our last meeting, he told me he intended to leave the army at the end of his tour.

He did not make it. The story was that he had landed to take two VC prisoner and was ambushed. That did not sound like Don Schroder. Later one of his officers told me that one of Schroder's company commanders, a young man Don cared for greatly, was wounded and on the verge of death. In a desperate effort to get the officer to a medical facility as soon as possible, Don attempted to land at the scene. The helicopter was shot down and Don and others were killed. In the way of these things, another officer took over the battalion. He was a competent man, but we were never to know each other as Don Schroder and I had.

I began to receive radio calls from Province regarding the movie *Doctor Zhivago*. At first they were questioning, but soon became strident and demanding.

"Bat Face One Four Six, this is Bat Face. Over."

"This is One Four Six. Over."

"This is Bat Face. I asked you last week what you did with *Doctor Zhivago* and I still don't have a satisfactory answer. Over."

"This is One Four Six. I told you it went out of here on a mail chopper a month ago. I believe One Three Six has it. Over."

"That's a negative, One Four Six. I say again, that's a negative. One Three Six doesn't have it. None of the others have it. We don't have it. You are signed for it and we want it. Over."

I received no assistance or commiseration from my fellow district senior advisors. I sat and squirmed through a polling as every district replied that they did not have *Doctor Zhivago*. Some of them were making cruel remarks, implying that I had probably traded it to a supply dump for a swimming pool. They did not have the connection with the engineers that I did, and I put their unkind comments down to jealousy. We had searched our advisor domain thoroughly. Everyone on the team was certain it had gone out on a chopper, but I did not have a signature to prove it. I did not have the faintest notion how many copies were in Vietnam or what a lost movie would cost me. Never take counsel of your fears, unless you are worrying about money. Imagination took over and financial fear gnawed at me. It would probably cost millions of dollars to remake *Doctor Zhivago*. Even if I stayed in the army until I was 120 years old, I would never get that movie paid for. Each time the province staff called, I frantically searched the house.

The Vietnamese mortar men were not sparing of the infantry battalion or artillery. On one attack they caught the battalion at a time when the troops had just returned from an extended stay in the field. I could see a number of medevac choppers landing and taking off. Towns, cities, and fortified camps are fixed targets. We needed to secure the places where the majority of the population lived—we needed to have troops there. It was not a matter of Americans sitting and waiting to be attacked. Day after day and night after night Americans made a determined search for the enemy; when he was found, he died. But all of these ground battles took place on the territory of our ally. When assassins are determined to kill someone, no matter the price, they will succeed. If your enemy can come to your house or office any time they choose and try to kill you, but you cannot go to theirs to put them out of business, you are in trouble. The mine, the booby trap, and the mortar round cost the enemy little, but they took a steady toll of American and South Vietnamese lives.

A wide variety of reconnaissance techniques were used by the Americans including electronics that would pick up enemy use and location of their electronics. Photographic intelligence would pinpoint their activities. Infrared devices probed the night to determine heat emission, and sidelooking airborne radar (SLAR) could spot movement. These components were blended together with men on the ground doing reconnaissance patrols to find the enemy.

Sometimes on night operations we would take up ambush positions near a Cao Dai temple. The Cao Dai select from the teachings of Buddha, Confucius, Brahma, Vishnu, Jesus Christ, Lao-tzu, Siva, and possibly Mohammed. Their spiritual guides include Babe Ruth, Victor Hugo, William Shakespeare, and Winston Churchill; it is the ultimate cover-your-ass religion. If we were close to the temple, we could see the flickering light from oil lamps dancing with the shadows of plaster dragons, cranes, and cobras among the ornate columns of the statue-covered altar. Above the altar, the all-seeing eye that was the symbol of the faith cast its baleful orb on the eerie surroundings. Priests in saffron robes performed the rituals of their prayer service at various times throughout the night, and the sound of gongs and chants would sweep across the rice paddies to the ambush positions where we silently lay in wait to kill. Rudyard Kipling would have understood. It was a haunting, mystical time and I loved it.

Captain Ray Byers had continued to work miracles in outfitting the team and district. He brought back fishing nets that were of great assistance to our people. Ray secured enough M-16 rifles that we were able to give firepower equal to that of the enemy to all advisors and a select group of Vietnamese. I longed for the time when we could equip all our Vietnamese with efficient weapons. Ray was constantly asking me to allow him to go on operations. The discussions became increasingly heated. He was the best scrounger I had ever known, and I worried that he would get shot. Ray knew his wounding would have made me somewhat sad, but the fear that I would lose the truckloads of matériel that I had become accustomed to was gripping. After a shouting match in which he threatened to transfer, I relented and allowed him to go into battle. Of course he distinguished himself in the very next fight.

The arrival of a new lieutenant on the team became my good fortune. His name was Ron Nelson, and he had a PhD in history. He was scholarly and introspective. He told me up front that he did not believe he belonged in Rach Kien. I felt that was likely, but asked him to give it a try. The first operation involved a long march through water-filled rice paddies under the boiling sun. Lieutenant Nelson collapsed and had to be carried home on a makeshift litter by Vietnamese troops. I expected he would ask for a transfer. He did come to me that evening, but only to apologize and assure me that he would not fail again. Ron Nelson was brilliant. He became the Lancelot of Rach Kien. Mike Primont's time in Vietnam was drawing to a close. Ron Nelson was assigned as intelligence officer and promptly went to work.

The country we knew as Vietnam had long been occupied by the French under the name French Indo-China. The French were meticulous record keepers, and many of the Viet Cong leaders had been revolutionaries who ran afoul of French law, which resulted in a dossier that provided useful information on someone we needed to find or keep an eye on. Ron Nelson could speak and read French. He was able to go into the old French criminal records and develop a list of suspects. We began to have the success I had hoped for.

Ron took some Regional Force troops and began setting up roadblocks in order to check identity papers of people walking on district roads or coming by bus or Lambretta. One afternoon he came to me wearing the tight smile of success. He had questioned the pregnant wife of the man Ron had identified as a Viet Cong official for the district, a man we could not find. Ron's smile broadened as he told me his meeting with the woman had been at the right moment in time. The wife had learned that her husband was cheating on her, and she revealed the location of the house in an outlying hamlet where the enemy official and his two guards were staying with the other woman. The Vietnamese knew the location of the house.

I talked with Captain Ngi, and we decided to go after the man at night, arriving in position to take him out at first light. At 0200 hours our small party slipped out of the compound and began to move across the paddy dikes. Some distance ahead were two members of the Provincial Reconnaissance Unit who knew the area well. The rest of the party was handpicked: a well-armed group from the Regional Force unit and National Police and four Americans.

Before first light we had made our way undetected to an isolated hut located in the center of a small but dense mangrove and nipa palm marsh. We established an L-shaped ambush and watched as dawn crept over us. The growth surrounding the hut had been thinned to prevent intruders from coming near unobserved. At the front doorway a small mud courtyard had been pounded solid by the foot traffic of generations. A man, rather large for a Vietnamese, stepped from the darkened interior. He wore thongs on his feet and black pajamalike bottoms. He took several steps forward, yawned, stretched, and prepared to urinate.

Captain Ngi identified the man, cupped his hands, and shouted for him to surrender. The Viet Cong official ran for the hut and died in a fusillade of gunfire before he reached the door. Automatic weapons fire came at us from within. I heard the familiar song of the bullet passing by. We quickly smothered the enemy fire and, in the silence that followed, moved cautiously to the house. The dead Viet Cong official lay on his right side, his arms and legs frozen in the position of movement from the last desperate dive for life.

The interior of the hut was sparsely furnished. A table and bench stood in the center of the room. Shards of broken pottery littered the earthen floor. The paddy mud bunker that served as a sleeping area was to the right. At its entrance lay a dead woman. Closer to the doorway was the body of another man.

It was evident that someone had torn their way through the thatched side of the house and escaped. A blood trail indicated that the man was hit hard. We went after him, but had only gone a few hundred meters when Ngi said we must stop—we had reached the boundary with another district. I thought this was insane and told him so. Not only was the American government saying you can't cross a border, but also the South Vietnamese. I now understood why the Viet Cong official had selected this house. With very little warning he could have been across the district border laughing at us.

We tied the bodies hand and foot and brought them back on bamboo carrying poles. One sergeant who was looking at the body of the dead official draped from a pole said, "Boy, she was an expensive piece of ass."

On return to the advisor house, I found the rest of the team in a state of high excitement. My request that a USO show be sent to entertain my small group had been approved and would arrive by helicopter the next day. We could not believe our good fortune. I told the men, "See, anything is possible if you really go after it." There was much speculation about how many round-eyed women would be with the show and just how patriotic they would be. This was a day of triumph and I was enjoying it to the hilt. We all had visions of seeing beautiful faces, ripe luscious breasts, and finely shaped legs. Would they dance for us? . . . of course. Would they sing for us?—most assuredly. Would they . . . ? Would they . . . ? Though it was only a dream, the real question was in the minds of most, if not all, of the men.

The advisory team burst into a flurry of excitement. The floors were swept and scrubbed. All sandbags were neatly stacked. Dishes were washed and beer put in the fridge. Some makeshift bunting was contrived and draped about the front porch. An electric air of expectancy fairly crackled with excitement. It was a night when we dreamed big dreams.

The next morning I arrived at the helipad early with a jeep and a three-quarter-ton truck to bring the USO troupe back to the advisor house. I looked upon the infantry battalion and artillery with an "eat-your-heart-out" air. A single Huey came from the direction of Province. That meant a small troupe, but that was okay as we were a small team. There would be enough round-eyed women to go around. The chopper settled on the battalion helipad, kicking up the usual cloud of dust. Two men exited the chopper. One was a staff officer from Province and the second wore military fatigues the way a civilian would wear them—sloppily. He had on a flak jacket and steel helmet. They walked toward us as we stood in stunned silence. I kept looking past them, hoping to see a shapely leg swing out of the helicopter door. The helicopter passenger area was empty.

The staff officer introduced me to the man and, in numbed shock, I shook his hand. I was told the name, but it did not register. I only remember the staff officer saying the words, "He appears on the *Lassie* show." A dog-show actor. They sent me a male dog show actor. I stood as though I were poleaxed until the staff officer suggested we visit the team. Now I was really in trouble. I could see the accusing gaze of my driver fastening on me. When we reached the house, I tried to make light of the situation. The men were not buying my performance. I learned a lot about body language that day. The well-meaning man shook hands with the team members, asked a few questions, and thanked them for their service. I walked him about town and talked briefly with him, speaking automatically with my brain in neutral. I took them back to the helicopter pad and they flew away.

When I returned to the advisor house it was wrapped in gloom. One of the sergeants gave me a look of disdain, shook his head in a wistful sigh, and said, "I wish they had sent Lassie."

Rats were in the house, big ones, who were inclined to go where they wanted and challenged our authority. Sometimes we surprised each other. In daylight we had the advantage, but they were the masters of the night. While on radio watch in the wee hours of a dark and stormy night, I stretched, yawned, and sleepily staggered out to the refrigerator to make a sandwich. When I opened the door, it startled a rat on top of the refrigerator and it jumped on my chest. I was not calm, cool, and collected. Both the rat and I were terrified and fled in opposite directions.

The helicopters we used on operations were not devoted to our exclusive use. The advisor took what he could get when he could get it. Sometimes we would start a ground operation in one part of the district and be picked up there to fly to another area, which was in some measure advantageous to us as it aided in concealing our true objective.

On one such occasion we had completed our search, came

up empty-handed, and were ready to move on. What followed was a routine extraction and insertion that was being repeated numerous times that day throughout South Vietnam. We established a 360-degree perimeter to make certain it was secure before the helicopters arrived. I watched the moving specks on the horizon grow swiftly into whirling, flailing machines that were dear to the feet and, therefore, the heart of every American soldier in Vietnam.

Identification was important to prevent the helicopters from being lured into a trap. We carried smoke grenades that came in white, green, purple, red, and yellow. White could show up like smoke from a ground fire and green blended with the foliage, so when we could we avoided using those colors. Some units disliked the use of any kind of colored smoke for identification as they felt it gave away their position. They preferred aircraft recognition panels. We had no recognition panels, so I pulled the safety pin on a smoke grenade, tossed it into a dry area, heard the pop and hiss, and watched as a stream of colored smoke built rapidly into a billowing cloud.

My radio transmissions to the oncoming commander of the helicopters were standard patter tied to frequently changing radio call signs.

"Red Leopard Five One, this is Metal Song One Four Six . . . over."

"Leopard Five One—go," said an emotionless voice.

"Ah, this is One Four Six. I have you in sight, smokes out—over."

In addition to serving as a means of locating troops on the ground, the billowing smoke also gave the pilot wind direction. On occasion the enemy had attempted to lure helicopters into traps by igniting captured smoke grenades. The counter was to vary the color of smoke and let the pilot identify the color he saw.

"Leopard Five One, roger. Identify purple."

"This is One Four Six. That's affirmative. Approach azimuth one three zero degrees, trail formation, lead bird vicinity smoke. Over."

"Leopard Five One, roger—out."

The critical stage in helimobile operations is when loading and unloading troops. The helicopter is especially vulnerable during those few seconds when the aircraft is stationary, either sitting on its skids or hovering a few feet above the earth. This is the optimum time for the enemy to destroy the helicopter and achieve maximum casualties. For that reason the approach and formation are tightly controlled.

As the helicopters descended, the cyclone force of the spinning rotors tore clouds of dust, mud, and/or debris from the earth. Our district troops were running in preselected groups of eight men to board the aircraft. A Vietnamese soldier might weigh 115 to 120 pounds, so we could get more of them on a Huey troop carrier, or "slick" as they were affectionately known. We loaded from the side and were quickly up, up, and away. Clouds of dust were left behind and the scene beneath became a kaleidoscope of paddies and palms as we held a mad race with the shadows of the hurrying helicopters that sped along the earth below.

Flying ahead of the slicks in the command and control ship (C&C), it was my job to pinpoint the location where the troops would be landed. A crew member handed me a U-shaped radio headset that allowed me to communicate with the pilot. I took a folded, acetate-covered map from my fatigue jacket and held it firmly to my knee against the onrushing air while I oriented the map to the ground. The route taken was circuitous. Using an airborne feint, we hoped to deceive the enemy, then turn and swiftly fly the final leg to the objective.

I gave the pilot landing instructions and watched while the ten helicopters carrying troops descended like locusts. As the C&C ship dropped to let me off, I could see pencil-thin Cobra gunships racing like greyhounds down the flanks of the insertion.

On this day the landing area was wet. The vicious downdraft of the helicopter rotors flattened the long grasses while the surface water rippled as it fled before the bludgeoning force of air. As the helicopters hovered several feet above the earth, men leaped clear, carrying their rifles one-handed while with the other briefly clinging to the mother ship to retain their balance. As we pushed free we struggled through calf-deep mud to clear the landing zone. As quickly as they had come, the helicopters lifted off and disappeared, leaving a sudden silence broken only by the rasping of our exertions.

This operation was a continuation of the effort to get local Vietnamese military into every part of the district. I placed considerable stress on the importance of district forces working toward the day when they could go anywhere and prove to the local people that the enemy did not control the land by remaining there. We had landed along that curious body of water they called the River of Ants. It was a difficult place with water-soaked ground and heavy vegetation encroaching the shoreline. A few thatched and decrepit huts had the usual collection of women, old men, and boys.

Near one of the huts stood four massive water buffalo. Several young boys frolicked on the broad back of one of the buffs. Nearby a boy approximately eight to ten years of age sat astride a ten-foot-long gray-black buffalo, scratching the animal's head and studying us with veiled eyes. Ngi called the boys to us. Separating them, the Vietnamese soldiers under Sergeant Kinh began to ask questions. It was not long before Ngi approached me, his hand resting on the shoulder of the boy who had been riding the buffalo.

He told me that the buffalo boy was a "crazy boy," ignored by the others. But the boy saw many things, and he knew where the enemy had buried weapons. This was a dream come true. The enemy frequently buried weapons in hard-to-find places. It was their resupply system. To find a weapons cache would cause the enemy considerable anguish.

The boy led us on slippery paddy dikes that wound inexorably toward the nipa palm growth of the riverbank. Periodically our young guide would leave the dike and lead us out into the mud-bottomed paddy. Initially he pointed out a scarcely visible fishing line that led to a fragmentation grenade booby trap. I was fascinated with this boy. His tattered rags, gaunt face, and exposed ribs spoke of a poverty that was a living agony. He talked continuously, in marked contrast to the other inhabitants of the hamlet who had stood watching, their faces betraying no emotion as the boy led us away.

The rice paddies that paralleled the thick growth were long unused and choked with high weeds. The area was periodically marked with crude signs portraying a skull and crossbones with Vietnamese lettering. I had seen them before. It was the enemy's manner of telling local farmers to stay out of this area. Occasionally the boy would point out a well-camouflaged punji pit, which was a camouflaged hole in the earth that had sharpened stakes pointed upward. A careless step and the victim would find his foot pierced by stakes whose points were often smeared with excrement.

While the boy served as our guide, we took all the precautions we could to avoid walking into an ambush. When we approached the thick growth, scouts moved ahead while the remainder of the force took up firing positions that provided security in all directions. After a few minutes one of the scouts reappeared. He held his hand and arm stretched toward us and moved his hand rapidly up and down on the hinge of his wrist, beckoning us forward in the oriental manner. We moved forward into the close confines of the jungle-like growth. The dense overhead palm leaves had starved some of the vegetation. Occasional lances of sunlight pierced the gloom, giving us sufficient visibility to allow progress and see the difficulty that lay before us.

I now saw why the waterway was called the River of Ants. The ground seemed alive and moving due to the vast swarms of small red insects that climbed quickly over our boots and into our clothing. They covered the palm fronds in multitudes around us; to brush against a broadleaf would result in a shower of ants. We slapped futilely, cursed, and struggled onward. The little boy seemed unaffected, his face being locked in a purposeful set. Suddenly he stopped and began clawing at the surface of the earth. His hands found the covering boards he sought, and he pulled upward a piece of plastic sheeting and a small wooden platform. Beneath was the circular shape of an upright fifty-five-gallon steel drum. The ants were forgotten as the boy walked about the area uncovering additional drums filled with the tools of war.

It is possible to be opposed to what the enemy stands for and yet admire certain aspects of his ability. I breathed a sigh of admiration for the skill of the men I was fighting against. The drums might well have been brought to Vietnam by the French, or sent by the Russians or Chinese, or taken from some pile of American refuse near a petroleum facility. They were ideal for the purpose. Digging the empty drums into the earth was clever, and the added touch of putting them under swarms of ants was genius. Few soldiers on routine patrol would face the attack of these insects in order to examine the area.

I was disappointed that no mortars were in the drums, but they did contain rifles and automatic rifles, all heavily oiled and wrapped in wax paper prior to being stored. We also uncovered rocket launchers, machine-gun parts, and a large amount of ammunition, including mortar rounds. We emptied each container and divided the material among the troops to carry to Rach Kien town.

Once the drums had been found, Captain Ngi seemed to take no interest in the boy. I made two suggestions to Ngi: that we return by a different route from the area so that local people could not observe our success, and that the boy be brought with us. He agreed. I also suggested that we booby-trap several of the drums. He liked that idea. We left most of the drums uncovered to show that they had been found. One of the drums was rigged to explode a fragmentation grenade when the cover was lifted. We restored the area around this drum to its original appearance. My hope was that the enemy, furious at the loss of weapons, would be careless and in a hurry to check the drum that seemed not to have been found.

I saw the weapons that we had found as an opportunity for

the district to make great strides. This was El Dorado, the wealth of a Spanish treasure galleon and the Lost Dutchman's mine rolled into one. To me, the boy who guided us to them was a hero; he had sacrificed his life at home to help us. I knew the boy could not go back to his hamlet since the VC would certainly kill him. When we brought the boy back to Rach Kien, I bought him clothes and fed him well. I provided the money to allow him to board with a family.

Several team members took an enemy weapon for a souvenir. I had one from Korea and passed on the opportunity. Captain Ray Byers took our captured horde to the supply dumps and got such a wealth of matériel in return that it staggered the imagination. We received vast quantities of supplies and large generators that ensured electric light not only for us, but also for the Vietnamese headquarters and even down into the marketplace. We got medical supplies that enabled us to open two additional dispensaries and staff them with Vietnamese women trained by our district midwife and team medic.

One of the sergeants had returned to the United States on emergency leave. We were anxious to learn about conditions in our homeland. What he told us was not reassuring. Young men at home were openly burning draft cards and carrying the enemy flag. Soldiers, even those wounded in battle, were harassed. Agitators were at work on the college campuses around the country. To use the benefits of freedom earned by others and to be against the effort in Vietnam was to be a campus hero. To run to Canada to escape service was considered a noble act of sacrifice. This was the best news the enemy could have had. Our own people were giving the enemy encouragement. I believed that, as in the Korean War, the majority of American people, if they did not have someone in Vietnam, simply saw it as a distraction. They were concerned with their own self-interest. It was up to the government to do the right thing.

It was impossible for the North Vietnamese military to drive the United States from South Vietnam through battlefield action. It was impossible for the United States to defeat the North Vietnamese when we were not allowed by our own political leaders to go into North Vietnam and crush them. The lessons of Korea had never left me. President Harry Truman had the courage to resist Communism in South Korea, but he was unwilling to risk a larger war in order to run the Chinese back across the Yalu. Now President Johnson had committed us to a war in Vietnam, and again fear of becoming involved in a larger war meant we would not win. People do not learn from the lessons of history. Time and again we make the same mistakes. Why send men to fight a war if you do not intend to win? I could understand why Americans were growing disillusioned. I could not understand why they would support the enemy and mock the Americans who were putting their lives on the line in the service of our country.

I don't know how Ray managed it—I knew better than to ask. He secured sufficient M-16 rifles that we were able to outfit the district troops with weapons that met the enemy on equal terms. He brought back a host of other items, including paint, which allowed us to paint our ammo box huts of "Primont Village" in white with green trim. We got educational materials to help the teachers, a spare radio, and batteries. I had also hoped we could trade for a copy of the movie *Doctor Zhivago,* but we were unable to do so and my ordeal continued.

I went with Ray on another trip. We stopped at the Saigon post exchange to replenish our shaving gear. I was astounded at the wide variety of items people were able to purchase there. It was the only PX I had ever seen where fur coats could be purchased. A generous government had decreed that I did not have to pay income tax on the first five hundred dollars of my salary. Since there was little to purchase in Rach Kien, I had a tape recorder, amplifier and speakers, and a large silver service shipped back to the States. While having a cup of coffee in the snack bar, I swapped experiences with a marine gunnery sergeant. He had used grenade volleys. Instead of one man throwing a grenade, the whole squad threw simultaneously. It would take a good resupply to do this, but would keep the enemy from throwing our grenades back. With ten grenades cooking off, no one could be so coordinated as to throw them all back.

I sat down and was approached by an officer with whom I had served in Germany when we were both majors. He was a graduate of the United States Military Academy at West Point, a superb school that has given the United States many men of outstanding leadership ability. A school that gave us Grant and Lee can be forgiven if it also turns out the occasional dunderhead. These few are men who have the tops of their skulls removed while living by the Hudson, the empty cavity being filled with reinforced concrete. They are the most inflexible of men. When I asked a brigadier general for his opinion of one, he replied, "He would do a good job counting postage stamps." Now and then we lesser mortals meet the rare academy graduate who is a boor but sees himself as a superior being. By their habit of tapping their academy ring on a desk or table when arguing a point, they have earned the appellation of "ring knockers." Not many such men exist, and their numbers seem to be declining. Unfortunately, the officer who joined me was of this ilk.

I don't know why he sat down at my table, as he knew I despised him. In Germany, I had a young first lieutenant working for me who was brilliant. He had a career ahead of him that far exceeded my potential. I was eager to see him remain in the service and did all I could to encourage him. The lieutenant was married to a lovely and well-educated woman who had a variety of interests. The wife of this major interfered with these interests. She wore her husband's rank in her mind and acted as though the wives of junior officers were under her authority. The wife of the lieutenant objected to this treatment and naturally complained to her husband, who complained to me. When I asked this major to have his wife cease her actions, he supported his wife and told me this was the way it was done in the army. I told him this was not the 1870s, and our conversation went downhill from there. The major's wife did not change her ways, and the lieutenant left the service as soon as he could and the couple returned to civilian life. Subsequently, this major and I were at each other's throats until he shipped out, and I took over his job as well as mine. Doing two jobs was commonplace when units in Germany were being gutted in order to send men to Vietnam.

Now this unwanted man was seated across from me, telling me that he was a staff officer at Military Assistance Command, Vietnam (MACV) headquarters. He asked what I was doing and where, and I told him. He replied, "You men in the field don't know how good you have it. I work long hours, and I have to climb seven flights of stairs each night to get to a bedroom that is not air-conditioned." I was stunned. I was looking at an infantry officer graduate of the finest of America's military schools. The odds were overwhelming that he would rise beyond me in the military. I was tired and did not feel like arguing. I gulped my coffee, wished him well, and drove back to Rach Kien.

Returning to the district gave me the feeling of coming home, perhaps more like Santa Claus coming home and bringing the elves more matériel. The materials we had gathered were immediately put to work, and it was pleasurable to know that we could now help the Vietnamese have light where there was darkness, improved medicine, and a better chance of surviving a fight.

The human race has many similarities, but there are differences in culture as wide and deep as an ocean. Flogging had gone out of style in the Western world, but in Asia, discipline, which often seems so lax on the surface, can be swift and terrible. On one occasion Captain Ngi, when angered by the action or inaction of a private soldier, picked up a length of two-by-four and beat the man to his knees. I could not understand their penchant for nepotism. A nephew of a powerful politician or general could be incompetent and yet be protected despite his actions. The lieutenant named Antoine was the obvious example.

I came to learn the intense feeling that Vietnamese have for family. If a man rose to high position, it was his duty to help other members of his family. They were a quiet people, often shy. The children gave more vent to their emotions. One street urchin yelled at me, "Vietnam number one! America number ten!" I had many conversations with Captain Ngi about the differences in our peoples. Ngi told me that all cultures find a way to get incompetence into their system of government. Considering the manner in which American political leadership was fighting this war, I agreed.

We decided that the issuing of new weapons must be done with ceremony. Each man would come forward from the ranks and recognize that he was now being treated as a first-class fighting man, and that his rifle and he would now be as one. Captain Ngi made a short speech, and we began to call the men forward. There is a "rifleman's creed," but none of us could remember it. As the rifles were being handed out, I overheard one sergeant saying an old army rhyme that is usually recited while holding a rifle in one hand and gripping one's crotch with the other, and it goes, "This is my rifle. This is my gun. This is for shooting. This is for fun."

We made a helicopter-borne (heliborne) assault near a village where the enemy was holding another proselytizing session to convert villagers to their cause. They fled as we landed, leaving numerous Russian, Chinese, and North Vietnamese flags hanging about; these added to our store of trading materials. We captured a young man who was known to be the brother of a Viet Cong leader. Under Captain Ngi's orders, the troops beat him viciously. They tied his hands and feet and upended him. Putting his head down in a pond until the man would nearly drown, they questioned him again. I objected and was ignored. This represented one of the difficulties of being an advisor. When their blood was up, the Vietnamese would not listen.

We tend to romanticize American wars, but what I witnessed in Vietnam was no different from many such events in the American Revolution or our Civil War. In Korea, American prisoners had their hands tied behind their backs and were executed, and many North Korean prisoners paid the price for that. War is cruelty and killing. I did not condone torture and wanted no part of it, but there were times when this was a private hatred and payback time between the South and North Vietnamese. Ngi had had members of his family murdered by Communist assassins. If someone tortured and killed my family, I probably would feel the same. I ordered my team members away from the scene, and we moved some distance to smoke our cigarettes until Ngi had finished.

I did not see the buffalo boy around town and asked Major Dong and Captain Ngi his whereabouts. Ngi replied that the boy was lonely for his family and had gone back to his hamlet. I was furious and told Ngi that they had made a terrible mistake, that the enemy would kill the boy. I was stunned to find that they agreed with me. They knew that allowing the boy to return home meant he would be killed, but they did not care. He had served his purpose. They viewed him as a traitor to the enemy cause and, if he had betrayed one side, they felt he would betray the other. Some months later we learned that the Viet Cong had made a horrible example of the boy, killing him with knives in their version of the death of a thousand cuts. I was heartsick. I felt that proper treatment of this boy might have encouraged others to reveal weapons locations. I believed that we had found our one and only cache of enemy weapons. I was right.

19

Tet

In mid-January, the province intelligence officer related indications that the enemy might launch a major attack sometime around the Tet holiday at the end of the month. I told Major Dong and Captain Ngi, but they discounted the possibility. A truce was to be in place during this greatest of Vietnamese celebrations, and they were more concerned with holiday plans. To be with their family at Tet was critical to them. If we were to put all the American holidays together, we might begin to understand what Tet means to a Vietnamese. That is what made it so dangerous when fighting a disciplined bunch of Communists.

I was concerned about Dong and Ngi's head-in-the-sand attitude and requested a meeting to discuss the Vietnamese leave and pass policy for Tet. The South Vietnamese and US commands had established a holiday cease-fire for the thirty-six hours from the evening of 29 January through the early morning of the 31st. The enemy proclaimed a seven-day truce from 27 January to 3 February. Despite the truce, I requested that strong forces be left in the district. Major Dong agreed and said that Captain Ngi would retain 75 percent of our force in the district. The remainder, headed by Major Dong, would spend holiday leave with their families, most of whom lived in Saigon. Voung begged me to allow him to go to see his family and assured me that Lang, the number two interpreter, would be with me. Lang was not fluent in English, but I would have Captain Ngi, who was constantly improving, so I agreed. Ba wanted to go with Voung to see her people, and I agreed. They both left.

On the morning of 29 January, I went to the district administrative office to wish Major Dong a safe trip home. I found him and Captain Ngi packing suitcases into the old district jeep. Both looked uncomfortable when they saw me. It was obvious that Ngi was leaving also, and I asked them pointedly what they were about. Ngi explained that there had been a misunderstanding and that I did not comprehend how important it was for a Vietnamese to be home during Tet. This was a time when the entire family, both the living and the spirits of the dead, gathered together to be as one. It was their responsibility to be with their families at this time and both of them must meet that responsibility. They told me not to worry, that plenty of troops were available whose families were local, and all troops had been informed that I would be in command while they were gone.

I told Ngi that this was bullshit, that they were shirking their responsibilities to their command. They nodded pleasantly and, as they drove off, Ngi called back, "We have much confidence in you." It was obvious that the troops who had family elsewhere were also paying no attention to the orders to stay. They were hiking out of town or riding away on bicycles or three-wheeled Lambrettas. I passed the word to the infantry and artillery, but they had their own perimeters. I spent time with the engineers, and plans were made to defend a joint perimeter with them. I visited artillery and planned defensive fires and worked out a signal-flare system for ground and medical support in the event radio and wire failed. By nightfall I felt that the American advisors and engineers could protect themselves in the event of a ground attack. I could not protect the town. Not enough troops remained for that.

I planned to position most of my team in the command bunker atop the Vietnamese military headquarters, from where we had better observation and communication. Lieutenant Rich Gaschott called from Trach An to inform me that his Vietnamese were also leaving. I ordered Gaschott to bring his team to Rach Kien and told him to be prepared to use the bunker at the rear of the advisor house. I could not find Antoine, but Sergeant Kinh was in the headquarters standing beside the beautiful Kim Trua. Using Lang to interpret as best he could, we did what we could with the limited troops available. As we spoke, a call came in on the Vietnamese radio from the commander of 627 Company. He requested that we fire artillery at VC south of My Le. However, this was insufficient information to bring fire to bear. I radioed the infantry battalion and Province, but they were unaware of friendly troops in that area. I was unable to get through to the advisor of the ARVN 47th Regiment and decided to investigate for myself. It took some rapid and apprehensive driving to get down the lonely and often mined road to My Le.

The moated compound was home and fortress to the members of 627 Regional Force Company. The Hoa Hao were warriors who had fought the French, Viet Minh, and the government of South Vietnam. Ngi told me the Communists had cut off the head of the leader of the Hoa Hao, an act many of the enemy regretted. That explained a curiosity. In the 627 Company area, enemy bodies were frequently found without heads.

The company commander guided me to the southernmost parapet and pointed off in the distance. He could not speak English and did not need to. When he said "VC," I understood. I looked through my field glasses over flat paddy land broken by clumps of vegetation, offering islands of concealment. To the south was the big river, the Song Vam Co Dong. Vegetation was heavier along the waterway, but I saw some open spaces.

Movement was visible, but the details could not be distinguished. From right to left I could see a long line of men moving in a single file along the paddy dikes. The line stretched across the open area and disappeared into the thick growth of vegetation. Whoever they were, they were too distant for me to identify. The captain spoke a single word, accompanying it with a thrust of his hand that indicated the direction this force was moving. "Saigon," he said with assurance.

My PRC-25 radio did not have the range to reach province headquarters, but I was able to relay the message through a sister district. The message returned that there were no reports of friendly or enemy troops in that area. I relayed a message for a helicopter to pick me up for a closer look, and that I believed enemy forces were moving toward Saigon. The return message stated that aircraft were not available. I switched frequencies to the infantry battalion and described what I was seeing. They told me they would try to get an aircraft over the area and try to contact the 47th ARVN Regiment to see if they had troops in the area.

I attempted to make Lang understand that I must be certain these were not South Vietnamese troops. I could not indiscriminately fire artillery on them. I suggested a patrol. The company commander had no intention of exposing his men to the force we were seeing. He said repeatedly, "VC . . . VC." I stayed on the radio, pleading for a helicopter, asking that some troops be sent to check this out. I asked that American forces in Saigon be alerted to this movement. With a distance of only fifteen miles to travel, if it was an enemy force, they could be there quickly. I was unaware of what they hoped to achieve against the powerful American forces there. I had never seen enemy movement of this size, and I knew that for them to move by day was completely out of character. Were they enemy or another South Vietnamese unit wandering through the district? If they were enemy, we could assemble the power to crush them.

Some ten minutes after the tail end of the line of troops crossed the open space, an OH-13 helicopter appeared overhead. We spoke by radio. The observers flew back and forth over the area but saw nothing. Once again I asked that the report be quickly passed up the line. My request was acknowledged. I had the feeling that my apprehensions were not getting through, that the report was not being taken seriously. I sensed that I would never forget that day.

We checked and double-checked our preparations, and I felt we were as ready as we could be. Voung had proven himself time and again; he was a full-fledged member of the team. That gave him the privilege of standing radio watch like the rest of us. But with Voung visiting his family, I decided to let Lang take a turn at radio watch duty. I believed that he now understood sufficient English to alert us in case of a problem.

In the small hours of 31 January 1968, I heard a pounding on my door and an excited voice calling me in both English and Vietnamese. I opened the door and found Lang looking up at me. He screamed, "Major! Major! Good news, good news. VC attack everywhere." I did not find that to be "good news," and it took me some moments to understand that Lang meant "important information." When I realized that, I began to laugh—I did not laugh long. Seconds later the first mortar round exploded nearby. It was a hit-and-run attack of about ten rounds on Rach Kien, but some of the other districts and the province capital were under both mortar and ground attack. It is likely we were spared ground attack because the enemy could not be certain whether the infantry battalion would be in Rach Kien or not. Furious attacks were taking place throughout the country. The next day the infantry battalion moved out and took most of the artillery with it. We were left with one 105-howitzer and crew for support.

That night they were back at us again in the worst shelling I have ever experienced. I heard later that one of their initial rounds landed close to the howitzer crew, taking them out of action. Priority of American fires was going to American units. As I had no supporting artillery or mortars, the enemy had a free hand to work us over, and they did a good job. We ran through a gauntlet of steel for the command bunker on top of the Vietnamese military headquarters. The engineers had a liaison party with me to coordinate our defense. They had also received some additional men and had requested to be allowed to share our protection until their bunkers were complete. These men were under fire for the first time.

This was not just an attack on the military compound. The explosions walked up and down between the streets and houses of the town in a calculated attack on the people. The incredible violence of high explosive was all about us. Shrapnel cut the pole antenna, and we could not communicate with Province. Shells fell like death's rain on and about the advisor house, our bunker, and the Vietnamese military headquarters as one shock followed another. In a momentary lull we could hear the teakettle-like sound of air whistling out of the punctured tires of our vehicles.

Fear is a natural emotion to a man in combat. A man who says he is not afraid is either a liar or a fool. It is not cowardice to be afraid. It is cowardice if a man allows fear to prevent him from doing his duty. Action is the best path from fear. I found it easier to control fear when I was a leader than a follower. In the hard days of training that precede a war, exhausted angry men would sometimes say, "When I get in combat, I'm going to kill that son-of-a-bitch." But when the desperate battle came, they would find themselves asking, "For God's sake, do something to get us out of this." As a leader, I knew I had to find a way to improve whatever circumstance we were in, and that responsibility outweighed the fear.

On this night the fear level was reaching the breaking point among these inexperienced young soldiers. In the darkness, with the thunder of war about them, I could hear them whimpering and I knew they were on the verge of panic. I had to do something.

"Ray?"

"Sir," Captain Byers replied.

"Give me a cigarette."

Ray did so, and I lit it with my Zippo, inhaled the smoke, and choked. "Goddamn it, Ray. You know I only smoke menthols!"

While this conversation was taking place, the young soldiers had fallen silent, eager to fasten their minds on anything that would replace their fear. Now, one of them could not contain himself. "Will you listen to that?" he asked incredulously. "Here we are getting our asses shot off, and that son-of-a-bitch is worried about what kind of cigarettes he smokes!" One of the soldiers laughed, then another; soon we were all laughing and someone started to sing. With the mortar shells bursting around us, we laughed, sang, and told jokes, and after a while the firing stopped. In his own inimitable fashion, Lang told me later that Sergeant Kinh and the Vietnamese downstairs had heard all this chatter and wondered if the Americans were crazy.

We had many repairs to make, but they had to wait as we had a number of townspeople wounded. A form of shock takes over at the sight of women's and children's bodies torn by shrapnel. It is not the shock that immobilizes—there is too much work to be done for that. This is a numbness and, for those of us without intensive medical training, a feeling of futility. We did what we could with bandages, and the team medic and midwives and their assistants worked diligently. We were all cursing, cottonmouthed, headachy, and covered with dust from the shrapnel-torn sandbags. Wherever we looked, people needed our help to repair broken roofs, punctured and leaking sandbags, and damaged vehicles.

We were filthy and the house was a wreck. Men were arguing over the few eggs that remained. We missed Ba terribly. One sergeant commented that he did not give a damn if anyone else came back as long as she did.

At the first opportunity I decided that, even though I had only filthy clothes to put back on, I was going to take a shower. The water system at my place was not operating, so I went into the advisor house, disrobed, and stood under the welcome spray of water. As I lathered my body with soap, mortar rounds hit in the street and behind the advisor house, and the VC attack was resumed. My reaction was instinctive. I jammed a steel helmet on my head, grabbed my weapon, and ran naked and barefoot to the Vietnamese military compound. This attack was brief and of less interest to the Vietnamese than my nudity. I would like to think that what they saw added to my stature in the community. Certainly my golden-red pubic hair fascinated them. This episode did nothing for my own self-respect, as I was not the calm, unruffled commander who set an example for the people. This emperor had no clothes. I don't know why I did not take the time to get dressed, probably because they caught me unaware and my brain momentarily shut down. It did not worry me. Roman gladiators often fought naked. David and Hercules fought their enemies naked. You don't have to have clothes on to fight. I was more concerned with action than embarrassment.

Combat leaders are not demigods. Most leaders give their best, but they are still only men, and in battle they are trying to deal with the most difficult circumstance that can be faced. The responsibility of a chief executive officer of a large corporation is nothing compared to that of an infantry platoon leader in combat. A few times in Vietnam, fatigue and tension shut down my thought processes. I was fortunate in that an infantry colonel, who had fought in the mountains of Italy, taught me that when your officers are staring at you, wondering what you are going to do, and you don't know, you say to them, "What do you recommend?" Someone may come back with a good idea, and even if they don't, it was my experience that just taking that action would jump-start my own thought processes, and I would be back in control.

On 3 February 1968, I began to see a trickle of strangers coming into town. The Vietnamese told me they were refugees from Saigon, and more were beginning to build up in my northernmost town of Trach An. My vehicles were out of action, so I took Sergeant Kinh and Lang for a ride north in a Vietnamese three-wheeled Lambretta. Traffic on the road was heavy, women and children and more men than I was accustomed to seeing walking toward Rach Kien. They were carrying large burdens of personal possessions. Bicycles, handcarts, and even a baby buggy had been pressed into service to carry their belongings. As I entered Trach An, I found myself in a crush of people so great that I could not continue.

I left the vehicle and climbed to the flat roof of a building. At the north end of Trach An, our dirt road joined with Highway 4, the asphalt lifeline that came down from Saigon to the Delta. The sight before my eyes was breathtaking. Coming down Highway 4 was a flood of humanity. Thousands of people were on the move, choking the highway and stretching as far as the eye could see—refugees fleeing the battles at Saigon. I learned later that some six hundred thousand people fled the city. I knew we would be overwhelmed. I remembered from Korea how the North Koreans had clothed their men in civilian garb and passed through our lines among throngs of refugees.

We had seven National Police in Trach An and a Popular Force unit, but at that moment these men were doing nothing. I had Kinh use the Popular Force troops to establish a roadblock at the bridge that led south to Rach Kien. They were told not to allow more refugees to pass the roadblock to Rach Kien until they had been screened for arms and ammunition and questioned. The National Police members were put to work establishing a checkpoint where they would interview people and then pass a portion of those who were true refugees through to Rach Kien. Priority would be given to those who had family or friends in the district. I did not have the means to assist the entire torrent of people pouring down Highway 4, but I could drain off part of the flow of refugees and make it easier for those districts and the province capital farther south. When our part of the task was working, I headed back to Rach Kien to inform Province and my sister districts and to establish a processing center.

The work seemed without end. We established a feeding center to provide the hungry newcomers with food. The team medic and all those we were giving basic first-aid instruction to helped as they could those who were injured. We made arrangements with schoolteachers to brief our newcomers and had the administrator providing shelter. A call to Province brought a helicopter carrying rice, blankets, and medicine. Although the American infantry and artillery were absent, some of their vehicles were left behind. Their rear party cooperated, and we used these vehicles to transport the refugees from Trach An to Rach Kien. I did not allow refugees to be housed in the military compound, but housed them in the town. The marketplace, school, Buddhist temple, and dispensary seemed to spew forth people in a massive regurgitation each time the communal feeding stations were established.

A second screening center was set up, where the police and intelligence interviewed the refugees and we gained useful information. Both sides make mistakes in war. The Communists had just made an error that would cost them dearly in men. They believed they could beat the American army on the ground. In their motivational propaganda, they were so convinced that the battle of Tet would inflict a stinging defeat on American ground forces that men, who for years had shielded their identities, came out from cover and openly proclaimed themselves as Communist leaders. We welcomed this information.

Several days passed while battles raged about the country, but we were not again attacked. As I returned to the advisor house after visiting the dispensary, I saw the district jeep followed by a two-and-a-half-ton truck loaded with rice bags. Captain Ngi and Voung were in the jeep and the Vietnamese military were gathered around. The American advisors only had eyes for the truck. Seated on a rice bag throne was Ba with her cheap, flowered *ao dai*, dusty face, and wind-scattered hair. Her two children were seated primly beside her. The men were cheering and applauding and Ba loved every moment. Her children carried the derelict, string-bound suitcase to their home in the village where she lived at the sufferance of her deceased husband's family. Each day she arose before dawn to care for her young boy and girl, and then worked seven days a week to clean and launder for us.

She went into the house, saw an empty beer can on the floor, and nudged it with her foot as she gave us a look of motherly chastisement. She surveyed the accumulated piles of dirty clothes and dishes with the air of a general surveying the site of an impending battle. She then grabbed her broom. The men cheered.

I secured the first available helicopter and flew with Captain Ngi to Saigon in the hope that we could get Major Dong. Ngi was familiar with the city and knew the suburb where Dong lived. Fighting was going on below us as American infantry mopped up a North Vietnamese unit. We flew too close over the enemy and a stream of tracer bullets appeared beside my door. It was an odd sight, like water from a hose. Very briefly I had the urge to reach out and grab it, but my temporary insanity passed quickly. Unable to land and with nothing useful to contribute, we departed.

We returned to Rach Kien to find that Major Dong had returned and was putting his considerable authority into helping the refugees. I did not lecture Dong and Ngi on what I considered their dereliction of duty. They knew how I felt and probably did not care. I was American and therefore did not understand what Tet meant to a Vietnamese—at least a South Vietnamese.

Several more days passed and fighting in Saigon ended with an American military victory. The whirring blades of a stream of helicopters returned the infantry battalion and the artillery came back down the road. They had been fighting hard but felt the thrill of success. Unlike the Communist leaders who cared little about how many lives victory might cost, American officers were always conscious of reducing casualties. That concern translated into firepower. The enemy was destroyed, but American television news reporters had filmed the action and presented it in the United States as a condemnation of the military for the destruction of private homes. Commanders were criticized for using "undue force." A disgusted captain, sweat-stained and tired, said in bewilderment, "The sons-of-bitches were using those houses to fight from, and we had men getting hit. What do those people back home want from us?"

I was beginning to see the captain's question as the crux of the Vietnam War. What did the American people want of the men they sent to war? Our soldiers went to war because the civilian leaders elected by the American people sent

them. These same leaders effectively tied the hands of our
military by forcing us to fight on the soil of our ally, while
invasion of the enemy homeland was not permitted.

There were complaints in the media about American casualties, yet these were coupled with complaints about the
use of American firepower that reduced the number of those
casualties. It seemed to us that many members of the press
saw the American military in Vietnam as the enemy. We understood that night after night broadcasters were filling the
screens with pictures of American dead. Few cared about
the sweat and blood that was going into attempts to help the
Vietnamese. Few wanted to see the marketplaces, dispensaries, or schools we were constructing. They wanted sensation—they wanted bodies. Those of us who remembered
World War II felt that we would not have seen that war to
victory had members of the American press conducted
themselves as they did in Vietnam. One of America's many
great treasures is freedom of the press. It plays a critical role
in the maintenance of our freedom, but there has to be a separation that can report the failures of the civilian and military leadership without giving assistance to the enemy and
harming the Americans who are fighting. It is a delicate balance. While watching a press seminar, I heard a famed television broadcaster say that if he knew of a military plan in
advance, he would broadcast it, even if it cost American
lives. He felt his duty was "the public's right to know." During World War II he would have been considered a traitor.

The Tet campaign cost the North Vietnamese dearly. Any
military success they had was brief and quickly snuffed, yet
it won them the war. Popular television broadcaster Walter
Cronkite announced that it was time for us to get out of Vietnam, and the decline of American home-front support became an avalanche. Americans who fought in Vietnam
would become the whipping boys for the failures of those
who sent them and those who should have supported them.
Some of the truest words ever spoken are MacArthur's:
"There is no substitute for victory."

Our difficulties were not only with American civilians. We

had brave leaders in the military; we also had military leaders who would sell their souls and their soldiers for advancement. I had a general officer visit Rach Kien with his spiffy horse-holder aide and a civilian delegation that he was seeking to impress. He began to berate me for not having paved the roads. I told him I was more concerned with basic needs, such as food, water, and medicine. I was tired and added I did not give a shit about asphalt. That made him angry. He locked my heels, telling me forcibly that I just did not understand the people or the problem. While he was at it, he took exception to the ballpoint pens that showed in my jacket pocket. When he had demonstrated his rank and impressed the civilians, he boarded his helicopter, treated me to a look of his war face, and flew off, logging some time for his air medal.

The Vietnamese had their share of visiting dignitaries accompanied by their "straphangers," which usually meant a banquet at the district headquarters where my presence was required. I'm a meat and potatoes guy and have no interest in adventure in food. The sight of a Vietnamese table was revolting to the extreme. The secretaries in their colorful *ao dai* dresses would smother me with courteous offers of food. I believed they did it just to watch me gag. I've spent enough time in the Far East to know how to ply chopsticks, and I like rice. I would cover my rice with *nuoc mam* sauce and politely nibble at the rest while wishing the evening would end. I have put my life on the line for my country, but my stomach is my own.

The Vietnamese loved to get us into drinking contests. When I was a young recruit I tried to show off in front of some old sergeants by consuming a vast quantity of beer. I became so ill that I thought, indeed hoped, I would die. From that time I have had a limited ability to consume alcohol. Many people seem to equate a man's ability to put liquor in his stomach with his manliness. Anyone can be a drunk—I chose not to be. The only time I ever took part in and won a drinking contest was when three Americans took on one Vietnamese official. He either did not know or did not care that he was drinking three toasts to our one. It took us a while, but we put him under the table.

At these functions it seemed that everyone to whom I was introduced had the name Nguyen. The Nguyen family must have been sexual fanatics. They were as numerous as grains of rice in Vietnam. We began to call our various items of equipment by that name. We had Nguyen latrine, Nguyen water can, and Nguyen Van sandbag. One night after a mortar attack we were listening to the air whistle out of the shrapnel-punctured jeep tires and one of the sergeants said, "Well, there goes Nguyen Van Jeep again."

The venereal disease rate was up in the battalion, and the commander was demanding that I do something about the whores. The one thing that I knew to do with a whore would have only contributed to the problem, so I limited myself to walking through Tin Pan Alley, showing the flag so to speak. This was ineffective and detrimental to the military courtesy and discipline of the United States Army in Rach Kien District. Military rank is no protection when a man is interrupted at the moment of ejaculating.

Americans have a schizophrenic attitude toward sex. We need it but the other guy doesn't. We believe sex is good for us and bad for other people. It is fine for the people back home, but we must do everything possible to keep the American soldier at war from engaging in sex. Beginning with the initial entry briefing on arrival in country, we heard preaching from on high about celibacy and "keep your hands off the local women." This is contrary to long-established military practice and the rights of man.

Wearying of struggling against the nature of humans, I made an arrangement with the American units and with Major Dong. We opened a district whorehouse with women the Vietnamese selected and who were passed by infantry battalion medics as being free of disease. The key arrangement was that the battalion surgeon would check them frequently to ensure they were risk-free. A woman would be taken off the line and treated if it became necessary. Except for worker salary and unemployment compensation, the whorehouse was a nonprofit charitable organization. Adding a small snack bar with American beer gave the place a touch of class. Though totally unauthorized by higher headquarters, this experiment greatly reduced the rate of venereal disease in Rach Kien. I suppose I could have been court-martialed, but I have no regrets. I think my action sent some healthy men back to the women of America instead of bringing them disease. I could also claim that I satisfied a revolution of rising expectations.

Drugs were beyond my understanding. I grew up in a generation when drugs were not a part of our lives. In the 1940s and 1950s, to smoke a cigarette or sneak a beer was the expression of teenage rebellion. Drugs may have been used by members of my team, but I never saw one of them appear high or unable to do his duty. I had no knowledge of what the commanders of the infantry battalion, artillery, or engineers were experiencing with troop drug use; aside from an occasional casual reference, the subject was not discussed with me.

I was working on the hamlet evaluation survey at the trailer desk when gunshots sounded so close by that I thought it must be a VC assassination squad at work. Grabbing my weapons, I exited and moved cautiously around the side of the trailer. The street was empty, but the locals were staring at a small Vietnamese tearoom that had been built for the military beside my trailer. I heard the thud of boots behind me and knew that other members of the team were coming on fast.

Though no stranger to the sight of wounds and blood, I was horrified at the sight before me. A small table had two glasses of tea on it, and behind that lay Kim-Anh, the intelligence secretary. Shot through the chest, her little body was sprawled beside an overturned chair. Her mouth was open, and flies were already beginning to settle on the blood that stained her sky-blue *ao dai*. A short distance away Sergeant Kinh lay on his left side, his face a mask of blood and brains. Stretching wide in agony, the fingers of his right hand had released the service revolver he had used to shoot himself and the girl he was not allowed to marry.

The team medic quickly checked both bodies. The boy appeared dead, but the girl was still breathing. I told a sergeant to call battalion and request that the surgeon be alerted while another brought a jeep to the scene. I carried Kim-Anh to the jeep, and our medic and I occupied the backseat with him trying to staunch the flow of blood while I cradled her body. Ray Byers carried Sergeant Kinh and held Kinh's body across his lap in the front seat. Traveling at a high rate of speed with the sergeant laying on the horn, we drove through the Vietnamese and battalion areas to the battalion aid station near their helipad. Men of the battalion, who did not know the circumstances, jumped from the roadway, cursing us as we sped by. The girl's blood was soaking into the front of my fatigue jacket. Her face was pale and her breathing labored. As we slid to a halt in front of the aid station, a sudden tremor ran through her small body.

"She's dead," said the medic.

The battalion medical people confirmed the deaths, expressed their condolences, and returned to helping the living. I felt like screaming at people—something had to be done to reverse this horror. I returned to the trailer and sat in solitude while I looked at my hands. They were stained with the blood of two young people whose love had been the hope of sanity in an insane world. Overcome by the futility of it all, I cried.

The rains were falling. Those who have never been in a monsoon land would find it difficult to compare it to that of which Shakespeare wrote, "falleth as the gentle rain from heaven upon the place beneath." The monsoon rain came in blinding torrents. As fresh water was always in short supply, we captured the runoff into a fifty-five-gallon drum under a downspout. I have seen that drum filled in a single rainstorm. Then would come the broiling sun that scorched our skin and the earth. It seemed that within an hour after the rain, the water had drained off and we could walk the dirt street and kick up dust.

The rains could quickly turn quiet streams and rivers into raging torrents. The rice paddies were filled, and the paddy dikes were slick and treacherous to walk on; this was especially difficult on night operations. Silent movement would be interrupted by a splash and a curse, as a foot slipped out from under one of us, who then went into the water-filled paddy. American physical strength became less important than Vietnamese agility. On several occasions, one or more of us would become so mired that the Vietnamese would be compelled to come to our rescue, dragging our exhausted bodies through the mud until we could reach a place to rest.

We had hard intelligence about a VC meeting place and intended to hit them in a predawn attack. They gathered at a hut that could only be reached by fording the River of Ants. The stream did not offer a challenge, as I had waded its knee-to-chest-deep waters on numerous occasions. A reconnaissance indicated that the water could be forded. Shortly after midnight we assembled in the darkness in front of the Vietnamese military headquarters. I had arranged for normal harassing and interdictory fires by the artillery, making certain these would not fall on our line of march. Parked facing west, the infantry had a tracked vehicle that mounted twin 40mm cannon. I arranged for them to fire several times throughout the night parallel to but avoiding our route. Their tracer shells would help me keep track of my location in the darkness and might lull the enemy into thinking we were not patrolling that night.

We moved through our perimeter and headed into the night, walking along the paddy dikes. A heavy rain descended upon us and made travel difficult on the narrow mud dikes. We frequently slipped off, but attempted to limit this to one leg. If a man fell, he would be covered with muck. I slipped and, to save myself from falling prone, jumped into the paddy muck. My interpreter Voung and a sergeant pulled me free. As suddenly as it began, the rain stopped and was replaced by a pale moon whose light glistened on the surface of the water and gave a ghostly appearance to our surroundings.

The paddy dike was easier to see in the moonlight, but the wet surface was slippery and the sound of a man falling was no longer covered by the rain.

We approached the narrow river and found it on the rise and moving rapidly. A powerful Vietnamese swimmer made his way across and affixed a rope to a palm tree on the opposite side. We tied off on our side and made ready to cross. Grabbing me by the sleeve, Voung whispered that he could not swim and felt the current was too strong. My Ranger training and experience had taught me to swim with equipment. Because we had a rope to cling to, I felt I could help him. I instructed Voung to climb on my back and I would walk him over. He did, and in the darkness I stepped into the water with my hand on the rope. At once the current hit me with a force that bowled me over as I lost my grip on the rope. Voung disappeared from my shoulders as I plunged into fast-moving water that was over my head. In a desperation move, I grabbed the leg of someone who fortunately had a grip on the rope. This enabled me to surface and catch the lifeline. Choking and trying to regain my breath, I made my way to the opposite shore. Voung had already arrived. When he left my shoulders, he caught the rope and pulled himself across. He was in better shape than I. I still had my rifle and equipment, but I had lost my map case and eyeglasses. Because of myopic astigmatism, the clarity offered by the moonlight was replaced by a blur.

It was my practice to carry spare eyeglasses, but after many occasions of not needing them, I had grown careless and left them behind. We soon came upon the VC hideout and engaged in battle. I was not effective in this fight since I could not see clearly enough to give direction or contribute fire. We killed some and wounded others without loss to ourselves. I radioed to the advisor house, and a Vietnamese patrol brought me another pair of glasses the following morning. The Vietnamese had generously held their laughter when I was nose to the ground, peering about trying to follow a blood trail.

We searched throughout the morning, but the survivors had made their escape with all weapons. The enemy did their best to move both their wounded and dead with them. When one of their men was killed and they could not take the body, they put themselves at risk to salvage his weapon.

On the march back home we passed through deserted rice paddies and thick palms. As we encountered a little-used road, a motorbike with two passengers sped toward us. The bike was driven by a young Vietnamese man, well dressed in civilian clothes. Riding on the back of the bike was a vivacious young girl with her arms around his waist. When we stopped them, we learned that he was taking the girl to visit her family. Ngi was obviously angry. He told me that the man was a "Saigon cowboy," one of thousands who evaded military service through family connections and bribes. Many were engaged in the black market, drugs, and prostitution. This smirking shirker, I decided, should join the army. When I suggested to Ngi that we draft this young man to military life, he looked surprised and then laughed. He told our men, and they roared approval. Ngi had courage. I am sure he knew that repercussions would abound from this slacker's relatives in Saigon, but he did not hesitate.

When the cowboy understood what was happening, he began to complain loudly and the girl started to cry. With the muzzle of a rifle pointed between his eyes, he was a willing volunteer. He pushed his bike back to Rach Kien. His beautiful girlfriend wept until she saw it was useless. In time he was rescued by family connections, but we had a crack at making a soldier out of him.

I had a serious morale problem. Somewhere, possibly on one of Ray's trips out of the district, a puppy had been obtained. It was a standard issue black-and-white pup who enjoyed pooping on the floor and licking people's faces. The team loved it, and husky men melted when they played with this little fellow. The pup would greet us at the door when we came home from an operation and would frolic about our feet. He disappeared one day, and it did not take a genius to know his fate—he ended up in a Vietnamese cooking pot. The fury of my team members was higher than I had ever seen it. If they could have identified the perpetrator, they would have broken his bones. For a time they wanted nothing to do with our allies.

20

The Roadrunners

A man could die a thousand ways in Vietnam. I felt that one of the most dangerous jobs was done by those who had to clear the roads each day. We learned so many ways that mines or ambush could take their toll. A useful trick for the enemy was to dig a hole in the dirt road. Our people would fill it in. That would happen again and again until one day there would be a mine in the dirt pile or lightly covered over in the hole. The enemy laid mines underneath mines, and mines that could be detonated from some distance off.

I had forgotten about the Roadrunners when a flurry of radio traffic at the infantry battalion caused me to visit them. Their tactical operations center was in an uproar. The word "ambush" was in every conversation. Early in the morning as they did each day, the Reconnaissance Platoon from the battalion had gone out to clear the roads of earthen road-blocks and look for signs of mines. They rode in two or more jeeps with mounted machine guns, a 106-recoilless rifle, also jeep-mounted, and troop-carrying trucks.

The road between Rach Kien and Can Giuoc had recently been opened with the aid of considerable security and engineer bulldozers and graders. The road was a good one that would be of considerable assistance to the people. Therefore it was a target of the enemy. And there the Roadrunners were ambushed and killed. One man had lived long enough to tell the reaction force what happened. The Roadrunners had found a number of palm frond piles across the road, more of a nuisance than something that would block a vehicle. The sides of the road in the area of the ambush looked no more suspicious than any other. The column came upon a place of several mud roadblocks that did not extend the full width of the road. One mud roadblock would come halfway from the left, while a short distance farther on, one would come from the right. This was routine and meant that a vehicle could pass the block by weaving through, but would need to slow down to make the passage.

When the Roadrunners' lead vehicle was performing this slow-motion maneuver, it was struck by a missile fired by an RPG (rocket launcher). The tail-end vehicle was hit in similar fashion, thus trapping the convoy on the road. All the vehicles were immediately taken under automatic weapons fire at close range and the Americans were slaughtered. The enemy swarmed over the vehicles to the point of jumping on the truck beds and firing into the bodies. They stripped the weapons and disappeared. In my view the men should have been off those trucks as soon as the roadblocks were spotted. They also should have checked the sides of the road before entering the roadblock area. They may have done that many times in the past and found nothing, but therein lies the trap. Be patient and wait for the enemy to be careless. It was a classic ambush. Though we hated them, we knew this enemy bunch was a well-trained and disciplined unit.

Periodically I would be called to Tan An to attend meetings with other district senior advisors. Other members of the team had occasional need to visit the province capital. We sometimes went by road, traveling north to intersect with Highway 4, and then traveling southwest over the Song Vam Co Dong at the Ben Luc bridge. We were temporarily inconvenienced when the enemy managed to blow the bridge.

The helicopter was the primary means of long-distance transport, and traveling through the infantry battalion to use their landing pad was time-consuming. My overriding concern was medical evacuation. The memory of the dying engineer remained. On numerous occasions, aid was required for those people whose bodies were torn by shrapnel from mortar attacks. Thanks to the engineers and the efforts of

Ray Byers, we had sand, cement, and reinforcing rod, so we all pitched in to build our own helipad.

The site selected was in a rice paddy behind our advisor house and latrine. The prop wash from the helicopter threatened the peace and concentration of the Vietnamese while they used their stilt-elevated crapper. Captain Ngi passed on complaints from office workers concerning the location of the helipad. I told Ngi that I understood their concern but saw the site of the helipad as advantageous. If a person is squatting to take a shit and a helicopter suddenly appears at the shoulder, the bowels may well be accelerated. I told Ngi it was likely his people would get their bowel movements done rapidly and spend more time at work. He was not amused.

Building the pad was an enjoyable experience. When the first helicopter touched down, I felt a kinship with the great architect Frank Lloyd Wright. It was team pride. No other district had a helipad like Rach Kien. Now the reconnaissance missions, the taxi to province headquarters, the mail, and the movies could arrive at our back door. We were still getting movies, but the threats regarding *Doctor Zhivago* had not diminished. I had the feeling that this correspondence was going to a higher level with my name on it.

On only one occasion was I called to province headquarters in Tan An with the requirement to stay overnight. A big meeting was held that night, with the district advisors and province staff gathered in a social environment. As the night wore on, someone ran into the room and yelled that my mobile assistance team was under attack at Trach An and needed support. An L-19 "Bird Dog" pilot volunteered to fly me to the scene. The L-19 was a light, fixed-wing spotter aircraft with room for one person to squeeze in behind the pilot.

I don't remember this pilot's name, but he was a man of action. A telephone call aroused his mechanic. We ran outside and the pilot jumped into the driver's seat of his jeep while I took the passenger side. We sped to another building and his sleepy-eyed, half-dressed mechanic climbed into the back. He was not settled in his seat before we sped away. The ride through the darkened streets of Tan An was done at a racetrack pace. We hit bumps that sent us flying and then crashing to earth. It took considerable effort on my part to remain in the vehicle. We roared onto the airfield and pulled up beside the aircraft. I then noticed that the mechanic was not with us.

"Where the hell is he?" asked my pilot. Then in answer to his own question he said, "Dumb son-of-a-bitch musta fell off."

He wasted no time getting his aircraft ready. I was stowed behind him and we took off. As an operations officer in Germany, I had frequently been a passenger in L-19s flying to meetings at division headquarters—that was in daylight. Now I was completely out of my element. All I could see was blackness. I was unaware of our location or altitude. "There they are!" yelled the pilot. Looking downward, I saw tracers but could not be certain who was firing them. We made radio contact with my team and began to direct fire. He was a professional at adjusting artillery fire from the air and I was not, so I told him to direct the fire and he did. He did not tell me that he was going to call for flares and, when the first one burst, it appeared to me as a great ball of light directly off our left wingtip. This concerned me greatly and I screamed "Jesus Christ!"—my reaction being of much enjoyment to the pilot. It was a windy night and we were buffeted about the sky, bouncing here and there, while he went happily about his work.

I maintained communication with my team and soon the enemy broke off the attack. The team was safe but I had sincere doubts about my coming through this night alive. It was a rough ride returning to the airfield. We slammed to earth, bounced, and slammed again, then taxied to a halt. I wanted nothing more than to get as far away as possible from that aircraft. "Great flight," said my pilot. "Great flight?" I exploded. "How can you call an experience like that a great flight?" The mechanic was waiting by the jeep and had the lights turned on, which enabled me to see the wry smile of the pilot as he said, "Anytime you walk away after flying in Vietnam, it's a great flight."

Competition is the first law of nature, and it was inevitable that district senior advisors would compete. We lived in separate worlds and saw each other about once a month. However, we always had the desire to brag about our own turf. Most advisors were trying to scrounge what they could, but I had an expert scrounger and had found a weapons cache. That combination made for high living in Rach Kien. Usually once a month a helicopter would make the rounds of the districts to pick up the district senior advisors for a meeting with the province senior advisor. Several of them would be picked up before me, so I showed off by having two of the best-looking Vietnamese secretaries from the district offices accompany me to the aircraft. One would carry my briefcase and the other would shelter me with an umbrella or sweep the path in front of me with a broom.

I became especially close to one other district advisor, a major, who I'll call Joe. That was not his name, but to preserve his marriage I'll call him Joe. We became friends at meetings and sometimes talked on the radio. We had decided to take our R&R together in Australia, as we had heard about the unrestrained living down under and had pent-up desires. The Tet campaign hit just at the time we were scheduled to depart, and our plans for Australia died in the sound of the first explosion. When we finally got to Saigon, we were told that Australia was fully booked. How a continent can be booked was not explained. We were offered the choice of Bangkok, Kuala Lumpur, or Singapore. We went to Singapore because its romanticism was irresistible to me.

We soon found ourselves at the Newton Towers Hotel. Joe had given way to my priority choice of Singapore, so it was only fair that he should determine our schedule. To my consummate disgust, he wanted to eat first. We asked at the desk for names of good restaurants and, armed with that information, found a taxi. The driver did not speak English, but Joe spoke slowly and loudly and was satisfied that his directions were being understood. We headed toward the waterfront and soon arrived at a large, disreputable-looking structure on a derelict street.

Joe said, "This is not a restaurant." I explained to Joe that some of the finest restaurants in the world are found in mundane surroundings. We were met at the door by one of the most vicious-looking men I have ever seen. He was Chinese, with a powerful build. Nude from the waist up, his face and body were scarred with what appeared to be knife slashes. Joe said, "This is not a restaurant."

The Chinese doorman ushered us to chairs, clapped his hands, and an ancient crone appeared with two cups of tea. There was an open space before us, and at a sign from the Chinese several women appeared and began to simper and make suggestive gestures. Joe said, "I told you this was not a restaurant." Alarmed at our lack of response, the villainous-looking Chinese clapped his hands again and again. I counted thirty-eight women before us. They were tall, short, slender, and fat, in a variety of races. The only things they had in common were their sex and that they fit the country expression "rode hard and hung up wet."

When he saw we were not interested, the Chinese snarled something and the women disappeared. The doorman then indicated that he would like us to accompany him. Joe protested, but his curiosity was as great as mine, and we entered into a hallway. There we saw cubicles for the women on either side of the hall, and outside of each cubicle were shoes. An aircraft carrier of the US Navy was in port, and the sailors' shoes formed a long black line outside the cubicles.

The Chinese was disappointed that this demonstration of his establishment's popularity left us unmoved. We went outside and found the cab waiting. Joe talked to the driver at some length, again using sign language to indicate that he wanted to eat. We stopped at two additional places but did not leave the cab. Seeing that we were Americans, the driver was convinced that our first priority was to get laid. He obviously felt it was un-American to think otherwise. At length we threw some money at him and left the cab. He did not take this gracefully and we were roundly cursed in Chinese. We responded in English, telling him to "F-off," advancing with threatening gestures. He began to yell at the top of his lungs and one of the words was in English . . . "Police!"

Not desiring to spend our R&R incarcerated in a Singapore slammer, Joe and I beat a hasty retreat. We ended up in a restaurant that Joe enjoyed; I thought it was a horrible meal. I began to be concerned that I'd made a bad choice of R&R partners. Joe had a goal in life of building a beautiful boat and sailing the world. He had refined this goal to the last dollar, and each time he spent money he complained that it was taking something away from his dream boat.

We returned to the Newton Towers in time to be part of the medically controlled evening lineup—the men on one side of the room and the women on the other. A small Australian soldier with red hair was unable to contain himself at the sight of all these women. He ran to and fro spouting an endless stream of excitement. The girls loved it. They all wanted to take him to bed.

Joe chose a dusky Indian woman who had striking features. When he paid the mamma-san, I heard him say, "There goes my air conditioner." I did not see the one I was looking for until I glanced into a side room. I got a glimpse of someone very attractive who dived behind a bed to hide from me. When I walked around the bed I saw a beautiful Chinese woman shaking her head, saying, "Not me!" Of course, that was the girl I chose. I laughed when I heard her name; it was "Lucy Er." She spoke excellent English and was skilled at her profession.

Lucy was a perfect companion for a man from war. We spent five nights together. Like a glass of water to a thirsty man, she satisfied a basic need. She was at times romantic, often hilarious, and frequently wild.

I enjoy meeting people who have gone beneath the surface of life. We talked for hours and I was impelled to ask her story. She said she was raised in a medium-income traditional Chinese family but fell in love with a British soldier and had a child by him out of wedlock. That combination ended her relationship with her family. In time the British soldier shipped out for "Old Blighty" with the usual promises, likely meant at the time, that he would send for her. But once back home in his own culture, the British soldier ceased to write. A young woman with no particular skill, adrift from her family, with a child and without a man, she went into the trade. She related that her young child was the keystone of her life. She talked at great length about the love this child had for teddy bears.

By day Joe and I toured the museums and wandered about the city. It was not long before we decided to find a golf course. As we left the taxi, we were surrounded by several dozen young boys, each insisting that we select him as a caddie. An oriental man appeared with a golf club handle and began to beat them while Joe and I stood watching in openmouthed astonishment. As the boys fled, the man announced in flawless English that he was the "caddie master" and would choose the best caddies for us. It cost twenty-five cents for a caddie.

Golf is golf and things seemed familiar as we rented clubs and shoes and began to play. On the sixth hole I was preparing to drive the ball when my caddie protested, warning me that there was a foursome of women to our front. I saw them as a long distance off and assured him that I could never hit a ball that far. I proceeded to hit the best drive I have ever hit in my life. It would have traveled at least 275 yards, if not for that woman who stopped it with the middle of her back. We hurried forward amidst cries of outrage and pain. I learned that the lady golfers were wives of British officers. They were not very ladylike and had a powerful command of expletives. At the conclusion of their "ugly American" remarks, they insisted that we play through. Without their interference the round was completed in a timely fashion.

We had dinner with our two girls and I learned the story of Joe's companion. She had been raised in a riverside village in India. One day raiders came by boat and abducted young girls to be sold into prostitution. She was taken to

Singapore and made a whore. She told her story in a matter-of-fact tone without complaint or hope of change. To be a whore was kismet, her destiny. She lived for the moment. A soldier in war could understand that story.

In the gift shop of the hotel I found a large and expensive teddy bear and purchased it for Lucy's daughter. I gave it to her on our last night together and she thanked me profusely, telling me it would make her child very happy. The next morning we said our good-byes. As I checked out of the hotel I happened to glance through the glass partition of the gift shop. Lucy was there handing the teddy bear to the Malay clerk. The clerk put the stuffed animal back on a display shelf, went to the cash register, withdrew money, and gave it to Lucy.

I came back from R&R to learn that in my absence Ron Nelson had had a very close call. Ron was inclined to downplay his effort, but other members of the team told me this aggressive and courageous officer had begun taking a couple of Vietnamese whom he trusted and going hunting at night. They would set off after dark and do reconnaissance to determine the location and actions of the enemy. The enemy took exception to this, and Ron and his duo found themselves being hotly pursued. Team members told me they were able to call in a chopper, but the fire was heavy and when Ron got his men on board the helicopter had to get moving. Ron came out hanging on a collapsible ladder. Ron would not confirm this to me, but others were certain it happened. Ron was inclined to stay ahead of the enemy in thinking, and he may have been angry at himself for nearly becoming a corpse.

The radio call came in the early morning, and it took some moments for me to recognize its source. The battalion commander of the infantry based in Rach Kien was on an operation and calling me from his helicopter. The battalion commander inquired if I had any elephants in my district. I replied that I had never seen nor heard of elephants in my area. A half hour passed and the radio crackled again. The battalion commander said they had contact and were driving a Viet Cong force westward before him. He offered to provide the helicopters if my district forces would be willing to insert to cut off the enemy escape route. I agreed and hurried to get Captain Ngi to round up 555 Company, the PRU, and Popular Force. Every advisor except one on base radio watch would participate. We made rapid plans on the disposition of our troops. The enemy could evade in the direction of My Le, so I requested that Ngi move 627 Company out of their compound and into a blocking position.

I was surprised and gratified when Major Dong said he intended to accompany us. It was rare for him to participate in combat operations. I did not doubt his courage. I had come to know and respect him as a quiet man who was trying to make life better for his people. Ngi was a proven military leader, and Major Dong's administrative efforts to improve the district seemed to be bearing fruit.

R&R was behind me and I was back at work. The command and control (C&C) Huey came in. Dong, Ngi, and I took off with our radio operators. I put on a headset to communicate with the pilot. Below me, I could see the Huey troop carriers, called "slicks," picking up the troops. I gave the pilot his direction, and the nose of the ship turned south. We were heading for the southern part of Rach Kien District where the Song Vam Co Dong formed our border. This was an area filled with streams and thick vegetation that made it difficult to maneuver and gave the enemy excellent cover and concealment.

We came in quickly without gunship support, but there was no enemy contact on the landing zone. We could see gunships in the distance supporting the infantry advance. The terrain was such that we needed to drive toward the Americans before establishing a blocking position. We had not traveled far when we began to flush Viet Cong, and the firing began. They were trapped, with the Song Vam Co Dong on one flank and open paddy fields on another. Some tried to escape by swimming the river, but they were easily eliminated. The rest were caught between the jaws of our pincers. We needed to clear a densely vegetated area before arriving at the stream that would mark our blocking position. With security ahead, Dong, Ngi, and I were traveling together on a path through thick vegetation. The trail turned frequently to bypass water areas where thick stands of bamboo made excellent places of concealment. The enemy frequently used waterways as hiding places or as a means of escape. We did not have the concussion grenades or gasoline that Americans sometimes used against the underwater enemy. Frequently our people went into the water after them. I wanted to search these areas and paused when I believed I saw a bamboo breathing tube projecting above the water. When trapped in water areas, the enemy was known to go below the surface of the water and breathe through lengths of bamboo or reed. When I stopped, Dong and Ngi hurried on.

Handing my rifle to my radio operator, I went into the water carrying a .45-caliber pistol in one hand and a knife in the other. The object that I had presumed to be a breathing tube had disappeared among the stands of bamboo. I searched in dark, chest-deep water without finding my man. He had been there. I located a tightly tied plastic bag secreted among the bamboo. I took the bag and waded back to my entry point, where I threw the plastic bag onto the bank. While I was getting out of the water, several Vietnamese tore the bag open and took the money they found therein. The bag also contained identification papers, some photographs, a crude knife and belt, and a small bottle made into a pocket-sized kerosene lamp. As I was examining these, a shot rang out farther along the trail. The shot was immediately followed by excited shouts in Vietnamese. One of my men hurried back along the trail and told me, "They shot Major Dong."

I ran forward to find Ngi and several Vietnamese beside the body. Ngi was trying desperately to restore life, but his grief told me there was no hope. I pushed closer and saw that Dong had been shot through the head. He was dead when he hit the ground. Ngi directed several soldiers to pick up and move the body to an open area. He then got to his feet and moved on. I tried to speak to him on several occasions, but he had only one purpose in mind. We did not stop until radio communication with the Americans informed me that we were moving into killing range of each other. Then we waited while a grim-faced Captain Ngi received reports from the Vietnamese.

When we could see Americans on the other bank, Ngi signaled his men and we moved northward to an area of open rice paddy for helicopter pickup. I don't know how many the Americans killed or captured. We had thirty-three Viet Cong, about half of that number in dead bodies and the remainder as prisoners. Captain Ngi personally supervised a group of wet and miserable-looking enemy who were under heavy guard.

Major Phan Van Dong was the only man we lost that day, but his death was a disaster for Rach Kien District. I could not understand what had happened. No one could tell me the origin of the shot. One man killed by a single shot? It sounded to me like a traitor was in our midst, an assassin who wore the South Vietnamese uniform and bided his time until the major exposed himself to battle. If Ngi suspected this, he would not tell me.

That evening we stood in front of the Vietnamese military headquarters talking about Major Dong and the funeral arrangements. An outgoing patrol from the 39th Infantry had come down from battalion and the men were making their final checks before going out. They were laughing among themselves, and I could see the impact on Captain Ngi. I shouted at them to be quiet and someone gave me a retort. The patrol leader told his men to be quiet and said, "Major Black's friend, Major Dong, was killed today." One of the men responded, "Hell, I've lost friends, too." But they sobered and Ngi thanked me.

The thought crossed my mind that Captain Ngi had killed Dong or had it done, but that thought did not stand inspection. Dong and Ngi were friends, worked well together, and had mutual respect. Even more telling was that Captain Ngi had nothing to gain by the death of Major Dong. Ngi was a political outcast. He was not going to get promoted. The wheels of the Vietnamese administration ground slowly, and for a brief time Ngi would be the only man I could work with. I knew someone else would come in, someone who pleased the politicians even if he was not worth a damn as a leader of men.

Ngi and I traveled to Saigon for the funeral of Major Phan Van Dong. A long line of mourners passed by a large photograph of the deceased. He would rest in an old cemetery that had trees and rows of markers where many soldiers were buried. Among the tombstones, some read "Mort Pour France" (died for France). I tossed the traditional handful of earth onto the coffin and saluted the passing of a man who had become a friend.

Back at Rach Kien, Captain Ngi did not move into the office of the district chief. He retained his simple desk in the military headquarters. An English-language copy of *Time* magazine usually lay on top of his desk, which he read from cover to cover. We attempted to keep up the pressure on the enemy, but Ngi seemed to be the lightning rod for Vietnamese displeasure. Now it was even harder to get supplies and other support from the Vietnamese at the province level. The team had a lethargy that was difficult to overcome.

I had to be wary of sudden unannounced visits from the American power structure or congressional tourists. One of these visits could ruin my day. One day I had a visit that had the potential for disaster. It involved my MAT (Mobile Advisory Team), headed by Lt. Rich Gaschott. The team was stationed at Trach An in the northern part of Rach Kien District, but living conditions there were beneath primitive standards. From time to time I would allow them to come down to Rach Kien for a shower and a decent meal and a movie. Since they knew their own schedule, I left it up to Rich Gaschott as to when he wanted to bring his team in.

In Vietnam we had a controversial figure named John Paul Vann. Vann had been a soldier, indeed a Ranger. He was the second company commander of the 8th Army Ranger Company in Korea. He came to Vietnam in 1962. As a lieutenant colonel he was senior advisor to the Vietnamese 7th

Division in the Mekong Delta. Vann spoke his mind, not always a healthy practice in the army. Critical of the Vietnamese performance and the American effort to assist them, he resigned from the army in 1964, then returned to Vietnam in a civilian capacity. Vann had power, carrying the authority of at least a major general and perhaps higher. I understood that in 1968 he was the equivalent of a three-star general and was ruthless in his dealings with those who incurred his disfavor.

I was making my rounds when Vann, in his LOH (light observation helicopter), suddenly landed on our district helipad. I hurried to report, briefed him on the district, and walked him around the town and perimeter, showing him the military situation and the efforts we had made to improve the life of the people. We were walking up the dirt street toward the advisor house when he said, "You have a MATs team in Trach An, don't you?" I replied that I did. "Let's go visit them," said Vann.

At that moment I saw Lieutenant Gaschott step out of a house wearing shower shoes and carrying a towel. My military career and its sudden demise flashed before my eyes. I had the distinct feeling that Vann had stopped at Trach An and knew they were not there. I was opening my mouth to stammer something when Vann's helicopter pilot ran toward us. "They want you in Saigon right away," he said. John Paul Vann gave me a baleful look. "I'll get you next time, Black," he said. I smiled and saluted, treating myself to a gloating thought: "The hell you will, mister." I had things I wanted to accomplish in Rach Kien and getting fired would not help. It had been close, but I never sweat the close ones. John Paul Vann did not return; he was killed in a helicopter crash in June 1972.

We continued in search of the enemy, coming in by foot, by air, and even by water, traveling the small streams on the boats of our fishermen. We did not make a habit of small-stream boating, which would have been asking to be ambushed. This was utilized only on rare occasions in the hope of surprising the enemy.

These operations had convinced me that the enemy was

building up forces in the far west of my district. One enemy area was near enough to the Song Vam Co Dong to facilitate transportation, yet far enough to give early warning in the event of attack by our riverine forces. They could also forage from the local farmers because it was close to farmland. This area was thickly vegetated and provided good cover and concealment. I had a gut feeling that someone was in there and in significant numbers. The province S-2 (intelligence officer) continued to assure me that there were no NVA (North Vietnamese Army) in Rach Kien District.

I recommended to Dai Ui Ngi that we launch a heliborne assault on the area using all district forces. He agreed, and I set about selecting a date and time and requesting the transport helicopters. I requested that Captain Ngi take every man we could spare, including 555 and 627 Regional Force Companies, the Popular Force, and the Provisional Reconnaissance. All advisors except the base station radio watch would accompany. We now had M-16 rifles for all the advisors and most of the Vietnamese. The powerfully built Sergeant Surbaugh carried an M-79 grenade launcher and the PRC-25 radio. Our machine guns were still of World War II vintage.

All of us carried fragmentation hand grenades and, for tunnels, some of us now had concussion grenades. The advisors carried at least four grenades each in addition to a mix of smoke grenades to signal in the helicopters. Most of us also carried knives and pistols and two canteens.

The helicopters were approved to take us to the objective area and bring us home. There would be no transport helicopter support at any other time. However, we would be able to call for medical evacuation assistance and, depending on availability, some gunship support. I spent much time with the artillery, who agreed to lend me a spare captain who would serve as forward observer. Having an artillery expert at hand was a luxury and a considerable comfort to me.

No infantryman likes to spend all his time sitting in a hole in the earth. Because the enemy had no indication that anyone was coming into the area, I believed that the enemy troops in the objective area would be screened from view by the palms, but would be out of the fighting pits cleaning weapons, making plans, talking with friends, eating, and answering the call of nature. They would be exposed to sudden attack. Just before our helicopters came into their view, I wanted to hit them with an artillery time on target (TOT). High explosives using variable time fuses and bursting at a height of twenty meters above the ground would slaughter anyone in the area. The artillery captain agreed. He would coordinate the fires, go over the map locations, and work out the procedures. I learned from artillery that this captain would not stay with me on the ground but would fly out and back on the command ship. Although disappointed, I felt that he would be of significant assistance. I requested all available artillery in one powerful strike and told him the area I wanted covered.

I had planned on calling for American assistance in the event that things got out of control. I was disappointed to learn that the battalion of the 39th Infantry was moving on that day to another location and would not be available. I understood that the 3d and 1st Brigades of the 9th Infantry Division were changing sites. It was rare to be able to get enough helicopters to move our three hundred Vietnamese, and I would not give up the opportunity. The battalion intelligence officer told me that enemy units were dispersing over wide areas to avoid being surrounded. To be effective, the Communists needed to bring their men together. I believed that their excellent intelligence would have determined that the Americans would be occupied elsewhere and they would use this time. I now felt it all the more likely that we were in for a fight, but I counted on getting in the first punch with artillery.

Ngi and I instituted strict security measures, with only a few Americans and Vietnamese being aware of the objective area. We tested-fired weapons, checked all equipment, secured spare batteries for the radios, and rehearsed helicopter boarding procedures.

Up from the ranks, I knew the experience of both the

enlisted man and the officer in war. In my opinion it is better to be an officer. The responsibility is present, but in most cases there is a greater opportunity for imagination and to influence events. I enjoyed picking up my weapon and stepping out in the street before the ranks of troops. It was a thrill to lead them. The wearing of an officer's insignia of rank does not make him something beyond a man. Infantry war is a walk in hell and it is done by men, not gods. We all suffer the bitter taste of fear, the nagging doubts, the lapses of memory, mind-bending exhaustion, the thousand shocks that an infantry leader is heir to. Ordinary men must deal with extraordinary events.

With operational briefings and checks complete, we waited for the dawn of another day in Vietnam. I felt I had done all I could to be ready and had a good night's sleep. With the morning sun, we strapped on equipment, picked up our weapons, and went off to work. The command and control ship came in first and picked a group that included Sergeant Surbaugh, the artillery captain, Captain Ngi, myself, and others of our command group. We lifted off, and I treated myself to the exciting view of the gaggle of helicopters landing in trail formation and the troops running to board them. We swung away with my attention given to communicating with the pilot and artillery observer. The timing of these insertions is critical, with little room for mishap.

"Fire the time on target," I instructed the artillery captain.

"Where?" he responded, looking frantically at his map.

His question left me aghast. All the planning and coordination, all the assurances, and now when we are airborne en route to the objective, he was lost.

"Where?" I yelled at him. "What the hell do you mean, where? Fire where we planned. Fire there." I jammed my finger at the objective area circled on the map. He looked at the map, looked out the door of the helicopter at the ground beneath, and then back at the map again. He was totally confused and disoriented.

"I don't know where!" he cried in a shaken voice.

"We don't have time for this. They're coming in," said the pilot. I could see the stream of troop carriers coming in behind us.

"Land them," I said.

We stayed aloft while the line of helicopters descended, landing in disused open paddy areas far enough from the objective to protect the helicopters from ambush. Usually we heard the sound of suppressive gunfire, but I have no recollection of gunships accompanying us on this mission.

Our command and control ship swept in for a landing and we jumped to the ground. The artillery officer remained in his seat. In a backward glance, our eyes met. His face filled with a look of shame. He lowered his head as they flew away. Now the roar of the helicopters dissipated in the distance. We were on our own but we were not alone.

Sergeant Surbaugh handed me the radio hand mike. Lieutenant Gaschott told me that men in brown uniforms and wearing pith helmets were in the tree line of the objective area. They were waving to our Vietnamese to come forward.

Other reports began to emerge from our Vietnamese. Ngi had a stony expression on his face. "They are North Vietnamese Army," he said. We compared reports and came to the conclusion that we were facing a confident force of considerable size. They knew it was Vietnamese that had landed, could count the troop carriers, and knew their capacity. The enemy was aware of the number of men we had and were not concerned. That concerned me.

I called Province and the S-2 came on the radio. I said, "I am in contact with an NVA battalion," and gave the map coordinates of the enemy position. The S-2 responded, "There are no NVA in your district." We had words, and there were assurances that assistance would be sought.

I called the 39th Infantry, but they were moving and did not acknowledge. Ngi tried the 47th ARVN, but they were occupied elsewhere. Our district forces were not designed to fight big battalions, but we could not just sit there. It was rare in Vietnam to know where the enemy was. I was aware that they would expect a pile-on of larger American or Vietnamese forces. Unless we held them there, they would vanish. So we attacked.

As we moved toward the heavily vegetated objective we crossed an open paddy. The periodic dikes would afford some protection, but we were exposed. I was not concerned since we were at long range. But as we closed, I was keenly aware of a parcel of unfarmed and heavily overgrown land that pointed at us like a finger. To continue moving as we were would place that finger of land on our right flank. The enemy held their fire, and I believed they did it for a good reason. They had chosen their ground carefully, and I suspected an L-shaped ambush. If we continued to move toward their line in the trees, they would allow us to get close and then take us under fire from the front and from our right flank. Though they were Vietnamese troops, Captain Ngi trusted my judgment. Ngi agreed with my analysis and we shifted our approach so that our line of attack would move up the finger of land. I had no intention of letting that piece of terrain be on our flank.

I called artillery, and gobs of vegetation and mud began to fly from the objective area, but this did not last long. The gunners were called upon to support someone else who had a higher priority than advisors. Just before reaching the tip of the finger, I halted our line, dropped them into firing positions behind a thick paddy dike, and instructed them to fire on the finger and the tree line. This is a technique called "reconnaissance by fire." By shooting at the area where you believe he might be, you encourage the enemy to return fire and reveal where he is. Recognizing that his ambush had failed, the enemy returned fire and the battle was joined. The air was filled with the roar of our rifles and the whiplash sound of bullets cracking by our heads.

We attacked directly up the finger of land, with the PRU and some of the Regional Force troops conducting themselves bravely. The enemy was well dug in and we took casualties. The Vietnamese *bac-si* (medic) was scarcely five feet tall and appeared to weigh less than a hundred pounds, but he was a man of courage. Time and again he sprinted into the open to assist wounded men.

While this attack was in progress, I attempted to flank the enemy position. I asked Ngi to send one Regional Force company to the left, swing wide of the enemy position, and strike them from the side. Ngi agreed and sent 555 Company under the command of the shifty little rat Antoine. I sent Lieutenant Gaschott and his MATs team to accompany them.

The action continued on our front, but we could not break through to reach the tree line by way of the finger. It is not the job of the soldier to die for his country, but to kill the enemy. I would not order men to attack over the open paddy in order to reach that tree line where the enemy was dug in. I was content to keep them in contact, holding them in position until the word spread and our powerful forces arrived. We kept them occupied while the hours passed by.

A burst of fire from the left flank told me that 555 Company had made contact. Most of the fire was the distinct sound of the Russian-made AK-47. I knew things were not going well. Lieutenant Gaschott radioed to me that Antoine had been careless in his movement and 555 Company had been hit hard. They were withdrawing and would rejoin the men with me.

The day wore on, with lulls and periods of artillery support and heavy firing. I felt that the enemy's position was worse than ours. To attack us he had to cross open terrain. We would have liked that target. Holding him there, we were like leeches, and he must have been aware that having his position known would be a disaster. An L-19 observation aircraft came overhead. The pilot looked over the situation and informed us that help would be forthcoming. I was happy to see him, since he was another tool to keep the enemy from breaking contact. He could not flee while the eyes in the sky were upon him. It was clear in radio traffic with Province that efforts were being made to provide assistance. Tension, battle fear, adrenaline pumping, and heat combined into exhaustion.

Province informed me that the helicopters that brought us in were needed for another operation, and we would have to be withdrawn. Surbaugh told me the L-19 had called for assistance. A Vietnamese fighter-bomber was en route and asked if I wanted an air strike. I did, but not at that moment. We were too close to the enemy to risk being bombed, but it was an excellent tool for breaking contact. We made one final effort on the finger of land to cover our intent. I was dragging a wounded Vietnamese to safety, and as we began to break free, Sergeant Surbaugh called in the fighter-bomber. We cleared the area as several five-hundred-pound bombs landed on the enemy position.

The next task was to move our people onto the helicopters, giving priority to the wounded, and then rounding up stragglers. After each aircraft was loaded, it lifted off and flew toward Rach Kien town. I had extracted all but approximately sixty men when a young American, a member of the MATs team, came to me with disturbing news. I remember him as PFC Aberly and believe he was from Ohio. He was a man of courage and an outstanding soldier. Aberly related that when Antoine had led 555 Company into ambush on the left flank, he had fled, leaving dead men behind and live men trapped. It is always best to bring back the bodies of men killed in action, but I did not believe that it was good policy to have additional men killed for a dead body. But the news that men were left behind who were still alive changed everything.

No commander worth the title would leave a fellow soldier trapped by the enemy if there were the slightest chance they could be brought out. Although my force was scant and had not been able to make a serious dent in the positions of this enemy unit, it seemed unlikely that I could achieve anything—but I had to try. Aberly said he knew where the men were trapped and could lead me to the area. Captain Ngi, who was beside me, agreed that we had to try. He explained this to the remaining Vietnamese, who looked at him numbly, obviously wishing they were on an earlier helicopter. Only a handful of Americans remained, but they knew what had to be done. My strange mix of fear and adrenaline became determination. I jumped on a paddy dike, waved my rifle in the air, and shouted, "Come on! Come on!" The Americans and Captain Ngi immediately started forward. The remainder of the Vietnamese stood silent with quizzical looks on their faces.

Suddenly the realization came home that I had spoken in English. These men did not speak my language. The words I had yelled sounded very similar to other words in Vietnamese. To their ears it seemed that this wild-eyed American was waving his rifle and yelling, "Thank you! Thank you!" It was all part of working in a strange land, fighting alongside, and, indeed, trying to influence men whose language I did not speak and whose customs were different from mine.

Uttering a strangled curse, I followed Aberly. We went in search of our lost men. Though a young man, Aberly had the wisdom of an old soldier. We followed a tortuous route that took us as close to the enemy position as possible. We waded in a ditch of waist-high water and muck that made movement difficult. We crawled on our bellies, trying to pick whatever concealment and cover we could find. Going beyond tiredness, we proceeded until I could see the bodies of our soldiers. I suspected and hoped that some of them were feigning death. As we started to move forward, bullets began to crack the air around us.

Two helicopters arrived on the scene. Sergeant Surbaugh handed me the radio handset and I directed them on the enemy position. They were not Cobra gunships, but they did carry rockets and side door machine guns. While they swept in firing, I moved our people forward. Glancing back at the men, I saw that most of the Vietnamese had lingered behind. At least a hundred yards back a man's face peeked around a palm tree, and the others were out of sight. I had fifteen men remaining, including all the Americans, Captain Ngi, a few PRU, and a couple from Regional Force. Our little Vietnamese medic was among that number.

Now a man raised his hand and other stragglers came crawling toward us. As I recall there were about six, and we hurried them behind us. One of the helicopters swerved suddenly and veered away. A pilot radioed that crew members were hit and bleeding badly, so they headed for a hospital. Another helicopter arrived from Province. I heard the familiar voice of Lt. Col. Bob Gilbert, who served as gunfighter for the province. By radio I gave him the azimuth to the enemy, and his lone helicopter swept forward firing.

I attempted to get to my feet and collapsed facedown in the mud. I was beyond exhaustion and so were the others. It was probably only seconds, but it seemed an eternity that I lay there pressed into the mud. I had to get up. I had to keep going. I will never understand why it happened, what fate directed it, but words came into my mind that have long been the guidepost of an American Ranger, "It is all in the heart and the mind . . . you can accomplish anything. It is all in the heart and the mind." I arose and the men followed. Bodies were sprawled about. Men had died in running positions. Some still wore the look of terror on their faces. Several of the trapped men came toward me. I remember Aberly, Surbaugh, and Ngi firing nearby.

Satisfied that no other men were alive, we broke contact, crawling free of enemy fire. Overhead, Bob Gilbert and his helicopter crew continued firing and survived several more passes. As we broke free, Lieutenant Colonel Gilbert brought in additional helicopters to take us home.

It was a sad night in our little town. This was war where the bad news comes when the man does not step from the helicopter. Wives were wailing, and children and family members were shrieking their grief at the loss of their men. Ngi told me his seniors would be launching an investigation. He knew that the heat would fall on him, not the politically protected Antoine, whose carelessness had caused the death of the men. To my chain of command, I praised Ngi and recommended him for a Bronze Star. I condemned the little scumbag Antoine, whom I despised. We were able to save

Ngi's job, but he had no influence with his seniors. No one touched Antoine.

I threw myself on my bunk and promptly fell asleep. Sometime later, I awoke to find my body acting strangely. I was on my back, and my right leg was raised in the air and shaking violently. It is a strange experience to have a leg acting independently of the rest of your body. It lasted for about fifteen minutes and I wondered if I was going to spend the rest of my life with a leg that had the shakes. It then stopped shaking and has been calm to this day.

Though I did not have the force to destroy the North Vietnamese battalion, my big brother did. The next day American infantry caught the enemy trying to get away and devastated them. It seemed to me that the North Vietnamese had hoped our district troops would walk into their ambush. They would dispose of us and be on their way. Instead they found themselves in a pitched battle and held longer in the area than they wanted to be.

By 1968 the enemy tactic of going back to the site of a battle was well known. This time no one was there when we returned. We recovered the bodies of our Vietnamese, and I explored the positions the enemy had occupied while fighting. Unlike us, they had been able to evacuate their dead from this battlefield. Bloody bandages and broken equipment showed that they had been hurt. Some documents were found; these along with letters and diaries found throughout South Vietnam revealed an enemy that was often lonely and frightened.

The men from North Vietnam were strangers to the area. They were not accustomed to the environment of South Vietnam and the people, who often looked upon them as foreigners. Few spoke the same dialect as was spoken in the South. Their health often suffered and, when possible, locals overcharged them just as they did the Americans. I found a bloodstained NVA pith helmet that showed the penetration of shrapnel. On the inside the former owner had scratched his name and a date several months prior. This helmet and flags captured on a previous mission would be destined for the Airborne and Special Operations Museum at Fort Bragg.

A sergeant from the 39th Infantry who came with us was excited by the evidence that our enemy had been hit hard. He cursed them as gooks and slopes. Most American soldiers thought the Vietnamese all looked alike. As advisors who lived and worked beside the Vietnamese, we knew them as individuals. When we talked about the enemy he was "Charlie," "VC," "gook," or "slope." The terms gook and slope had been used in Korea as generic descriptions of orientals and were carried over to the next war. Colorful nicknames for the opposition have been used since warfare began. When fighting the British our ancestors called them "lobsterbacks" or "limey," while Germans were the "Boche," "Hun," and "Kraut." No matter the nickname, most soldiers had respect for the fighting ability of the enemy. Death drew its share of slang. It was possible to be greased, whacked, snuffed, or zapped or to do likewise to the opposition. From the traces on this battlefield I believed we had covered all the definitions for this enemy unit.

21

A New War

My promotion to lieutenant colonel came through. Lieutenant Colonel Bob Gilbert jokingly told me that I would now have to stop packing a rifle. I would have felt undressed without a shoulder-fired weapon and retained my M-16. I received a letter from the army telling me that my next assignment would be ROTC and requested my choice of universities. Ray Byers suggested I ask for "Suntan U," which was totally unfamiliar to me. Ray explained that it was a nickname for the University of Miami at Miami, Florida. This would be my first choice.

I walked to the marketplace and felt a surge of satisfaction. The marketplace was the centerpiece of life in Rach Kien. The oriental understands that the basis of all fine cuisine is fresh ingredients. I have been in restaurants in Hong Kong and in mainland China where the fish entrée is selected while still swimming. Throughout Asia the vegetables and meats are left in their natural state as long as possible. Thus daily shopping is a way of life.

The market was also a gathering place, an opportunity to chat with friends and exchange information. Rach Kien was a food-rich land. The marketplace was crammed with cackling chickens and squawking ducks, colorful vegetables, and freshly butchered meat. The vendors still squatted beside their merchandise, but now much of the meat was in screened cages and vegetables were displayed on low tables. Although there was no resemblance to the antiseptic cleanliness of an American market, for Vietnam it was a model of sanitation and cleanliness. It gave me a sense of accomplishment to see these improvements that could extend a life.

I continued to have problems improving the water supply. Like the *Rime of the Ancient Mariner*, we had "water, water, everywhere, but not a drop to drink." The waters of Rach Kien were brackish. Fresh water had to be carried long distances. Each day the women would pass to and fro before the advisor house, heading for a spring. They moved in a shuffling gait, the long carrying poles over their shoulders and a five-gallon can on each end. The process was centuries old. I talked at length with engineers and province officials about drilling a well. The consensus was that a very deep well would be required, and even then it was unlikely that we would have fresh water.

Cisterns are a viable option in monsoon country. Only a privileged few in the better houses had cisterns. We welcomed the water truck from the American infantry battalion and treated its driver well. To return from a patrol through deep mud or boiling sun and enjoy the pleasant sting of a cool shower was to live in the lap of luxury.

Someone suggested that we build a cistern that would service the marketplace. The idea caught hold. The marketplace had a lengthy roof, one with sufficient area to catch rain during the monsoon months. A concrete catchment, gutters, and drains would be needed. We could solve those problems. The operation in which Major Dong died had furnished enough trading material to resolve the problem of getting water for the marketplace.

Once again I turned to the engineers. They had done a remarkable job. One new school had been opened in Rach Kien and another was being built on the road to Can Giuoc. Much admired by the townspeople, the engineers often gave of their little free time, as did the medics of the infantry battalion, to help improve life in the district. Thanks to engineer design and Vietnamese and American volunteer labor, we were able to build a giant-size catchment system that brought clean water to the marketplace.

Improvements were made while battles raged about the

district. The American forces had become very adept at using a pile-on concept of locating and fixing enemy units, and then bringing in overwhelming force to encircle, then kill with superior firepower. Enemy losses were vast and there was terror in their ranks. Not all were heroes prepared to sacrifice themselves for the cause. Sometimes the Americans or South Vietnamese captured diaries or documents that revealed the serious morale problems the enemy had. They maintained discipline at the muzzle of a gun. A great many soldiers of the North Vietnamese Army had been rounded up and sent to war, knowing if they did not go they would be shot, and some resisted that. Captured documents showed that some North Vietnamese defied their government and hid out. The political leadership in North Vietnam was prepared to take any number of casualties and was ruthless in rooting out dissenters. They understood better than we that as long as the homeland was not invaded, they could hold out. They could lose a thousand battles knowing that the outcome of the war would not be decided in South Vietnam, but in Washington, D.C.

To counteract encirclement, enemy forces began to disperse over larger areas. Sometimes when Americans had one element of the enemy surrounded, they would find themselves under mortar fire or ground attack from the rear.

The American infantry began a tactic of establishing base camps in outlying areas. From these camps, troops would be flown out in various directions much like the forming of the rim of a cart wheel. Then these troops would close inward toward the base camp. If contact was made, troops from the base camp would move to seal off escape routes and pin the enemy beneath American firepower.

Road improvement became a major goal for advisors. Throughout the province new roads were being opened, making it easier for people to travel and move produce to market. I was eager for laterite to arrive in Rach Kien. The red dirt was a composite of certain rocks and used to construct our roads. It arrived in convoys of trucks driven by Vietnamese. In order to exercise better control, the enemy wanted to keep the people isolated. They did not want a prosperous economy because prosperous people seldom want revolution. So the enemy ambushed the dirt convoys and killed several drivers. We rode shotgun, ran patrols and ambushes, staggered convoy times, and armed the drivers, and kept the number of attacks low. The enemy could not prevent us from doing the work, but they were an annoyance. I doubt that we ever killed a sniper, as they fired and fled. They were a part of life in Rach Kien.

We continued to be mortared on a regular basis, but everything was now solidly protected. Unless we were caught in the open, the mortaring was routine. Several attacks brought thunderous explosions. Judging from the size of the craters, I considered these to be 107mm rockets. They would have defeated our preparations, but the rockets landed on the fringe of our perimeter and served only to enhance conversation. The enemy mortar men lacked the skill of the original gunners or no longer cared about winning the hearts and minds of the civilians. Initially they had hit in the military areas with astounding accuracy. Now their rounds frequently landed in the area of civilian housing, killing and wounding people of both sexes and all ages.

After one attack a Vietnamese man came running to me, carrying the body of his wounded daughter. She was about eight years old and her little body was torn and bloody. Our team medic began emergency treatment for her wounds while I called for a medevac. Our private helipad saved time, since the helicopters could now be brought closer to the town. As the chopper was en route, other wounded arrived. We did what we could, but it was the ability to have rapid response in getting people to American hospitals that saved them. Although she was scarred, the child survived. These actions in which all members of the advisory team participated were of particular satisfaction. I never had qualms about killing the enemy, but it is of greater satisfaction to save a life than take one.

We were making progress on the enemy infrastructure, the shadow government that was so essential to his goal. Tet had been a serious military defeat for the Communists. Their overconfidence had caused them to make foolish mistakes. So confident were they of military success that many of the shadow leaders came out into the open, exhorting the people to support the attack on the American and South Vietnamese forces. This placed them in the position of being known to a number of people who would talk, and they soon lost their cover.

One local VC leader had written his sister a letter proclaiming that their campaign would drive the Americans from Vietnam and crush the puppet government. It was not difficult to discover his identity and end his letter writing once and for all. Hundreds of infrastructure members were rounded up. Key men at the province, district, village, and hamlet level were identified and taken into custody or killed. The enemy lost leaders and workers at all levels.

The enemy wanted to promptly launch a follow-up offensive, but the military failure of their Tet offensive was a major setback. They were forced to reorganize. There was a sense of exhilaration on our side.

I now noticed a disturbing sign in the American forces in Rach Kien. When I had arrived there, the men of the infantry battalion had been a proud and confident group. Many were drafted, but they were good soldiers who believed in our cause. Whether it was for God and country or, more likely, for the friendship with the man next to them, they fought well. But now a new breed was coming from the United States. It resembled watching a cancer being introduced into the body. Discipline problems began to arise and we heard reports of officers being murdered. They called it "fragging." The murderer would wait until an officer was asleep and toss a fragmentation grenade into his tent.

When I became aware of this I believed that the killer would be tracked down, convicted, and shot by a firing squad. However, a new phenomenon began to surface. Under attack for its inability to end the civilian-inspired and -directed war, the army felt it could not afford to incur more wrath from the American public. Many junior officers felt betrayed by senior officers of the army. They felt unsupported, and investigations ended without results.

A great tragedy of a no-win policy in war is the loss of respect for leaders. Vietnam left a lasting imprint on how Americans look at political leadership and how soldiers look at military leaders. Many of us who served in Vietnam came away with no respect for Lyndon Johnson, Robert McNamara, and their ilk, and little respect for the senior generals. We had serious debates about our senior military leadership. I believed they should have publicly opposed the insanity of giving the enemy safe haven. They should have gone public against fighting the war on the territory of our allies. Had they threatened to or resigned en masse, they would have kept us out of Vietnam or brought it to a different conclusion.

Others disagreed with me and said that if one man resigned, he would only be replaced by another; there is always the honest belief that the mission can be done. I understood that philosophy. There are no simple answers to these questions.

The use of drugs in the infantry battalion became tragically apparent. I was standing on the front porch of the advisor house looking across the street. I had assigned Matthew, one of the old Vietnamese carpenters, to repair a picket fence beside the dirt street. He knelt as he placed a new board. Suddenly from around the corner came a jeep with an American driver. He was traveling at a high rate of speed, weaving back and forth across the road. The vehicle slammed into the pickets, shearing them, struck and crushed the body of the old carpenter, and finally crashed into a building. The driver was unhurt and unconcerned. High on drugs, he had no concept of his actions.

I called for the team medic as we ran across the street. Men from the battalion had followed the driver and hustled him away. I am not aware of what became of him, but it was fortunate that they took him away quickly. When we saw that Matthew was dead, both the American advisors and the Vietnamese were filled with rage. He was only a small man, but to all of us who cared for him, it was a great loss. I made apologies to his family on behalf of my country and gave them what was called a "solation" payment. The men of my team and the engineers contributed, but we knew money could not heal the hurt. The Vietnamese were silent but I felt their thoughts. The Americans whom they had turned to for help had caused a tragedy to another Vietnamese family.

Discipline was going. I was riding in my jeep through the battalion area when two black soldiers came toward me. In the military the salute is a two-way gesture of respect. I had learned early in my career as an officer that if an enlisted man does not salute, salute him first. Until that day in 1968 it had always worked, the response being a prompt salute in return, often accompanied by a sheepish grin. These two raised their fists in the air and pumped them skyward while looking at me with hate. I was not amused.

We continued to hear about a replacement district chief. It was obvious that the Vietnamese administrative structure was on hold. Several operations I proposed to Ngi were accepted by him and rejected at Province. When we again were permitted to take the offensive, I could tell he was under restraints.

The enemy was efficient and well-disciplined. They had early-warning systems, and going overland often resulted in a fruitless march. Month in and month out they lived with assault by helicopter and had developed their early-warning techniques well. I tried a ruse using a large supply helicopter called a Chinook. Putting Ron Nelson and some of the best men aboard, we made what must have seemed a routine supply run, then quickly landed near a hamlet of which I was suspicious. The Viet Cong were present. I could see men running among the houses, but the targets were too fleeting to get a shot. By the time my troops got off the helicopter, the enemy had disappeared. Despite an intense search we could not locate the tunnels they entered.

I had long wanted to do an amphibious operation, going into the outlying areas of the district by water. In order to do so I would require the cooperation of the men who lived and fought the river war. One of the great stories of warfare in Vietnam was that of the Riverine Force that operated in the Mekong Delta. The French had employed an active campaign on both the Tonkin Delta in North Vietnam and the Mekong Delta in the south. The most powerful of the French river craft were primarily armed with .50- and .30-caliber machine guns, 20mm cannon, and 81mm mortars. They proved their worth on the rivers of Vietnam and set the stage for a superb example of cooperation between the United States Army and Navy. The navy developed what to a landlubber was a bewildering variety of small craft. These included sixteen-foot Boston Whalers and "Swift" boats that were fifty feet long, could travel at twenty-eight knots, and were armed with mortars and machine guns. They also had the thirty-one-foot, fiberglass-hull PBR (patrol boat, river) that was driven by a water jet system that allowed it to operate in shallow water. The World War II LSTs (landing ship, tank) that had served to take our Ranger companies from Pusan to Inchon during the Korean War were back in action serving as mother ships. The navy also had armored troop carriers and monitors that carried 40mm cannon and 81mm mortars, and some were equipped with flamethrowers. This naval force was joined by the 2d Brigade of the US 9th Infantry Division which, when not out in the muck, lived in floating barracks. The soldiers even had floating fire support from 105-howitzers mounted on barges.

Those who thought the navy had the good life were not familiar with the Riverine Force. These men went in harm's way. Water was a principal means of moving personnel and supplies in the Mekong Delta and nearby areas. The adaptable enemy quickly learned a variety of tricks to lead Riverine Force boats into ambush by mine and gunfire.

Through 9th Infantry Division contacts, I proposed an amphibious operation that would bring us in from the river and allow us to come at the western portion of the district. After considerable coordination and planning, a joint operation was agreed upon. The 9th Division forces would land on our left flank and press inward several kilometers, seeking to roust out an enemy force and put us in position to account for any who were trying to get out of the American path. Ngi and I trucked our two Regional Force companies, the PRU, and the Popular Force troops from Rach Kien in the early morning and traveled down Highway 4 to the Song Vam Co Dong, where we joined with the 9th Division troops and the navy boats.

The Americans were going in with guns roaring. Unless taken under fire, we would land quietly. No fire support would be used that could signal the location of our landing. We sailed downriver. To our north we heard the staccato roar of machine guns and the crumping sound of mortars and grenade launchers. We struggled ashore through deep mud and began to search the desolate area filled with thick vegetation, empty huts, and fallow rice paddies. We then pushed inland, meeting no resistance.

A PRU, who was lead scout, was moving about fifty meters to my front when he stopped and looked closely at the ground. Obviously puzzled, he took the muzzle of his rifle and poked at whatever aroused his curiosity. There was a thunderous explosion and the man was hurtled backward. He was one of our most experienced men, but in a careless moment he had triggered a booby trap and paid the price. It was little short of a miracle that he did not die on the scene. I called for a medical evacuation helicopter and he was taken away. I later learned that he did not survive.

Choosing our path carefully, we continued on. The area was heavily booby-trapped and there were places where the enemy had placed signs with a crude skull and crossbones to warn the few local inhabitants not to enter. We found prepared fighting positions useful for ambush; these were relatively fresh diggings. Although we were not making contact, we knew the enemy had been present recently or was close by.

We began to find some rice fields and occupied huts. One such hut was near a Vietnamese graveyard. Beside this open space was a plot of thick vegetation and large-boled palm trees about the size of a basketball court. Our troops were spread out in a wide perimeter around this space. I was talk-ing on the radio to our base camp. Ngi moved to the hut to interrogate the old woman and man who were its occupants. Ngi had gone up the right-side paddy dike around the wooded area, so I proceeded left. For reasons I do not re-member, two of my sergeants were temporarily delayed. I was not concerned, since I was in the middle of a perimeter and the paddy dike that lay beside the vegetation was open. As I moved down the path I noticed that a broken palm frond hung across the trail. There are times when training and experience become automatic. I was not suspicious, but I stepped off the paddy dike into knee-deep mud and made a difficult, wide detour around the area before coming back to the path.

I joined Ngi, who was completing a brief conversation with the elderly couple. They explained that many foreign-ers were coming into the area who were not kind to the local people. I thought he meant Americans, but he told me they were referring to people from North Vietnam, people not of this area, people with a strange accent. This confirmed our belief that the enemy was committing still more troops of the North Vietnamese Army into Rach Kien.

Our conversation was interrupted by an earsplitting ex-plosion close at hand. A grenade had exploded in the area I had just left. Ngi and I ran to the corner of the wooded area to be met by my two sergeants, who were wide-eyed and ashen-faced. They had come down the paddy dike. One of them brushed aside the palm frond I had avoided. Going back to the area of the explosion, I came to the conclusion that the frond contained a length of hidden fishing line at-tached to a hand grenade. The grenade had been placed in the fork of a low palm at head-high level. I could see slight marks where it had been hidden. The safety pin was loos-ened to allow a push movement of the frond to pull the pin and arm the grenade. When one of the sergeants pushed the palm frond, the pin did not release entirely. The grenade swung out of its position and, still attached to the fishing line, went into a pendulum motion. It came free just at the time when it was propelled into the vegetation. Fortunately for the two men, it exploded behind the bole of a large palm that was deeply scarred with shrapnel. The odds of these circumstances coming together are incalculable, but I could find no other explanation. It was a miracle they survived without harm.

Vietnamese soldiers of their 47th Infantry Regiment were involved in a land portion of this operation. We made contact and joined them on what would be a long, wet march home. Shortly after the linkup we received fire from our left flank. The men of the 25th Division were sometimes ridiculed as the worst division in the South Vietnamese army, but these men performed well. Like a door swinging on a hinge, the Vietnamese came on line in the assault and used marching fire to silence the enemy. Several dead VC were found and the rest fled.

We made the long, muddy march back to Rach Kien while my fortunate sergeants marveled at their narrow escape. For three weeks I had two devoutly religious, deeply introspective, soft-spoken, kindhearted, and generous sergeants. Then they recognized they were still alive.

The American infantry was justifiably concerned about the large number of Vietnamese who passed through their perimeter, including those on buses and Lambrettas and everyone from Rach Kien town who wanted to get to Highway 4 and Saigon. I decided to build a bypass road. The infantry battalion commander was in full support, but the most important man was the captain who commanded the engineer detachments. He was a good man who did everything he could to help, but he had other priority missions from his headquarters. The gifts obtained from our relationship with the engineers had worn thin. I could no longer expect a truckload of lumber. The road was built, but I had a very angry engineer officer snarling at me when I commandeered one of his road graders in his absence.

Despite the loss of the district chief, Captain Ngi did what he could to keep us on the offensive. We ran frequent operations, constantly expanding our reach into areas that district forces had never occupied. These were often small-unit operations of a reinforced platoon. Lieutenant Rich Gaschott and his MAT team and several of my team sergeants were busy training the Regional Force companies. Rich was down south with 627 Company at My Le. In Rach Kien we had the rifle and pistol range in operation south of the administrative headquarters. The team medic was working with the midwife and the battalion surgeon to develop more dispensaries in the district.

This concern over fighting battles with friendly forces had a good cause. The 39th Infantry had this misfortune. Two of their companies lost contact one night and engaged in a firefight with each other. Men died or were badly wounded. It is a serious business to be roaming the dark in a kill-or-be-killed environment. Clashes between friendly forces, artillery and bombs falling on their own people, occur in all armies in war because to err is human. Some wordsmith called this tragedy "friendly fire."

Knowing your location is a critical part of being a soldier. Being in the wrong spot can put a person in a body bag. It sounds simple, and when you are moving over terrain that has definite features it is not difficult. The peculiar shape of a hill, a line of mountains, or a lake helps pinpoint a location on a map. When operating in plains, desert, rice paddies, or in forests, where there are no reference points, it is a difficult process. Now soldiers utilize satellites to pinpoint position, but in the wars I fought, indeed over thousands of years in hundreds of languages, the eternal complaint of soldiers was "Where the hell are we?"

I used every technique I could and asked almost everyone to help me move our district forces to the outlying areas. A mechanized unit began operating in Long An Province, and I prevailed upon them to take one of their companies and the Vietnamese on a scout using armored personnel carriers. We moved west and came into a wide expanse of paddy area. After some time, one of my officers asked our position. I told him, but he disagreed by pointing to another location.

Ray Byers believed that we were somewhere else, and the infantry commander disagreed with all of us. As the only field grade officer on the scene, I had the dignity of my office to uphold. I told them to go about their business and that I intended to prove my point by getting the artillery to fire a marking round. I radioed the artillery and asked them to fire a round of white phosphorus (WP) at a selected set of map coordinates, having the fuse explode at two hundred meters' altitude. From a distance it makes a beautiful white puff in the air, and this can be used to confirm a location on the map.

While sitting on top of an armored personnel carrier, I selected a spot some eight hundred meters to my south and called in the map coordinates to the artillery. After a short time, the radio crackled and a voice said, "On the way!" As I looked south to locate the burst, the round exploded directly over my head. Terrified men dived for cover. I practically defecated in my fatigues. Fortunately the explosion was at two hundred meters above us and no one was hurt. The officers ran toward me as I recovered my wits.

"See that?" I yelled. "Don't ever tell me I don't know where I'm at!" They were properly awed.

The artillery could be fallible. On one occasion when working with the infantry, their commander called for a WP marking round at two hundred meters. The round went off over our heads, but the artillery had fired high explosive. A Vietnamese sergeant came running up to me juggling a large piece of shrapnel that had torn the earth beside him. "Number ten!" he cried, "number ten!" All I could do was nod and say, "You're damn right, it's number ten."

Word came down from Province that a technique was available to remove the enemy's hiding places in areas of dense foliage. This involved aircraft flying over an area and spraying it with a defoliant. They called it Agent Orange. When the planes came to Rach Kien, I watched clouds of this substance spew from their bellies. We believed it would not harm the district or us, but only the foliage where the enemy was concealed. Years later I became the only member of my family to be diagnosed with prostate cancer.

I was informed by Province that the matter of the *Doctor Zhivago* film was now in the hands of higher headquarters. I had come to hate *Doctor Zhivago*. I doubted he was licensed. I could not remember if the Communists had killed him—I hoped so. I could afford to root for them on this occasion.

As I slept soundly, there was a pounding on my door. My caller was Captain Ngi and he was clearly angry. "They have a family and they are raping," he said. I thought he meant the Viet Cong were in the village. Hurriedly I dressed and grabbed my weapon. By the time I had finished I understood he was referring to Americans from our infantry battalion. I called the battalion and requested immediate assistance at the village.

Vietnamese were in the street and several of my team were aroused and followed me. I asked Ngi to have a guide available for whoever would arrive from the 39th Infantry. We proceeded into the village. The sounds and voices emanating from one house were obviously of American men out of control. They were not off-duty soldiers. These men had been assigned to conduct a night patrol as part of the defensive posture of our district town and their unit. High on drugs or alcohol, they had shirked their responsibility, broken into a Vietnamese house, terrorized the family, and assaulted one of the daughters. They did not know me and ignored my orders. They were even difficult to control when their own officers and sergeants arrived on the scene. Of course, the battalion officers and senior NCOs were ashamed and apologized. They promised compensation pay, and they promised punishment, which I doubted would occur.

These men were part of the breakdown in society that was occurring in the United States. When I arrived in Vietnam in 1967 the army was confident and disciplined. By the fall of 1968 many of those men had returned home. Some of the new men now filling the ranks were a disgrace to themselves and their country. The sergeant major of the battalion and I shared a sense of despair at what was happening to our country and our army.

I received a message that an officer from the inspector general's office would be arriving from Saigon the following week to investigate the missing copy of the film *Doctor Zhivago.* That was agreeable with me since my tour of duty in Vietnam had ended and I would ship out before he arrived.

I packed my bags to leave Rach Kien. With my orders in my hand, I said farewell to Americans and Vietnamese whom I was very proud to know. Ed Surbaugh had the last night radio watch, and I did not want to disturb his rest by waking him to thank him and say good-bye. I have often regretted that.

22

Welcome Home

I had received no letters from my wife while I was in Vietnam. I came home with the hope that time would have healed her. I thought how wonderful it would be to see her waiting as the plane landed. It would be one of those reunions where husband and wife run to each other's arms. My hopes were in vain. I was met at the Harrisburg, Pennsylvania, airport by my sister-in-law. She drove me to a home I owned near Carlisle. I thanked my sister-in-law for her kindness, and as she drove away I opened the door that led to the kitchen. My wife was standing at the kitchen sink doing dishes. She looked over her shoulder at me, said, "Oh, hello," and returned to her work. Though divorce was not what I married for, I knew this marriage offered nothing but despair and it was time to end it.

I wound up in Miami. Sunny days are not infrequent in Florida, and the campus of the University of Miami. As I walked across the campus in uniform, I was surprised that most of the students I passed looked at me with open hostility. Seeing my insignia, a young woman yelled, "Hey, Ranger, did you kill any babies today?"

Performing Reserve Officer Training Corps (ROTC) duty at a university could be one of the most rewarding experiences of a military career. There, young men could enter a program of instruction leading to the gold bar of second lieutenant. But in 1969, ROTC duty was another combat tour. This was the dawning of "the age of Aquarius," so the students sang, an age of harmony and understanding, an age of humanity coming together, and an age of self-expression.

Like the war, the age in which it was fought became something different from that envisioned at its beginnings. It became rebellion for the sake of rebellion, a self-seeking, self-serving, anything-goes time of anarchy when the demonstration and the sit-in replaced reason as a form of expression in America.

The heroes for these youth and the adults who supported them were those who did drugs, resisted any form of authority, burned the American flag, and openly praised those who were killing American soldiers. There was no justification for the way those of us who fought in Vietnam were treated by our country. Whether volunteer or draftee, those who went to Vietnam went at the orders of the elected government of our nation. Whatever the faults of getting involved, it was not the men who fought the war who put us there.

The war in Vietnam was the spark, but in the early going, most Americans felt that the spread of Communism by force should be opposed. It was the stupidity of the conduct of the war in Vietnam that brought us to national grief. Why would we send men to fight a war on the territory of our ally and grant the enemy safe haven in his homeland? Why fight a war in which concern for the possible action by another country, such as China or Russia, would dictate what we could or could not do? Our political leadership learned nothing from the lessons of the Korean War, where we allowed the Chinese homeland to be a safe haven while they sent armies against us. If concern for Chinese entry into the war in Vietnam was preventing us from sending ground forces into North Vietnam, then we should not have entered the war.

The seeds of Vietnam were sown in the Korean War. Revisionist history has made Harry S. Truman a hero, largely because he fired Gen. Douglas MacArthur, but the people who lived in the early 1950s knew better. Truman was not popular when he left office. There was never a legitimate question of whether an American president had the right to fire a general. Of course he did. The significant question was not addressed—that being MacArthur's "There is no substitute for victory." "Police Action" Truman sought a substitute. Like President Harry Truman, President Lyndon Johnson put us in a war that lacked victory as the only acceptable goal. There is a biblical quotation, "If the trumpet sounds an uncertain call to battle, who shall follow?" Those of us who fought in Korea and Vietnam believed in our country and our government. We followed the uncertain trumpet. We fought those wars and paid the bitter price.

Courage comes in varying forms. It took courage to be a student enrolled in ROTC during the late 1960s and early 1970s. Some students in the program did so out of patriotism, others for the scholarship money the program provided. They were scorned and harassed by many of their fellow students. During drill periods anti-ROTC banners hung from dorm windows, loud music was played to interfere with the instruction, and catcalls were frequent. Some professors openly insulted ROTC members during class. Excellent students told me their grades suffered due to these activist faculty members. Anyone with short hair was suspect of being pro-military. We were the enemy.

The University of Miami ROTC program had a female auxiliary known as the Princess Corps. Suntan U had a plethora of beautiful women, and this dozen-or-so-member corps had its share. Many of them were daughters of military families. Even they were not spared the ridicule of other students. I asked one of these young women to carry a paper to the university printer for reproduction. She was rebuffed and told, "ROTC is not relevant."

The so-called Students for a Democratic Society (SDS) and their allies challenged our academic credentials. The university administration caved in and sent a team of faculty members to see our methods of instruction. The American military has been teaching since the foundation of our nation. Officers are teachers. We use the time-proven method of "tell them what you're gonna tell them—tell them—tell them what you told them." When I showed the professors our instructional methods and tools, they confessed surprise and several took examples for their own use. We retained our accreditation.

We were called upon to defend the war we had fought before students and faculty members who were not there to listen or discuss, but to harass. At one such gathering a student shouted at me, "You are in Vietnam to steal the diamonds!" How does one respond to such a closed and ignorant mind! I thought back to Rach Kien with its dirt roads, lack of electricity and potable water, flies covering the meat in the marketplace, the efforts to get medical treatment besides a midwife for thousands of people, and the effort to get schools teaching beyond the fourth grade. These American students were not interested in learning. Their minds were closed.

When Miami or Miami Beach had a parade, they often sought military representation. On one occasion I was riding in the backseat of an open car with Claude Pepper, the venerable, red-nosed congressional representative. As we drove slowly along, a woman ran from the crowd and pursued the car, shouting something. As she drew closer she began to shake her fist at me and shouted, "Killer! . . . Murderer! . . . Get out of Vietnam!"

On Memorial Day the Jewish War Veterans would hold a commemorative service at the Cenotaph on Miami Beach. They were passionately patriotic, vocal, and argumentative, so I got along well with them. My first year in Miami, I was invited to be the guest speaker, an opportunity I welcomed. I was angry as hell, and my speeches were fire-and-brimstone denunciations of those Americans who did not support the men and women whom the United States had sent to war.

It seemed I had hardly left my car before the old veterans were in some scrap they wanted me to resolve. They had served in World War I and World War II. One octogenarian claimed he had been a corporal with Pershing in the Mexican campaign. He felt that was worthy of respect and that a form of precedence was due him. Several aged warriors from World War I took exception to this and the arguments were vociferous, with many appeals to me. It was a challenge in diplomacy to appease both sides.

My speeches were outdoor, open-air talks that attracted others, including the longhair opposition. The veterans turned up the volume on the sound system and prevented the longhairs from drowning out the sound of my voice, but they shouted their displeasure and this greatly angered the cane-carrying elders. My rage was increasing. When I spoke the second year, I again denounced those standing on the sidelines. That resulted in one sign-carrying member of the opposition trying to get through the crowd. He probably wanted time on the microphone, but my gallant defenders would have none of it. Men in their seventies and eighties turned on this unfortunate wretch, pummeling him with their fists and trying to hit him with their canes. When one of my supporters had a heart attack, the scene dissolved. Our side rushed to his aid. By the time the crisis had passed and I concluded my speech, our opponents had drifted away.

Bitterness filled my soul. It was not enough to have fought in Vietnam. I was now required to face the hostility—indeed, utter stupidity—of those who had no understanding of what we had experienced and no desire to listen. These students, faculty members, and members of the general public were convinced that we were the enemy. Many of them openly praised the Communist leaders of North Vietnam. They never understood and few tried to recognize the philosophy of the totalitarian rulers of these so-called Communist states. General Vo Nguyen Giap, commander of the enemy forces, had said, "Every minute, hundreds of thousands of people die all over the world. The life or death of a hundred, a thousand, or tens of thousands of human beings, even if they are our own compatriots, represents really very little." This butcher was a hero to many American youth who flew the flag of North Vietnam on American college campuses, taking full advantage of the American freedoms that others had fought for and won.

In previous wars, the news of death in battle came with the arrival of the dreaded telegram. That was not the system in

Vietnam. Now it was those of us in uniform who had to seek out the family and inform them of the death of their loved one. Whatever this system did for the family, it was destructive to the combat veterans who were required to perform the duty.

Some family members reacted in stunned silence. Unable to comprehend their loss, the inevitable reaction occurred after I departed. But that did not always occur. Some people took out their anger on the symbol of their government who stood before them. At times they cursed me and, on one occasion, a grieving mother tried to attack me. Conversely, I visited a man whose son had been a medical evacuation helicopter pilot. He had a model of his son's aircraft and would frequently visit the ROTC Department, carrying the model and asking the same questions over and over again about medical evacuation procedures.

I was breaking the news of a son's death in battle to a woman who lived alone. She denied having a son. I went over all the information I had, confirmed that I was at the correct address, and told her that military records indicated the deceased soldier had recorded her name as his mother and next of kin. She angrily denied that he was her son and told me to leave. I do not know why I did this, but as I reached the door I turned to her and said, "I'm sorry to have disturbed you. We need to locate the next of kin, as there is insurance involved." The woman looked startled, suddenly sobbed, and cried out, "Oh, my poor boy!"

It is wearing on the body and mind to fight a war and not reasonable to have to justify it to others, but to return from the battlefield and then be required to inform families of the deaths of their sons and daughters is an injustice to the soldiers who fight our country's wars. It would be better to have the corps of chaplains enlarged during wartime for the purpose of notifying families of their dead. To require those who fought and carry their own scars of war to be the messengers of death is a cruel thing.

My thoughts often turned to the words of a young man who lost his life in Vietnam, a man who wrote in his diary,

"How frustrating life is! To whom should I unburden myself? In whom should I confide? Who can possibly understand my pent up feelings? No one could possibly, except us, the soldiers!" Those words were written by a man I never met; his name was Mai Van Hung. He was my enemy, yet we were closer in feeling than we were to many of our own countrymen.

Epilogue

The remaining years of my military service were little different from working at the headquarters of a large civilian corporation or in a city hall. The army that I love is found in the training area or the battlefield. Being part of or close to the men in ranks were my most memorable times as a soldier. At senior headquarters the bonding does not occur in the close contact and shared experiences of those who fight.

The closer I got to the top, the more uneasy I became about the wisdom of some who lead us. I served under a general who assembled his officers to tell us that the saddest remembrance of his life was that, growing up in a country club atmosphere, he never got to play tennis with a black man. I was serving at CINCPAC, headquarters of the commander in chief, Pacific, in Hawaii, when my senior said to me, "Black, you are a historian. The admiral wants a report on the battle of Stalingrad, the one the Germans won." I replied, "The Germans did not win the battle of Stalingrad." His response was, "They must have. The admiral said they did." I looked forward to the time when I would not have to work for other people. I am comfortable with my own ignorance but cannot abide it in others.

Over the past forty years I have spent countless hours researching the nearly four-hundred-year-old history of the Rangers and have spent twenty years trying to preserve it from an army that believes history is whatever the current army chief of staff wants it to be. I've watched the army falsify the historic lineage of the Rangers and carelessly destroy proud traditions, such as when Gen. Eric Shinseki, army chief of staff, killed the tradition born in the Korean War of Rangers wearing black berets. That which Rangers endured so much to earn became an item of issue to other soldiers in the name of fashion. The once-proud black beret is now handed out like underwear. How can someone be proud of being given something that another soldier earned?

Unable to continue marriage to a mentally ill woman, I got a costly divorce, remarried, and retired from the army. While I do not blindly love it, the army gave me the adventure I sought and the opportunity to answer questions I had about myself. These were questions that could not have been answered to my satisfaction in a civilian career. I did not feel trapped while in uniform, yet the day I retired from the service I felt suddenly free, almost like jumping into the air and clicking my heels together. Still, had the cold war gone hot I would have rejoined in a heartbeat.

In examining my life, I came to the belief that combat in Korea and Vietnam were not the most trying experiences I knew. I could take meaningful action at those times. The times of greatest challenge were within my family. I could do nothing to cure the mental illness of my first wife. Medical care did not cure her nor did prayer. The impact it had on my career was nothing to the loss she endured and that of our family.

A new life as historian beckoned, but tragedy dogged my trail. When the doctor speaks the word "terminal," life changes. After twelve years of marriage, my second wife developed lung cancer. Then began two years of pain, ending in five hundred days of horror. We owned an eighteenth-century brick-and-stone farmhouse, which some called an estate. It was winter in Pennsylvania, the days were gray and gloomy. I did not want to sell the home I loved, give up the family dog and familiar surroundings, but my wants were not important. When a spouse is dying, what they want is all that matters. The home was our passion, but in her grief, she asked me to take her to Florida as she felt she would improve in the sun. I could not deny the request of my dying wife. We sold out, moved to Florida, and found ourselves alone in a different environment. We had only ourselves and doctors we did not know. She had a simple wooden cross that she prayed over each day, and each day the cancer advanced.

In the beginning my wife prayed that she might be cured. Later she prayed that she might find a peaceful acceptance of her fate. That is the type of prayer I hope I can always make to my God. It is the one most often answered. For my wife and me, her dying was a loving time. In the dying, there was a loving gentleness to our relationship that had not been a constant in our marriage. She made a long hard fight.

In the end, she told a nurse, "Bob can't take this anymore," and she let death take her. I held her hand in the passing, and the last words she heard were "I love you." Leaving the deathbed, I walked out under the stars of an empty world. It seemed as though everything in my life was gone. My wife was gone, my home was gone. I was totally adrift and had to start anew. It was all in the heart and the mind. I determined to come back, but I would never again be tied to material things. My body is the house I live in, knowledge is my goal, and travel is my path.

To finance my wanderings, I became a travel writer and roamed the world from Morocco to Antarctica and from the Galápagos to the fjords of Norway. I've searched Mayan ruins in the jungles of Belize, been mugged in Rio de Janeiro, haggled with vendors in the bazaars of Istanbul and Cairo, watched the lions feed in South Africa, saw the night sky of the Sahara Desert, walked the Great Wall of China, and sailed down the Amazon and the Nile. I've ridden horseback in Monument Valley and been stirrup deep in wildflowers in the Alpine meadows of the Grand Tetons. I've been on cattle and bison drives and swam with sea lions. I've done hot air ballooning over Napa Valley and in Africa. There were great adventures in travel. Macquarie's Island is located in the Tazman Sea between New Zealand and Wilkes Land in Antarctica. Shrouded in mist and pounded surf, Macquarie's Island is a jagged rock that leaps from the sea. Its slopes and beaches are covered with thousands of king penguins. These are beautiful birds about three feet tall appearing as gentlemen in formal wear but wearing a bright orange collar. Their companions on the island are giant elephant seals, massive creatures that come up from the sea like a pickup truck driving from the surf.

We rode rubberized Zodiacs in through the surf, then sat quietly on the beach while the penguins surrounded us. They could not comprehend who or what we were. Hoping I was edible, one pecked at my backpack while another tried my boot. Losing interest, they went off to stand beak to beak, talking with one another or pecking at the elephant seals as they humped their way up on the beach.

We went back to the Zodiac and began coasting around the island so that I could do photography. I was taking photos from the bow of the boat when I heard a warning cry from the helmsman. Looking over my shoulder, I saw a towering rogue wave sweeping toward us. When the wave hit, I was off balance and was thrown overboard. There is a rope that runs around the top of the craft, and I had the sense and good fortune to grab that rope as I was airborne. I was fully dressed with boots and parka and encumbered with cameras. In the sudden transformation I went from being in the boat to being under it. It was rough water, and my white-knuckle grip on the rope was likely what saved me. The helmsman had a difficult time dragging my water-weighted body back on board. He succeeded, to my effusive thanks. It was a close call, but I never sweat the close ones.

In Africa my guide, driver, and I were watching a bull elephant eat a tree for lunch. To get closer photography, we took the Land Rover down a sandy creek bed. I took the shots, and the elephant began to indicate he was aware of our presence and preferred that we be elsewhere. When the driver stepped on the gas pedal, the wheels spun in the sand and began to bury themselves. The noise seemed to have an unsettling effect on the elephant, and he began to threaten. Men do not outrun elephants. The guide and I jumped from the vehicle and with magnificent inspiration heaved the vehicle free. My sundowner martini had a special flavor that night.

I was a widower for ten years. In time I met Carolyn. She is all things wonderful to me: lover, companion, friend, and wife.

Cancer came for me. I believe in preventative medicine and was being checked twice a year. Despite that, I was diagnosed with a fast-moving, high-grade prostate cancer, and I had to make a fast decision. "You may end up incontinent and impotent," my urologist told me. "I have things to accomplish," I responded, and on my sixty-fifth birthday went into surgery. Then followed healing and a month of radiation. Misfortune is easier to deal with when it happens to oneself rather than a loved one. I went from radiation to the gym and lifted weights. Cancer left me deeply wounded, but the Ranger spirit brought me through.

After the collapse of the Soviet Union, I sailed the Elbe River in what had been Communist East Germany. I found an army post that the Russian army had occupied. The buildings were desolate and ruined, and on its rusting barbed-wire gate hung a red star, battered and askew. I felt a sense of satisfaction that during my time on watch I had contributed to a temporary victory of freedom over tyranny. The victory is not permanent, the issue is not settled and may never be. There will always be wolves in the world. I can only hope that the United States will look out for its own interests and follow the old adage used by President Theodore Roosevelt, "Speak softly and carry a big stick; you will go far."

Life plays out in slow motion until you are looking backward at it. Korea and Vietnam were a couple of wars that already seem to many as distant as the conflict between the Trojans and Greeks. The sacrifice of years of the cold war is scarcely remembered. Only those who serve and their families carry the true memory of war. The hot wars and the cold are always just one surprise away. The first law of nature is competition—it is unlikely that will change. In all our centuries of social and technological advancement, we have not developed one new emotion. We are operating with the same jealousy, love, hate, fear, and anger as those who lived five thousand years ago. We should be telling the story these emotions create and learning from that story, but we don't. We write history, and then rewrite history to make it what we want it to be to fit our present mood. We very seldom learn the lessons of history.

Mine was the eternal experience of the foot soldier. The same winter cold, the broiling sun of summer, the dust, the rain, and the mud that the Greek hoplite and Roman legionnaire endured were mine to share. I carried in me the same emotions that were at Hastings, Waterloo, and Gettysburg. Technology is a necessary veneer, but it is that which is inside the soldier, that mix of spirit, training, will, and tradition, that brings victory on the battlefield.

The defining period of my time as a soldier, indeed of my life, was to train and fight with the 8th Airborne Ranger Company. I will never forget those few, that valiant brotherhood of Rangers, that I was part of. Purely American, with a rich and vibrant history that extends deep into the 1600s, the Rangers are a river of courage through time. Their philosophy that "It is all in the heart and the mind, you can accomplish anything" is not just military code. It is applicable to the lives of all of us.

Through the mist of time, I can see the boy who roamed the green hills of Pennsylvania, his mind so filled with hopes and dreams. He sought adventure, not riches. He found humor practically everywhere and believed that anything was possible. I'm proud of that boy. He never rose to fame, but in his own way he met his challenges and accomplished what he set out to do. It's been a long way from there to here, and the final destination is not far distant. That, too, can be faced. It is all in the heart and the mind. I'm a Ranger born, a Ranger bred, and, when I die, I'll be a Ranger dead.

Glossary

KOREAN WAR

A-frame A carrying device used on the backs of Korean laborers.

Ash and Trash A soldier's work detail. Carrying cans filled with ash or trash from the work area to trucks, then on to a disposal area. Heavy lifting.

BAR The Browning automatic rifle. A gas-operated, air-cooled, magazine-fed American shoulder weapon. It weighed twenty-one pounds without the sling. The twenty-round magazine weighed one pound, seven ounces when full. First used in World War I, the BAR was also standard in World War II and Korea and with some Vietnamese units. During Korea it was usually assigned on the basis of one per infantry squad. Ranger squads had two.

Barracks Guard The soldier who remains behind in barracks when the unit is in training or at work. Duties include cleaning the barracks and latrines.

Brownshoe Army The pre-1950s army when brown boots and shoes were worn and many work chores were performed by enlisted soldiers.

Bug Out The Korean War term for the flight of an individual or unit in panic.

C ration The basic food of a soldier when in the field in lieu of garrison.

Call Sign Radio identification system frequently consisting of several temporarily used words picked at random

347

and a number: for example, Red Bandit 6. This is the call sign that identifies the unit, and 6 traditionally is the identifier for the commander. Used in all wars since radio transmission began.

Carbine Lightweight (6.60 lbs. with a thirty-round magazine), magazine-fed, air-cooled, gas-operated, shoulder-fired weapon of the US Army. Useful for close-in fighting when the M-2 automatic or semiautomatic version was used.

Charge of Quarters The individual, usually a noncommissioned officer, who in a rotation of duty answers telephones and otherwise represents the commander of a unit in a garrison during nighttime hours.

Chogi- and Chiggy-bearers Korean laborers.

Deep Kimchi Serious trouble.

DRO Dining room orderly. The best job when assigned to Kitchen Police. Places the napkins and coffee and maintains the dining room.

Flying Ten The ten-dollar bill paid to soldiers whose pay records were mislaid or lost.

Foo Gas Fifty-five-gallon drums filled with napalm (jellied gasoline), used with detonators and trip wires by American infantry in defense.

Foxhole The protective/fighting hole dug in the earth by an American soldier.

Frag Fragmentation. Usually used to describe a corrugated cast-iron grenade used in WWII and Korea.

GI Government issue. A term applied to matériel and soldiers.

Gook Derogatory slang for an oriental.

HE High explosive.

Jody Cadence A singing accompaniment to marching, done with calls and responses.

LST Landing ship, tank.

M1 Standard shoulder-fired weapon of the infantry in World War II and Korea, a gas-operated, semiautomatic, self-feeding, .30-caliber rifle weighing 9.5 pounds. It used an eight-round clip.

Midnight Requisition   To steal what is needed.

MLR   Main line of resistance. The line of battle of the army, also called "the front."

Mortar   High-angle-of-fire weapon of the infantry, used by both sides.

Napalm   Jellied gasoline. Incendiary used by Americans in Korea and Vietnam, primarily dropped from aircraft but also used with flamethrowers. The substance adheres to that which it burns and takes the oxygen from the air. While denounced as inhumane by those whose lives were not at risk, it was one of the most effective and therefore most popular weapons used by US forces.

Night Fireman   A soldier's work detail. The barracks in a battalion or regiment were heated with coal-fired furnaces, and these had to be maintained throughout the night.

Number Ten   Used in both Korea and Vietnam by Americans and Asians to describe the lowest or worst. Number One was the very best.

Police Call   To clean up an area.

PRC-10   Principal platoon and company radio of the Korean War. Often referred to as a "Prick-ten."

Quad 50   Four .50-caliber machine guns mounted on a halftrack. The machine guns could be fired individually or together. One of the most effective weapons of the Korean War.

R&R (Rest and Recreation)   A program, usually a week in length, to give personnel a break from the combat zone.

Recognition Panel   A brightly colored plastic panel with tie-down capability. Approximately two feet wide by eight feet long, used to identify friendly units for friendly aircraft or other units.

ROK   Republic of Korea.

Satchel Charge   Explosive packaged in a canvas bag and activated by a pull cord. The Chinese attempted to blow the treads off American vehicles with these.

Short Round   Artillery or mortar shell fired by friendly forces that falls short of the enemy position, often with harmful effect to our troops.

SOP Standard operating procedure. That which is established routine procedure.

Special Duty A soldier removed from regular duty rosters, often to participate in sports.

Squad The basic formation of the infantry, usually consisting of ten men.

Truman Extension The year of involuntary service added by President Truman to enlistments at the beginning of the Korean War.

White Phosphorus Called Willie Peter from WWII radio phonetics, or WP. A highly effective burning agent used by both sides.

VIETNAM WAR

Airburst Detonation of shell or bomb aboveground. Particularly effective against troops who are aboveground and unprotected by overhead cover.

AK-47 Since 1949 the principal assault weapon of the Communist bloc nations, including the NVA. Steadily improved, this 7.62mm weapon was based upon the German World War II MP44. It was relatively inexpensive to produce, reliable in battle, and accurate in ranges of 275 yards or less.

Ao Dai The traditional dress of a Vietnamese woman.

Ap Vietnamese designation for small communities that Americans called hamlets.

Arc Light One of the most effective tactics of the war in Vietnam; it consisted of B-52 bombers each dropping 108 five-hundred-pound bombs in area coverage. Though much feared by the enemy, they dug deep and many survived these attacks.

ARVN Pronounced "arvin." The acronym for the Army of the Republic of Vietnam (South Vietnam).

Cadre Those who served as a nucleus for revolutionary activities for both north and south.

Cao Dai A Buddhist (reformed) sect with wide-ranging

religious practices. The faith had its formation in Cochin China in 1925 when a spirit appeared before a group of civil servants and pronounced itself the "Cao Dai," the supreme god of the universe.

Chieu Hoi An "open arms" amnesty program established by the South Vietnamese government in 1963. It encouraged insurgents to change to the side of the government.

CIA Central Intelligence Agency. The primary American intelligence service. Founded in 1947, it replaced the World War II intelligence service, the OSS. A major opponent of Communist subversion, the CIA was a major target of Soviet Union disinformation programs.

Civic Action A program designed in 1955 to assist the South Vietnamese government to develop communities.

Co An unmarried young Vietnamese female (miss).

Cold War The competition between the Communist bloc and the Western nations that occurred from the close of World War II to the demise of the Soviet Union.

COMUSMACV Commander, US Military Assistance Command, Vietnam.

CORDS Civil Operations and Revolutionary Development Support. Under the control of MACV, this agency began in 1967 with the mission of coordinating the American pacification effort.

CRIP Combined Reconnaissance and Intelligence Platoon. Specially recruited and trained force to capture or kill members of the enemy infrastructure. They worked from the province level. An effective program that was started too late in the Vietnam War. They were often former VC or NVA who knew how the enemy operated.

Counterinsurgency An American term describing counterrevolutionary activities.

County Fair Similar to cordon-and-search. A tactic in which American and South Vietnamese troops would surround a village. The South Vietnamese would enter and entertain, question, and provide South Vietnamese government propaganda to the villagers. Cordon-and-search could be done by troops of either country and was more direct action.

District In Vietnamese, *huyen* for the Communist or *quan* for the South Vietnamese government. Roughly comparable to an American county.

Dustoff A medical evacuation by helicopter.

Free Strike (or free-fire) Zone An area evacuated by the South Vietnamese. It was presumed that anyone found there was the enemy.

Gaggle A line of troop-carrying helicopters.

Geneva Accords The 1954 agreement that divided North and South Vietnam along the 17th parallel and established a demilitarized zone (DMZ) between the two. The north skillfully used the partition to send cadre south in the guise of refugees. The division was intended to be temporary until elections scheduled for 1965. The election did not occur, and the country remained divided until the Communist victory.

H&I Fires Harassing and interdictory fires. Fires directed against possible enemy routes or positions at irregular times. Wishful thinking fires.

HES The hamlet evaluation survey. A report designed to rate hamlets and villages on the degree of pacification obtained.

Hoa Hao Pronounced "wa-how," a reformed Buddhist faith begun under the leadership of Huynh Phu So. It stressed internal faith instead of outward symbolism and ritual.

Horse Holder An aide to a general.

Infrastructure The Communist political and administrative apparatus within South Vietnam.

M-16 In various models, the standard weapon of the US infantryman in Vietnam. The 5.56mm M-16A1 weighed six pounds, five ounces unloaded. It carried a thirty-round detachable box magazine. The M-16A2 could fire single shot, a three-round burst, or automatic.

M-60 The standard machine gun of US forces in Vietnam. It was belt-fed using 7.62mm ammunition. Much of its design was copied from the superb German MG42 of World War II.

M-79 A 40mm, single-shot grenade launcher.

MACV Military Assistance Command, Vietnam. Established in 1962, it was the senior American military headquarters.

Medcap Medical Civilian Action Program.

MAT Mobile Advisory Team.

Neutralize To take the enemy out of battle by their capture or death.

Nuoc Mam The fish sauce that Vietnamese add to their rice. Not suitable to the taste or nose of most Americans.

NVA (North Vietnamese Army) The American description of the enemy army they called the People's Army of Vietnam (PAVN).

PF (Popular Force) The village military force (militia) of the South Vietnamese. They were paid little and were poorly led and equipped. Much effort went into improving training and life for these troops and the Regional Force soldiers in Rach Kien.

Phoenix A program initiated in 1968 designed to gather information on and eliminate the Communist infrastructure in South Vietnam.

Piaster Currency used in South Vietnam. Called "P" by Americans. In 1968 the rate of exchange was 118 P to one US dollar.

Plain of Reeds Dong Thap Muoi, or Rung Sat Zone.

PRC-25 Radio used by small units and the principal radio of advisors at district level. Often referred to as a "Prick twenty-five."

Proselytizing In Vietnam, the propaganda campaigns waged to convert the thinking of the people. Communist units used speakers, flags, banners, and executions.

Province *Tinh* in Vietnamese. Roughly comparable to an American state.

Provincial Reconnaissance Unit (PRU) A small, highly motivated intelligence-gathering and strike force. Many had lost family members to the enemy and some had defected from the Communist cause. They were the most effective South Vietnamese fighters in Rach Kien District during 1967–68.

PSP Pierced steel planking. Used to reinforce the roofs of bunkers and construct airfields and bridges.

Punji Stakes A field-expedient weapon of the Communists. Bamboo stakes sharpened to a point and often covered with human feces to encourage infection. They were placed in holes and were intended to penetrate the foot or leg.

PX Post exchange, the army and air force military department store. The navy and marines use the term BX for base exchange.

Quan South Vietnamese name for district. The supervisory level of government over the villages.

R&R Rest and recreation. A program to give soldiers a break from the combat zone, usually a week in duration.

Regional Force Called the RF, or Ruff Puffs, by the Americans. The district military forces of the South Vietnamese, organized into companies and sometimes by religion. In Rach Kien, 555 Company was Buddhist and Cao Dai, while 627 was Hoa Hao.

RPG Communist-bloc antitank and antibunker rocket launcher.

Search and Destroy Staff term for a military operation to find and eliminate the enemy.

Sitrep Situation report, usually informally given by word of mouth, face-to-face with a commander or by radiotelephone.

Slick Nickname for a Huey helicopter. Usually those used for troop transport.

Smoke Grenade A canister-type hand grenade that emits smoke in varying colors. Primarily used to mark the location of friendly forces to be extracted by helicopter or to give fire support.

Spider Hole A well-camouflaged, one-man fighting position used by the enemy. They would frequently allow US forces to pass by and then strike from the rear.

Spooky Reliable old C-47 or twin-boomed C-119 aircraft equipped with fast-firing Gatling guns. They provided excellent overhead support to ground forces.

Straphanger A lesser being that accompanies members of Congress or military entourages.

Tet The Vietnamese lunar new year. The most sacred holiday for the Vietnamese, a time when family and the spirits of their ancestors gather together.

Tru Gian The Communist program to kill those they considered traitors.

Trung Nong A peasant farmer.

USAID United States Agency for International Development.

Viet Cong The description used by the South Vietnamese government and the Americans to describe those in the South who supported the Communist cause. Their leaders were often men who had been planted at the time of the separation of North and South.

Viet Minh A front established by the Communists in 1941, employed against the French. Many continued as leaders and members of the Viet Cong. French records were of value in identifying and eliminating them.

Warning Order The preliminary order that allows units to begin initial preparation for a mission.

Waste To kill.

White Mice A derogatory American term for the white-shirted South Vietnamese police.

WIA Wounded in action.

WP White phosphorus. Used in grenades and artillery rounds. Often used as an airburst in the flat land of the Mekong Delta to determine one's location.

Zap American jargon for wounding or killing, usually the latter; "I zapped him" or "Sam got zapped." Other descriptions were "wasted," "greased," and "snuffed."

Index

Relentless daring,
Heroic sacrifice.

RANGERS IN WORLD WAR II

by Robert W. Black

From the deadly shores of North Africa to the invasion of Sicily to the fierce jungle hell of the Pacific, the contribution of the World War II Ranger battalions far outweighed their numbers. They were ordinary men on an extraordinary mission, experiencing the full measure of the fear, exhaustion, and heroism of combat in nearly every major invasion of the war.

With first person interviews and in-depth research, author Robert Black, a Ranger himself, has made the battles of WWII come to life through the struggles of the men who fought to win the greatest war the world has ever seen.

Published by Presidio Press
Available wherever books are sold

The war the world didn't want to remember, fought by the men the world will never forget.

RANGERS IN KOREA
by Robert W. Black

In the Korean War, one group above all others distinguished itself, a small elite band who volunteered for action behind enemy lines. They were the men of the U. S. Army's legendary Rangers.

This is their story, told here for the first time—based on military records, interviews with survivors, and the author's personal experiences as an American Ranger in the Korean War.

"A tribute to [Darby] and his men, whose contributions to victory deserve everlasting recognition and thanks."
—Martin Blumenson
Army Magazine

DARBY'S RANGERS
We Led the Way

by William O. Darby
with William H. Baumer

From the moment they hit the beaches in North Africa to their last desperate struggle at Anzio, Darby's Rangers asked for only one thing in World War II—the chance to fight. Experts at amphibious landings, night attacks, and close combat, the Rangers were the spearhead for advancing U.S. forces. And at their helm was William O. Darby, a forceful, charismatic man who inspired, and was inspired by, his troops. Against overwhelming odds in Tunisia, through the concentrated hell at Gela, on to the final kill at Messina and the Italian mainland, Darby and his Rangers led the way.

Published by Presidio Press
Available wherever books are sold

The riveting true story of the first African American LRRP team in Vietnam

SOUL PATROL
by Ed Emanuel

When Ed Emanuel was handpicked for the first African American special operations LRRP team in Vietnam, he knew his six-man team couldn't have asked for a tougher proving ground than Cu Chi in the summer of 1968. Home to the largest Viet Cong tunnel complex in Vietnam, Cu Chi was the deadly heart of the enemy's stronghold in Tay Ninh Province.

Team 2/6 of Company F, 51st Infantry, was quickly dubbed the Soul Patrol, a gimmicky label that belied the true depth of their courage. Stark and compelling, Emanuel's account provides an unforgettable look at the horror and the heroism that became the daily fare of LRRPs in Vietnam.

Published by Presidio Press
Available wherever books are sold